JOAN OF ARC
AND HER SECRET MISSIONS

JOAN OF ARC
AND HER SECRET MISSIONS

Pierre de Sermoise

Translated by
Jennifer Taylor

ROBERT HALE · LONDON

First Published in Great Britain 1973

ISBN 0 7091 4105 x

Robert Hale and Company
63 Old Brompton Road
London, S.W.7

PRINTED IN GREAT BRITAIN
BY EBENEZER BAYLIS AND SON LTD
THE TRINITY PRESS, WORCESTER, AND LONDON

CONTENTS

I BIRTH

1 Demystification 13
2 France and the Hundred Years War 16
3 The Fruit of Adultery 22
4 The Flight to Domrémy 27
5 The d'Arc Family 32
6 Childhood and Adolescence 36
7 Charles VII's First Coronation 40
8 Education 44

II THE BEGINNING OF THE SAGA

9 The Reception at Chinon 53
10 Honours 59
11 The *Book of Poitiers* 63
12 The Sword of Louis of Orleans 67
13 First Miracle at Orleans 71
14 Faithful Friends of Orleans 75
15 The Liberation of Orleans 79
16 The Heraldic Proof 83
17 The Coronation 87
18 The Trap 93

III THE TRIAL OF CONDEMNATION

19 Pierre Cauchon of Sommièvre, Lord Count-Bishop of Beauvais 103
20 English Policy and the University 107

21 From Beaurevoir to Rouen 110
22 Prison 114
23 France and Burgundy 117
24 Cauchon's Forgeries 119
25 *In Nomine Domini . . . Amen* 123
26 Torture 128
27 The Abjuration 131
28 The Judgment 136
29 The Stake 140
30 The Substitution 144

IV THE END OF THE SAGA

31 Exile 155
32 Elizabeth of Goerlitz, Duchess of Luxemburg 162
33 The House of Armoises 170
34 1436 174
35 The Marriage Contract 178
36 The Pseudo-Siege of La Rochelle 182
37 Gilles de Rais 187
38 The Town of Orleans' Gratitude 192
39 The 'Swindler' Rewarded 197
40 Nicolas Louve the Franciscan 201
41 The Tomb at Pulligny 205

V THE MAKING OF A LEGEND

42 The Rehabilitation 215
43 Canonization 221
44 Joan and Knighthood 226

Addendum 232
Bibliography 235
Index 243

ILLUSTRATIONS

facing page

The Paris of the Middle Ages: the Hôtel de Sens and the façade of the Hôtel de Clisson 32

Extract from the accounts of the Hôtel Saint-Pol showing the presence of the d'Arc family at Charles VI's court 33

Clothes given to Joan by Charles of Orleans 48

Royal grant of arms to Joan 49

Bishop Pierre Cauchon, from the statue on his tomb 112

A veiled woman going to the stake 112

Joan's coat of arms 112

Bouvreuil Castle before its destruction in 1809 113

Plan of a sector of the tower of Bouvreuil Castle where Joan was imprisoned 113

Painting of knights in combat from the Templar's oratory, Metz 128

Nicolas des Armoises ('The Bawler') 128

Hispano-Peruvian painting showing Joan the Maid with a standard 129

Extracts from the *vidimus* of the purchase of 'the ¼ of Haraucourt' 184

between pages 184 *and* 185

Medallion at Jaulny showing Joan the Maid, Lady of Armoises

Louis de Maele, Count of Flanders

Medallion of Robert des Armoises at Jaulny

A sketch in the Paris Parliament register showing Joan and her standard

Joan's tomb and the sculpture of an angel in the church at Pulligny-sur-Madon *facing page* 185

page

TABLE I The relationship of the Plantagenet and the Valois lines 233

TABLE II The Sermoise branch of the Armoises family 234

To my maternal great-uncle
His Eminence Cardinal François-Désiré Mathieu
Archbishop of Toulouse
Ambassador of the Vatican to London
Member of the French Academy
Doctor of Literature—Professor of History

† London, 1908
In Memoriam

I

BIRTH

1

DEMYSTIFICATION

> . . . If lying is forbidden, it is none the less licit to hide the truth, in special circumstances, by means of a good fabrication or equivocal expressions . . .[1]

These incredible words, spoken in Notre-Dame Cathedral by Master Guillaume Prévosteau, attorney of the d'Arc family,* more or less amounted to a justification of expedient lying in the fifteenth century.

Today, the process of mystification is near its peak. In an attempt to force down their 'truth' more easily, a number of conformists to the legend narrow their field of investigation instead of broadening it, and purposely limit their knowledge to the two Trials of Condemnation and Rehabilitation of Joan. To these autocrats of intelligence, the only scientific attitude is to submit unconditionally to a 'one-way learning', with the result that discussion never even gets under way.

The present stage of distortion in the dispute has been reached because of the indiscriminate use of such methods. Yet how is it possible to trust Prévosteau and his brothers in religion after reading these texts where they proclaim the deceit right from the start, and make a doctrine of dissimulation?

Relying on exploiting simpleness, the legend of 'Joan the Maid' was staged in its every aspect and made pregnant with edifying examples and symbols likely to sway the masses. The legend's persuasiveness can be judged by this summary of the official version published in Orleans in 1894.

> Old Merlin, the ancient seer, had foretold the coming of Joan of Arc, and she came at the time predicted.
>
> She was born in 1412 in Domrémy, a small village in the former Barrois, on the borders of Lorraine. Her parents, worthy farm-labourers, cultivated their small domain. . . . One day, when she was still young, and tending her flock in the solitary fields, mysterious voices spoke to her under the Fairies' Tree and in the shade of the chapel of Notre-Dame of Bermont. These voices eventually identified themselves as

* Translator's note: This was at the opening ceremony of the Trial of Rehabilitation, on 7th November 1455.

those of St Michael, St Catherine and St Margaret. They ordered her to leave for Chinon where Charles VII, the unfortunate king of France, was then residing, to lead the French army and drive out the English who had just laid siege to Orleans.

After much hesitation, and after overcoming everyone's incredulity, she left at last, equipped as a man-at-arms and arrived in Chinon on 6th March 1429. She convinced the indecisive king, won over captains and soldiers alike, and marched on Orleans at the head of 3,000 men. . . . She delivered the town; dislodged the English from the bastions; chased them from the fortresses along the Loire; crushed them at Patay; and led the king across country terrorized by the enemy garrisons to be crowned at Rheims.

Though she then wished to retire and return to her father's fields, she was forcibly detained, and soon found herself without support and hampered in every endeavour as a result of the jealousy of the courtiers and mistrust on the part of the captains. . . . After her failure to take Paris, she was abandoned and betrayed and maliciously made to fall into the hands of the English at Compiègne on 24th May 1430.

She was dragged from prison to prison and eventually to the tower of Rouen, where, despite La Hire's efforts to deliver her, she was judged in an iniquitous trial, a masterpiece of malice and villainy. Condemned as a witch, she was burnt at the stake in Rouen on 30th May 1431, by the English and a few even more infamous Frenchmen, to wit Bishop Pierre Cauchon and his assessors.

She was officially rehabilitated by the victorious Charles VII, in agreement with Pope Calixtus III, on 7th July 1456.

She has just been declared venerable by the Church. The heroine of Orleans has frequently inspired artists, orators, poets and historians, but it is doubtful whether her chaste and heroic figure has found an interpreter who could rival history's sublime simplicity.[2]

Could any of this be disputed? Yet all I knew, from study, from family traditions and documents, pointed to some other version of the facts. Wishing to ascertain the truth, I explored every possibility, with the aid of all auxiliary disciplines relevant to the subject—namely induction, deduction, symbolics, psycho-analysis, and factorial analysis of events, individual and collective behaviour.

Sometimes in conflict with my own case, I remained obstinately and rigorously faithful to the one method which permits the right conclusions to be drawn and which has been defined by the mathematician Henri Poincaré: 'To doubt everything and to believe everything are two equally easy solutions, both of which dispense with the need for thought.'

Endless checking and cross-checking confirmed this second version, which seems so much more natural yet equally attractive: Joan was in fact the bastard daughter of Queen Isabeau and Duke Louis of Orleans, and she appeared in Domrémy on the night of Epiphany 1408. Subjected to the Machiavellian skills of Bishop Cauchon yet protected by them, she escaped the Rouen stake, and after a marriage to Robert des Armoises which was never consummated, she endeavoured to the last to accomplish a FIVE-POINT MISSION, of which only the first two points have been retained by history.

2

FRANCE AND THE HUNDRED YEARS WAR

By reason of its importance, the King's secret was not of a nature to be openly revealed . . .

(Jehan Bréhal, Grand Inquisitor of France, at the Trial of Rehabilitation, 1456)

To understand the events of the first half of the fifteenth century, one must go back in time and seek their original causes. The secret of the birth of Charles VII, and the disintegration of the kingdom of France in the face of the English occupation were by-products of a return to social chaos. Manifested first of all by an unprecedented dynastic rivalry, disorder soon resulted in a conflict, the long-term effects of which are still to be felt in the twentieth century.

For the balance of the western world had been rudely shattered in the course of a few years by the dissolution of the Knights Templar, which came soon after the failure of the Crusades. In 1314, two years after he had suppressed the Order, Pope Clement V settled in Avignon, thereby seriously dividing the Church. In the midst of a society based on faith, ecclesiastical anarchy made possible the election of several popes at the same time. The way was paved for the Great Schism, and foundations laid for the Reformation.

Conflict, sometimes hidden, sometimes open, arose between Franciscans and Dominicans over the dogma of the Immaculate Conception. This was a revival of the cult of the Mother-goddess, represented by the 'Black Virgin', which took its inspiration both from the East and from the Western Druids. Reinstated by St Bernard, this cult was then taken up by the Franciscans, as well as by the Celtic movement which flourished in both France and England. The conservative Order of St Dominic reacted and, as stricter members of the Church, it was but one step from anxiety to an intensification of inquisitorial practices.

After their dispersion, the surviving Templars had been rapidly absorbed by orders settled outside French territory: by the Orders of the Thistle in Scotland, of Calatrava in Spain, and of Christ in Portugal.

A state of complete confusion then prevailed in the West, and the ensuing general relaxation gave particularly to monarchs and to prelates of the Church total freedom of action wherever their personal interests were at stake.

Although rivalry had always existed between Capetians and Plantagenets, who originally came from Anjou, the conflict had never before assumed such proportions. But in 1328, fourteen years after the death of King Philip the Fair of France, the Capetians were without a direct descendant, and the throne went to Philip VI, the representative of the junior line of the Valois. Nothing more was needed to whet the appetite of the King of England and especially of his entourage. By his mother, Isabella of France, a daughter of Philip the Fair, Edward III was indeed a descendant of the Capetians, and by virtue of English law, a direct descendant. This distinction made him feel justified in claiming the French crown from the junior line. The result was the Hundred Years War, which involved political, religious and economic factors.

Ten years passed. The Valois were the first to attack by seizing Guyenne, and French and English started killing each other. The Emperor of Germany intervened only later and incidentally in the war, by lending troops for a little money.

Unfortunately the respective stands taken were inflexible because of a legal misunderstanding over the application of the Salic Law, the only parry to the English claims the French jurists could evolve—or so it has been said.

Issued under Clovis* in 486 but fallen into disuse, this code of laws comprised a rule whereby women were excluded from succession to 'ancestral land' (*terra salica et aviatica*) and thus from succession to the throne. This enactment of *droit privé* only applied to France and had never even been used. Nevertheless for the occasion it was claimed to be *droit public*. As it was not recognized by English law, the dispute was a dialogue of the deaf and degenerated into a conflict in which each sovereign was vindicated by the law of his state.

What followed was not to France's advantage. The English, with their civic sense of responsibility, organization and discipline, boosted by superior armament, scored impressively from the outset of hostilities. Edward III indeed had the full support of his subjects, who were keen to export to the continent their wool and produce. This would, in the main, be absorbed by the flourishing weaving industry of the Flemish middle classes. In 1340, he assumed the title of King of

* Translator's note: Clovis, king of the Franks, 466–511, the first Christian king of Gaul.

France, and had the fleurs-de-lis quartered with the English leopards on his coat-of-arms.*

In the first big sea-battle outside the port of l'Ecluse, the French fleet was more or less wiped out as the Valois troops, massed on their ships, were decimated by the English archers' arrows.† The coasts were no longer protected, and King Edward's armies could now land anywhere along the coastline.

Six years later, French knighthood suffered another traumatic disaster at the battle of Crecy, where the English used bombards—the first tactical use of gunpowder in the West.

In 1356, a decade later, a new defeat for the French at Poitiers was marked by the capture of their king, John the Good, who was taken prisoner to London. An exorbitant ransom and Draconian conditions completed the financial ruin and dismemberment of a country already ravaged by the Black Death of 1348 which had come from the Orient via Italy. In under a year, half the population had perished and labour became so scarce that prices soared. War and plague combined were responsible for the ruin of many families, at all social levels, and for the emergence of social troubles.

It was an almost desperate situation that the young Charles V inherited on his father's death in 1365. He was, fortunately, exceptionally intelligent and well-balanced. He first endeavoured to restore his finances, so that he could reconquer his lost dominions without any financial worries. Admirably seconded by Bertrand du Guesclin, the Breton *routier*, or leader of mercenary bands, whom he promoted to the rank of constable,‡ he revised military tactics; and he succeeded both in regaining most of his dominions, and in ridding the countryside of the *Grandes Compagnies*. These were bands of rapacious lords, men-at-arms and unemployed mercenaries who lived by brigandage, battening on almost the entire kingdom. Thus, at the end of his 15-year reign, France was virtually restored to its condition under the last Capetians, prior to the devastations of war and the plague. But his premature death in 1380 came at an unfortunate time.

The halfway point of the Hundred Years War had been reached.

* Translator's note: For over sixty years the fleurs-de-lis of the French quartering were 'scattered over the field', but following the example of the King of France, Henry IV in 1405 reduced their number to three. This gave rise to the heraldic term 'France Modern'. The three fleurs-de-lis remained in the royal arms until 1801, when they were replaced by the arms of Hanover.

† Author's note: The English troops were equipped with the Welsh long-bow, a swift and precise weapon with a very long range. It was so deadly that it could pierce any type of armour, rivet a rider to his saddle, and sometimes kill man and horse in one shot. Out of bravado, the French knights did not use archers, 'footsloggers' whom they regrettably despised.

‡ Translator's note: A constable—*connétable*—shared the high command with princes of royal blood and some of the greater vassals.

There followed a catastrophic sequence of events which again plunged the country into such straits that by 1429 it warranted the use of a last resort: 'Operation Joan-the-Maid'.

Before his death, John the Good had made the bad mistake of giving the Duchy of Burgundy in apanage* to his fourth son, Philip the Bold, for, exceptionally, it did not revert to the crown at the Duke's death. Burgundy became a truly dynastic and hereditary state and a cause of division amongst the French.

This new line of 'great Dukes of the West', said to be 'of the second Burgundian race',† in turn coveted the throne of France. It did not obtain the throne, but through John the Fearless, Philip the Good and Charles the Bold, the heritage of the Bourgogne–Valois descended to the Emperor Charles V of Austria, as a result of the marriage of Maria of Burgundy, daughter of Charles the Bold, and Maximilian of Austria.

Charles V was succeeded by his 12-year-old son, Charles VI, and the kingdom fell victim to the Regency Council formed in the circumstances. The four overlords, called 'Princes of the Fleurs-de-Lis', three of whom were brothers of the late king, and one his brother-in-law, were jealous of each other; and they soon hated each other so bitterly that their own interests always took precedence over the nation's welfare. In no time the treasury was depleted, the country divided, and once more ruin brought in its wake widespread social unrest, which lasted until the coming of Joan.

Some time after this, acting upon the astute advice of his uncle Philip of Burgundy, the young Charles VI married a German princess, Isabeau of Bavaria. The young queen who had grown up in the gloom and traditional austerity of the German courts, was now plunged into the dazzling luxury and diverse, uninhibited pleasures of the Valois court.

Besides being beautiful, Isabeau was seductive and sensual, to the point of being irresistible—and insatiable. It was only natural that at this time the king should have been passionately in love with his ravishing wife whom he tenderly called 'his own Isabeau'. As Auguste Bailly writes,[3] their union may have been arranged and concluded by diplomats, but it was also the most ardent of love matches.

Despite the intrigues of his uncles, Charles VI's vision was clear. He started to fight the hold of the Regency and had the wisdom to

* Author's note: *Apanage*: a portion of the royal domain that a sovereign gave a younger son or brother to provide him with a source of income and compensate him for his exclusion from the throne. An apanage was not normally hereditary.

† Translator's note: The 'first Burgundian race', or first House of Burgundy, was descended from the King of France Robert the Pious (996–1031), a son of Hugh Capet, and died out in 1361.

surround himself with the *marmousets*, advisers chosen from the most intelligent and enlightened members of the bourgeoisie. This first period, which alone constitutes his real reign, began most promisingly.

Unhappily, he had by no means inherited his father's equilibrium. At first given the nickname of the 'well-beloved', he was soon, to the country's great misfortune, called 'Charles the Mad'. For, debilitated by unbridled festivities, all kinds of excesses brought about by Isabeau's temperament, and worries about the power of the throne, his mind gradually deteriorated and in 1392 cracked suddenly, during a ride in the Mans forest; it was Charles VI's first attack of raving lunacy.

A year later, at the *Bal des Ardents*, he fell into a sort of stunned lethargy which afflicted him intermittently for the rest of his life. If this famous royal party-cum-fancy-dress ball had not ended in tragedy, it would have been rather comical. But, as Bois-Bourdon, one of the Queen's favourites, later confessed, this horrifying accident was in fact the result of a plot. It was organized by Isabeau and her brother-in-law Louis of Orleans who, in an effort to usurp the power of the throne, made an attempt on the mad king's life.

Having just recovered from his first attack, Charles had decided to lead the ball at the head of about ten of his favourites. In order to disguise themselves as savages, the dancers had donned close-fitting tunics coated with pitch with tow stuck on in simulation of hair. The party was at its merriest and most drunken, and the musicians had launched into a *sarrasine*, a mimed dance consisting of grotesque, obscene gestures. Suddenly there was a blood-curdling cry. A valet, carrying a torch, stumbled and fell at the sovereign's feet. In a few seconds, the savages' costumes were alight, and several of them were writhing in terrible agony.

Charles the Mad owed his safety only to the presence of mind of the Duchess of Berri who had immediately covered him with the wide folds of her skirts. A few moments later he emerged from under the dress, half-naked and unscathed. But, in a sudden stupor, he murmured as though in ecstasy: 'Oh! where are the pretty flames which were running all over the dance?'[4] He pursued these flames to the end of his wretched life, passing from incoherent dreams to fits of fury.

Thirteen years had passed since the death of Charles V and his wisdom was replaced by debauchery and madness, while a notorious liaison was established betwen Queen Isabeau and Louis of Orleans.

The King's more or less incurable insanity meant that his uncle Philip the Bold, Duke of Burgundy, once again had to sit on the Regency Council, and this second time he came into contact with the handsome Duke of Orleans. Systematic opposition sprang up instinctively between them and their rivalry quickly degenerated into unrelenting hatred between the Houses of France and Burgundy.

Often prudish, history has insufficiently stressed the Queen's liaison with her brother-in-law. Yet on closer examination it explains much. The birth of the future Charles VII in 1403 was one of the most controversial and fiercely-debated events of the period. But there is now little doubt that Charles was the love-child of Louis and Isabeau for the heraldic evidence is provided by Jeanne d'Orliac in her book on Yolanda of Anjou.* 'We know through Dufresne de Beaucourt that Charles had two cradles, bearing only the Queen's arms. Is this a clue to the mystery surrounding the birth of this child who was the youngest but one? The arms of Bavaria only: was Charles then not the King's son?'[5]

More recently, this possibility has been brilliantly confirmed by data produced by Professor Jean Bosler.[6] His tabulation of the Queen's pregnancies in relation to her husband's periods of lucidity, proves categorically that Charles VII was not the son of Charles the Mad, but of Duke Louis, his brother.

* Translator's note: Yolanda of Anjou was the widow of Louis II, Duke of Anjou and King of Naples and Sicily. She was in her own right Duchess of Bar and Queen of Aragon. Her daughter Marie married Charles VII in 1422.

3

THE FRUIT OF ADULTERY

> The misfortunes of France, come from abroad and from certain branches of the Lily, and nourished by its sap . . .
> . . . a poisonous viper [Isabeau of Bavaria] will smother the roots of the sacred plant . . .
> But a Virgin, rising from where the brutal poison had spread, marked with a small red spot behind the right ear . . . will liberate France.[7]

It was commonly believed in the fifteenth century, according to Bosler, that people of royal blood were born with such a red sign on the body, and so the Grand Inquisitor of France's allusion to this 'red sign' in the course of the Trial of Rehabilitation would have pointed categorically to the truth, except for those who chose to disregard the obvious.

Furthermore, Professor Bosler suggested that Bréhal and the 'daughter of the king of Hungary' were but one and the same person, that is to say that Engélide never existed. He thinks Bréhal used the pseudonym to impart this information in a veiled fashion as it was impossible for him to do so any other way. 'It is up to you to understand, if you are able,' said the Inquisitor.

The teaching of history often reminds one of a prayer-wheel that some people follow through sheer laziness of mind. Others lose interest because of the lack of objective information, political expediency having caused documents to disappear in its attempt to influence public opinion more easily.

Twelfth-night of the year 1412 was chosen by the Vatican at the turn of the twentieth century as the official date of Joan the Maid's birth in Domrémy, Lorraine (Acts of Pius X). I contest both time and place, associating myself in this with all 'non-orthodox' writers. We have good reason to do so, as a comparison, marshalling and analysis of texts will show.

In the fifteenth century the village of Domrémy-Greux was not situated in Lorraine but in France. It straddled the two countries and depended essentially on the crown, one half being in the *Barrois-mouvant*—under French jurisdiction—the other in the Duchy of

Lorraine, which was only joined on to France in the eighteenth century. A few miles south began the Duchy of Burgundy, whence the frequent devastating incursions of Burgundian troops into the region.

As for the date, Joan's official age—barely 17—is glaringly incompatible with the maturity of mind and body which she showed from the start—unless of course one attributes this to supernatural causes. The only evidence for 1412 is one very evasive declaration uttered by the Maid in the course of her Trial of Condemnation in 1431: 'I am 19 years old, or thereabouts, as far as I know . . .'

But two years previously, according to Béroalde of Verville who later gave an account of the meeting, she had said to Charles VII: 'My age adds up to three times seven,'* which made her 21 at the start of 1429.

This claim is confirmed by other sources: the contemporary chronicles which are unanimous, Article VIII of the Rouen trial, and the two wholly valid depositions at the Trial of Rehabilitation. The year 1412 is therefore ruled out, and 1407 it is, beyond a doubt. Ever since the fifteenth century, the protagonists of the false date have of course only made use of the data supporting the version imposed by dynastic and political dictates.

Would we give credence to the so-called biography of one of our contemporaries if the author relied entirely on the documents of a big political trial? Can we credit a fantastic tale, in the knowledge that the Trial of Condemnation was rigged from the start, and that it took several years to draw up copies of the proceedings, the original minutes having disappeared?

In 1407, in the Paris district of the Marais, there was a rich private *hôtel* situated near the Porte Barbette; two pointed turrets framed its ogival portal. It was the love nest of a queen of France seeking to escape her husband's sometimes wild and demented aversion for her.

Isabeau had bought it a few years previously from Montaigu, Grand Master of the King's Household. Already then, the public muttered its disapproval of the notorious scandal, for it was bruited that the Queen eagerly received her lover, Duke Louis, there, in the company of bawdy revellers. Their liaison was long-standing, possibly even going back to the time of Isabeau's wedding. The mere name of Barbette was a byword, if not for orgy, at any rate for great moral laxity in the course of 'joyous suppers'.

* Author's note: 'Three times seven' not only indicates Joan's real age, but is also symbolical. In medieval number symbolism, the number three alluded to the Trinity, and four to such quaternities as the elements of Earth, Air, Water and Fire. The sum of three and four gave seven as the symbol for man, whose nature is both spiritual and physical.

Six months before this haven became the focal point of important events, an occurrence was recorded at the King's residence, the Hôtel Saint-Pol,* which is surprising to say the least:

'On 12th June 1407, a "village-woman" called *Jeanne DARC*† came to offer garlands of flowers to Charles VI, for which she received recompense of eighteen *sols.*' (*Accounts of the Hôtel Saint-Pol*, Archives Nationales—see Illustrations.)

Even more of a coincidence is that this honourable Jeanne Darc, sometimes addressed as 'lady-in-waiting' was sister-in-law of Jacques (or Jacobus) d'Arc, future official father of Joan the Maid.[8]

In this way, the King's court paradoxically provided a first 'Joan of Arc', even before the second Joan—Joan the Maid, 'called d'Arc' —was born.

Some research on these two namesakes might prove interesting. Indeed, various contemporary chronicles narrate first of all that on 10th November 1407, Queen Isabeau came to the Hôtel Barbette to give birth, and at the last moment did not return to her husband's palace as she had done on previous occasions. It was understandable, for the King was more or less normal at the time. 'And there,' says Monstrelet,‡ 'delivered of a child who was deceased, lay the Queen who had not yet been purified [was still in confinement].'

This is confirmed by Father Anselme's royal genealogy '. . . A child named Philippe, born in Paris on 10th November 1407, was taken the same evening to Saint-Denis.'§ And the *Chronique du Religieux de Saint-Denis* adds 'that the Queen was violently affected by the premature death of this child (Philippe) and was in tears for the whole of her confinement . . . and the Duke made her frequent visits to assuage her grief.'

There is no doubt that at this point Isabeau had not yet become dissolute. She was still seemingly enamoured of her brother-in-law

* Author's notes: The Hôtel Saint-Pol was in fact a collection of *hôtels*, juxtaposed without any overall plan, on a site now surrounded by the Hôtel de Sens, the rues Saint-Antoine and du Petit-Musc, and the Seine. Charles V had bought them after he had converted the Louvre into a luxurious palace, but had found it too gloomy a place to live in.

These *hôtels* were linked by galleries, courtyards, cloisters and gardens, and were richly appointed. The fact that there was a menagerie, with cages for lions, as well as aviaries and an aquarium, is recalled by the modern street-name rue des Lions; there is also a street called rue des Jardins Saint-Paul.

† Until the revolution, spelling did not have the importance it has since acquired. Proper names in particular frequently varied, sometimes in the same text, as indeed will be seen later on. For the name *d'Arc* for instance, the following variations have been found: *Darc*, *Dart*, *d'Art* and even *Day*.

‡ Author's note: Enguerrand de Monstrelet (*circa* 1390 to 1453), appointed chronicler of the dukes of Burgundy, particularly of Philip the Good.

§ Translator's note: The abbey of Saint-Denis, near Paris, traditional resting-place of the kings of France.

and was faithful to him. Similarly, her maternal instinct had not yet deserted her, and this is confirmed by history.

Suddenly, thirteen days after Philippe's death, there were no more tears but instead 'a joyous supper' at the Hôtel Barbette, writes the monk of Saint-Denis. Indeed he insists on the fact twice, stressing that the Duke's last visit was followed by a feast which ended tragically. Such rejoicing is unusual, especially in the Middle Ages when, however lax morals were, pleasures invariably gave way to the religious respect accorded to death.

As it was not in the interests of the monk-chronicler to dwell upon the scandalous nature of a carousal amongst these eminent people, his aims are inexplicable unless there is some purposely veiled explanation for the feast. This revealed by the texts when put in the right sequence, as follows:

1. The first official genealogies, according to Jean de Saint-Jean* who was particularly well-placed to obtain this information, gave one child only, named Jehanne.

2. In the fifteenth-century Saint-Denis chronicle, and in the eighteenth-century *Grande Généalogie de la Maison Royale de France* by Father Anselme, the Christian name is modified to 'Philippe who lived only a day'.

3. Then, without saying why, Abbé Villaret, who as Secretary to the Peers was in a good position to have knowledge of confidential documents, corrected Father Anselme's work and changed Philippe into Jehanne, writing 'Jehanne who lived only a day'. Abbé Villaret retained the correction in the following editions, showing that he was confident of its accuracy.

4. Isabeau spent thirteen days crying over Philippe then suddenly 'treated herself to a joyous supper'. The reason why she was so soon consoled was simply that Jehanne was not only alive, but now in safety.

The problem of Philippe has two solutions. The majority of non-orthodox authors are in favour of a substitution: Jehanne, born of the Queen, was well and truly alive, but to prevent possible complications, a dead baby (Philippe) was substituted for her in the course of the day, and buried at Saint-Denis. It is a perfectly plausible hypothesis. The operation would have been easy enough to carry out for in the one month of August 1445, for instance, an epidemic in Paris accounted for over 6,000 deaths of children.[9]

But having investigated this theory myself, I do not support it. It was to my mind a far more natural affair, namely that Isabeau had

* Author's note: Jean de Saint-Jean is the pseudonym of M. Bernard Daulon, a descendant of Jean d'Aulon who was Joan's equerry. He is the author of *Jehanne, 1407–1432*, a first-rate booklet on the question, in which this vital fact is revealed for the first time.

twins. This would explain the uncertainty about the Christian names: Jehanne, Philippe, Jehanne.

There are very few twins in the history of dynasties. They always create problems and so they are camouflaged. In this case, Jehanne and Philippe were fortunately born outside the Hôtel Saint-Pol, and one of them thoughtfully died after having been baptized privately. That same evening, he joined his ancestors at Saint-Denis, and the semi-official ceremony, taking place with some degree of pomp, was a godsend for the lovers. Only the dead would have to be declared, and Jehanne's concealment would be all the easier.

For prudence was now well and truly necessary. Charles VI was unfortunately going through a lucid period and could well realize that he was not the father of this baby girl. That was why, for thirteen days until the solution took shape, Jehanne's presence only added to the Queen's unhappiness and anxiety. An indiscretion on her part could easily cause the mad King to have a relapse, or, by way of revenge, to have the Parliament of Paris decree her deposition.*

The best way out was to separate from the child, and Louis found the means at the court. He knew that, of his faithfuls, the d'Arc family bore the utmost loyalty to the crown, the Orleans party and the House of Anjou. He therefore assigned the 'first Joan of Arc' to take care of his daughter and be responsible for her fate. These events are so inextricably involved that a fanatical supporter of the legend, Siméon Luce, has written in all innocence that the first Joan of Arc 'was one of the Maid's godmothers, the one in fact to give her her name'.

Henceforth, in Domrémy, Duke Louis' daughter would be called 'Jehanne' or 'Jeannette'. At Chinon, by reason of her origins, she became *La Pucelle*, 'The Maid', 'of Orleans' being added later.† And last of all, not before 1456, she came to be called Joan of Arc, to substantiate the legend.

'Before continuing with the narration of events concerning this strange girl,' says Abbé Villaret in a foreword to his account of the saga, 'it is right to warn readers to make their own assessment of the facts.‡ We will keep to a simple exposition of attested facts.'

This is indeed what must be done, so long as nothing is left out in the process.

* Translator's note: This indeed happened some years later, in 1417. Queen Isabeau was no longer allowed to sit on the Council, and her establishment was considerably reduced.

† Translator's note: In the same way, Dunois, Joan's half-brother, was called 'the Bastard of Orleans'. He was an illegitimate son of Louis of Orleans by one of his numerous mistresses.

‡ Author's note: Despite diverse opinions of Villaret as a historian, a study of his text establishes that he had grave doubts about the legend. In all likelihood he adhered to it only for political reasons.

4

THE FLIGHT TO DOMREMY

They had all their pleasure in delights of the flesh . . .
(*Chronique du Religieux de Saint-Denis*)

That is precisely what they were up to at the Hôtel Barbette, on the evening of 23rd November, thirteen days after Philippe's funeral.

With the consolation of daily visits from Louis of Orleans, the Queen had soon overcome her grief. All necessary instructions had been given, so that little Jehanne, now in the safe hands of her future godmother, Nicolas d'Arc's wife, would be immune to the death threats made by John the Fearless against the Duke's progeny.

Isabeau's confinement was not yet over, but an intimate party was organized in her room, the guests including her brother, Louis of Bavaria.* Orleans came incognito that evening, unarmed and escorted only by two equerries and a handful of servants. The supper was at its merriest around seven when there was a knocking in the night. At the door was a servant called Thomas de Courtehouse.

'My lord,' he said to the Duke, 'the King sends you word that you should go to him without delay. He would speak with you urgently about something which much affects him and you.'[10]

Having taken leave of his hosts, Louis mounted his mule and departed. He led the way, flanked by his torch-bearers, with his equerries following at a short distance behind. As he turned the corner of a narrow street, he was set upon by eighteen men who shouted: 'Kill him! Kill him!'

'I am the Duke of Orleans!' he cried, thinking this was an attack by cut-throats.

'The very man we're after,' replied his assailants, redoubling their blows.

One of his hands was severed at the wrist and the unfortunate man fell from his mount. A blow from a mace cleft open his skull and he died almost instantly with his brains spilling out onto the road. One

* Translator's note: This is Louis the Bearded, who became Duke of Bavaria on his father's death in 1413. There was another Louis Duke of Bavaria, the 'Red Duke', who was son of the Emperor Rupert. He married Blanche of Lancaster in 1402, which made him Henry V's brother-in-law.

of his equerries who had tried to intervene and make a shield with his body was also butchered.

It was well known that John the Fearless had compassed this gruesome assassination—indeed he never sought to deny it, the rivalry between the cousins having ended in a feud. There were a number of reasons, mainly political, which had made him organize the ambush. But the History of Burgundy[11] mentions another reason which could well have been responsible for making the growing animosity turn to murderous intent. '. . . It was the outrageous mortification he [John the Fearless] suffered when, whilst in Louis' study, the latter showed him, amidst portraits of ladies who had granted favours to him, that of the Duchess, his wife . . . who was looked upon at the court, and elsewhere, as a model of good behaviour, modesty and faithfulness to her husband . . .'

'It was the most dolorous and piteous affair to happen for many years in the Christian kingdom of France,' affirms Monstrelet. This was especially so as the Duke of Orleans had a first-rate mind and was beloved of a large part of the nation, despite his prodigality. There was no doubt he would have made a better king than his brother.

The survivors of the killing took refuge at the Hôtel Barbette, so that Isabeau was immediately alerted. 'And,' says the Chronicle, 'the Queen conceived so great a fright and horror, that notwithstanding that she was not yet purified [recovered] had herself placed on a litter by her brother, Louis of Bavaria, and others of her people, and carried to the Hôtel Saint-Pol, in the chamber next to the King's. And likewise, several noblemen, such as the Count of Saint-Pol, grouped and armed themselves, knowing not what business might ensue . . .'

This precipitate return to the royal residence shows that Isabeau was then intent on keeping up appearances of respectability and on making people forget, if possible, the merrymaking at the Hôtel Barbette.

Anxious to protect the life of her son Charles after these recent events, she lost no time in entrusting him to her relation, Queen Yolanda of Anjou, although she was not on the best of terms with her. Is this the reaction of an unnatural mother, as has been suggested?

She had done the same for Jehanne, having agreed to Louis's suggestion to entrust her to the 'dame Darc'. The latter had now to make a speedy return to Domrémy, where her sister-in-law, Isabelle d'Arc, would be charged with bringing up the child of royal blood.

At this point everything begins to fall into place, for Yolanda of Anjou was a *Grande Dame Discrète* of the Franciscan Third Order the mainspring of which was Colette de Corbie. And Colette, who frequently travelled round the eastern part of the country, was, as it happened, a close friend of Isabelle d'Arc.

Monstrelet concludes on the subject of the Duke's murder:

> This dolorous death was in the year of the great winter, the year one thousand four hundred and seven. The frost lasted sixty-six days, with so savage a hold that when the thaw came, the Pont-Neuf in Paris was swept into the Seine, and many floods and frosts did great damage in various parts of the kingdom of France.

It was obviously out of the question to undertake a 70-league journey in such intense cold with the responsibility of a new-born child. Jeanne d'Arc, her godmother, was forced to wait awhile. At last, towards New Year's Eve, departure was considered possible and the ten-strong party set out. It was a treacherous journey. Since the suppression of the Order of the Temple, forests and open country were unsafe, although the *Grandes Compagnies* had been mopped up by Du Guesclin. Scores of more or less organized brigands would attack and ransom anybody, cutting throats if necessary. And of course it was in the shortest days of mid-winter, with icy north winds blowing over the snow-covered or hard-frozen ground.

The last stage was one of the longest and explains the arrival at Domrémy in the middle of the night. For they found themselves within an ace of their destination and decided to carry on; especially as arriving at this time would be far more discreet. Indeed hardly anyone would know what actually happened. The only existing account is that of a chamberlain of Charles VII, Perceval de Boulainvilliers,* in a letter to Philip-Maria Visconti, Duke of Milan. He wrote it 21 years after the event, shortly after Joan the Maid had said to her brother the Dauphin: 'My age adds up to three times seven.'

It must be remembered that Visconti too was a close relation as Louis of Orleans had married his sister Valentine.† And this long letter, dispatched to Milan a month before the Rheims coronation is far more like an account of the unfolding promotional campaign decided on to save the kingdom, than the naive historical narration it has so often been called.

The author describes the end of the journey as follows:

> On the night of Epiphany, torch-bearers disturbed the usual quietness. Invited to celebrate the event, the villagers, ignorant of the birth

* Author's notes: Boulainvilliers was therefore an important personage in close contact with the King. He later became Seneschal of Berri etc.

† Their legitimate son, Charles of Orleans, was therefore half-brother to both Joan the Maid and Dunois, Bastard of Orleans. Made prisoner at the battle of Agincourt in 1415, he spent most of his life in captivity in London, and there wrote some delightful poetry.

of the Maid, went here and there to find out what had happened. Moreover, the cocks started to flap their wings, and crowed for two hours, as though having a premonition of this happy event . . .

Even this short extract bristles with strange contradictions. For instance, it was a rule that torch-bearers were reserved for the escort of royalty; Louis of Orleans had been escorted in this way on the night of his assassination.

Other than the Maid's arrival, there is no record, for either 1408 or 1412, of any move made by a prince. Who then was being escorted in this corner of the kingdom on the night of Epiphany? Was it the second visit of the Three Kings in the course of the Christian era, returning on Twelfth-night this time for Jehanne? I am willing to suspend my disbelief but it does not seem the most natural solution. In this connection, the experts inform us that Christianity has likened the Dauphin to 'Jesus-Christ the Immaculate King', making him intervene directly in symbols linked with Epiphany . . . Considered a royal fish in ancient times and endowed with superior intelligence and qualities, the dolphin symbolizes 'the Christian who has taken refuge in God's bosom'.

But it was only after 1130, in the time of St Bernard, that the title of *Dauphin* was given to the eldest sons of the Counts of Viennois and Auvergne. It was later adopted by the kings of France, and it is interesting to note that the first royal Dauphin was Charles V, a Valois.

These symbols, linked with the official manifestation of Jehanne at Domrémy, point at any rate to the secret plot surrounding her birth. Moreover, despite the fact that it was Twelfth-night, and that Isabelle d'Arc, wife of the first notable of Domrémy, was supposed to be pregnant, the whole village was sound asleep. In a community of thirty homes, if the mayor's wife gives birth to a child, surely no-one ought to have to 'find out what was happening'. This is the first paradox of the legendary account. And the sudden 'awakening, torches, general agitation and surprise', establish that there was no birth that night.

On the other hand, there is no doubt that Jacques and Isabelle d'Arc welcomed someone of importance according to instructions received: Jehanne. This is confirmed by the fact that Boulainvilliers gives no date in his letter—neither 1407 nor 1412, of course. This lacuna is odd to say the least as his text is otherwise teeming with all kinds of details. The only possible reason for this forgetfulness is political expediency. The family secret soon became a dynastic one, especially after the decision taken at Poitiers to use Jehanne to inspire the troops of liberation. When Boulainvilliers wrote this letter to the Duke of Milan Orleans had been delivered and Charles VII had just given a coat of arms to the Maid—but for herself alone, with no idea of associating the d'Arc family with it.

In fact the questionable legitimacy of Charles the 'so-called dauphin' would demand silence until the end of the Ancien Régime. It was simply a question of divine right.

5

THE D'ARC FAMILY

> Azure a bar fesswise Or charged with a sheaf of arrows, the points upwards, two gold barbed and feathered argent, the third of the last barbed and feathered of the second. On a chief argent a lion passant gules.
>
> (*Charte du XVII siècle*, in the Bibliothèque Nationale, quoted by Quicherat.

When these armorial bearings of the d'Arc family were confirmed by a charter of King Louis XIII, they were recognized as being pre-fifteenth century. This is not surprising. The *Gallia Christiania** mentions a Jean d'Arc, Bishop of Mende—*episcopus mimatensis*—as early as 1331, and this scholarly work also reveals that in 1357 Marie d'Arc married Duke John of Burgundy, 'of the first race'.

Thorough research has brought to light that the d'Arc family originally came from Arc-en-Barrois, and in the late 1370s still owned a few small fiefs in the area.[12] It was only at the Trial of Rehabilitation in 1456 that, for reasons of dynastic security and religious policy, it became a matter of necessity to reduce their rank;† they would have been made into serfs if it had been possible. The legend of Joan the Maid, springing from a background of poor and humble peasantry, would then be sure of obtaining the support of the church-going proletariat that was indispensable for it to be fully effective whenever necessary. And indeed the nineteenth century took advantage of this distortion.

And yet, in 1407, the choice of the d'Arc family living in Domrémy had not been lightly made.

Situated on the old Roman road linking Verdun and Langres, the village was small but of real commercial importance. It straddled Barrois, which was under French jurisdiction, and the Duchy of Lorraine—which had close family ties with Yolanda of Anjou—with the stream of Trois-fontaines acting as boundary. Also, in the event

* Translator's note: The *Gallia Christiania* was an ecclesiastical history of France by provinces. It was first published in 1626, with subsequent editions in the eighteenth century.

† Author's note: This evidently motivated Charles du Lys' petition in the early seventeenth century. Claiming to be a direct descendant of Jean d'Arc, he asked for his nobility to be recognized.

The Paris of the Middle Ages

(*above*) The Hôtel de Sens which once formed part of the Hôtel Saint-Pol, and (*below*) the façade of the Hôtel de Clisson built in 1370. The Hôtel Barbette stood 200 yards away.
(Photo by Michel de Sermoise)

Dons.

The presence of the d'Arc family at the court of Charles VI is attested by this extract from the accounts of the Hôtel Saint-Pol. The sixth item concerns a *Jehanne dart* (or *darc*) who was given 18 *sols* for offering garlands of flowers to the king; the seventh and tenth items concern gifts made to *Guillaume hart* (or *harc*) for having lent money to the king.

(Archives Nationales. Photo by Societé Française du Microfilm)

of an attack from the Burgundians, escape could easily be effected by crossing a small bridge over a tributary of the Meuse which flowed by the village. At the time, there was much traffic on this river: Burgundian wines bound for the North and Flanders, Flemish cloths and manufacture bound for the Mediterranean region.

Great lords, monks, minstrels and yokels all stopped at Domrémy-Greux, doubtless knocking on the door of the dean, Jacques d'Arc. Born in Ceffonds, Champagne, in about 1375, he came from a family of long-standing nobility which had made advantageous marriage alliances, on occasion with the entourage of kings. But it was unfortunately one of the many to be ruined by the economic consequences of the Hundred Years War and Black Death of 1348. Nevertheless, life had to continue, and the impoverished younger sons had the option of making a rich marriage, or of taking up manual work. In the second case, they would derogate, though this forfeiture of their noble status and prerogatives was not irrevocable.*

By 1400, Jacques d'Arc had married and shortly afterwards settled in Domrémy. With the money arising from the sale of a few small fiefs, he rented some arable land: he had chosen to derogate.

His wife, Isabelle de Vouthon† was a woman of great virtue, endowed with the kind of human piety which is extolled by the Franciscan movement. Indeed she belonged to the Third Order, and later became an intimate friend of St Colette of Corbie. Like her husband, she came from a family impoverished by war. Her brother, Henri of Vouthon, who had brought about their marriage, was nevertheless an influential person, being *curé* of the small fortified town of Sermaize, near Bar-le-Duc. There had moreover been some good marriages in this Vouthon branch, and there were more to come, with families such as Beauvau, Nettancourt, Ludres and even des Armoises.‡ The d'Arc and Vouthon families therefore had similar origins and had made similar alliances: to use a modern expression, they were of the same class.

After settling in Domrémy, which was not far from Vouthon, Jacques d'Arc willingly accepted honours and responsibilities. He was both dean and head of the archers when in 1419 he became 'farmer-general' of the district, quite an important post. At about the same time, he leased, jointly with a man called Jean Bizet, the lord-

* Author's notes: It could be abrogated by royal decision. *Déchéance* (degradation) on the other hand was infamatory and its consequences permanent.

† Isabelle (or Isabeau) d'Arc was often called *Romée* because of a pilgrimage her mother had made either to Rome or Puy-en-Velay: these were the two places which entitled pilgrims to use this name.

‡ There are many spelling variations to be found for *des Armoises*: des Ermoises, de Sermoises, often in one word or lacking the final 's'. One can sometimes find three different spellings in the same document. See part IV, bibliography and archives.

ship of Domrémy, so that he managed the castle and its domains and collected the rents.

His ability and honesty earned him such trust from those under his administration that on the occasion of several important trials, he was appointed procurator before Robert de Baudricourt, captain of Vaucouleurs. So, if he had lost his noble status by taking up manual work, he had on the other hand gained a number of prerogatives. Where is the humble peasant of the ludicrous legend?

In 1428, Jacques d'Arc was a notable whose position had picked up and improved miraculously in the previous twenty years—as soon as Joan the Maid had been entrusted to him by Jeanne d'Arc, first of the name, wife of his brother Nicolas. Similarly, several members of

Fig. 1

Armorial bearings of the d'Arc family, to be seen on a sculptured stone in the church at Ceffonds, and in old texts.

his family made an appearance at the courts of Charles VI or Yolanda of Anjou, strangely enough, after January 1408. Guillaume d'Arc, lord of Cornillon, was the King's chamberlain and councillor and the Dauphin's governor.* Raoul d'Arc was the King's chamberlain, before becoming a seneschal in Aveyron. In 1409, Yvon d'Arc, a bailiff† in the Grésivaudan, became the Dauphin's councillor.

The sum of these facts gives the fundamental premise that as soon as Joan was placed under the protection of Jacques and Isabelle d'Arc, the Dauphin of France was also entrusted to members of the same family, whose loyalty to the King, to the Houses of Anjou and Orleans—that is to say the Armagnac party—needs to be stressed.

Thereafter nothing in this affair comes as a surprise. The link

* Translator's note: Then Louis, Duke of Guyenne; born in 1397, he became dauphin on the death of his elder brother, but died in 1415 in suspicious circumstances. Having married the Duke of Burgundy's daughter, he had pro-Burgundian sympathies, and was probably poisoned by the Armagnacs.

† Translator's note: A bailiff, or seneschal, was an official representing royal authority with full powers.

would be the all-powerful Queen Yolanda, with her *éminence grise*, St Colette, Mother Superior of the Franciscan Order of St Clare. It is hardly surprising that after 1412, and possibly before that, Mother Nicolette, as she was often called, frequently went to Lorraine and Barrois. The reason usually given is that she was visiting the Clare convent at Toul, about 13 miles from Domrémy. It was certainly not the only reason. In Domrémy, everything links up perfectly; everyone knew each other and met up at the opportune moment. Isabeau's last two children, in particular, entrusted to the d'Arc family, were guided at an early age by Yolanda and the Third Order.

Joan was able to recognize her brother Charles VII at Chinon so easily because everything concerning him had been revealed to her by the *voices* assigned to the task . . . And when she said at Rouen: 'My mother is called Isabelle', without specifying the surname, it was no lie. She had the choice between 'of Bavaria' and 'd'Arc'.

6

CHILDHOOD AND ADOLESCENCE

> One would not have said this young girl had been brought up in the fields, but at schools, in the cultivation of letters.
>
> (Alain Chartier, secretary to Charles VII)

> She rode on horseback and could wield a lance like the best horseman.
>
> (Marguerite la Touroulde, *Trial of Rehabilitation*)

At birth, Jehanne had been baptized privately at the same time as Philippe. A few days later, acting on her lover's advice to separate from her daughter, Isabeau of Bavaria entrusted her to Jeanne d'Arc, Jacques' sister-in-law, whom she asked to see to the child's education and be her godmother. This accounts for the name 'Jehanne' given to her.

As soon as she had arrived in Domrémy, steps were taken by the d'Arc couple for the official christening of the little princess—for such was her title. For those who remain unconvinced, this was confirmed at the time of her entry into Orleans. One of the most important people in the town, Jacques Boucher, who was treasurer-general of the duchy,* had received instructions to provide lodgings for the Maid at each of her visits. He welcomed her by these astounding words:

'Noble Princess, how does my lady Jehanne?'

This expression, in court etiquette, denoted great respect. It seems highly improbable that Charles of Orleans' treasurer would dare to use the title of 'noble princess' lightly at a time when the town had not yet been liberated and Joan had accomplished nothing.

In accordance with royal custom, Joan was surrounded, at the

* Author's note: He was the brother-in-law of a rich tradesman and notability of Orleans called Jean Luillier. Luillier supplied the cloth for the splendid garments in the colours of the House of Orleans offered to the Maid in 1429, and had them made up. This was on the orders of Duke Charles. In 1439, Luillier was one of those to officially recognize Joan, by then Lady of Armoises. They are both quoted, together, in the town's account-books. Who was better able to recognize Joan than her draper and tailor?

baptismal font, by the otherwise abnormal number of at least four godfathers and five godmothers. Their names are known to us.

After this, to uphold the Maid's birthplace as Domrémy in the midst of the d'Arc family, is completely illogical and renders subsequent events inexplicably absurd. Descartes was wrong in saying that common sense is the most common thing in the world. Every kind of writer and historian, linked by the bond of enthusiasm, has expatiated on the subject. And yet, two fundamental facts, supported by a few unquestionable testimonies, corroborate and complete Boulainvilliers' text.

The whole problem lies in recreating the atmosphere of 6th January 1408. It was bitterly cold. Isabelle d'Arc was not on the point of giving birth, otherwise some villagers, at any rate, would have been on the alert. A sudden commotion, the arrival of the torch-bearers of royal escorts, the crowing of cocks and the unexpected appearance of a two-month-old baby—surely such a night should have stuck in people's minds. Nothing of the sort. Fifty years later, when they came to testify at the Trial of Rehabilitation, they obeyed the instructions to keep silent: no mention of these facts, not a word about the date!

Alone amongst the witnesses, two intimate friends of the Maid innocently revealed some of the truth. Otherwise, the reading of the statements brought the first crop of platitudes and generalities that were to embellish the fable.

However, Article VIII of the Trial of Condemnation drawn up by Bishop Cauchon marks the beginning of the trail which goes back to the Hôtel Barbette and the birth of 10th November 1407: 'At the time of a journey to Neufchâteau, in 1428, Jehanne was in about her twentieth year.' And not in her seventeenth.

Secondly, Monstrelet declares in his chronicle 'that in the aforesaid year (1428), there came towards the King of France at Chinon a Maid, a young girl aged twenty years or thereabouts, named Jehanne, who was dressed in man's attire'. And Jehan Chartier, one of the Court chroniclers, says the same.

Finally, who are in a better position to tell the truth than Joan's two best childhood friends? Isabelle Gérardin d'Epinal was born in 1405. Under oath, she said that Joan was more or less the same age as herself.

Hauviette de Syna was 45 in 1456, and so was born in 1410 or 1411. While all the other statements sound well-rehearsed, hers strikes a note of sincerity.

> I know this because I was often with Joan at her father's house and slept with her. She was my friend. But I do not remember her godfathers and godmothers, except by what I have heard, for Joan was older than me by three or four years, so it was said. That is all.

1410 minus three gives 1407.

It is because of this secret that the first years in Domrémy are obscure. The less they were talked about, the better. However, the true facts are surprisingly supported by a local legend which long prevailed in the Bar country and which is reported by the Franciscan Tertiary Bessonet-Favre.

> St Colette of Corbie, passing by Domrémy in 1412, left a mysterious ring in the young Joan's bed. This ring had been given Colette by St John the Evangelist once when he had appeared to her, as a pledge of the mystical union she was contracting with Jesus![13]

This mysterious ring was supposed to bear the same inscription as was painted on the Maid's banner at Orleans: Jhesus-Maria and three crosses—a rallying sign of the Franciscan movement.

Fig. 2

In fact, the mystery only existed for the masses, not for the Rouen judges. The ring's very precise political significance led to close questioning in 1431.

Continuing her narrative, Bessonet-Favre added that Isabelle d'Arc 'had been warned, some time after August 1412, that the Lord had specific and mysterious views on the child of benediction'. At first sight, one wonders what they could be. But the question of 'specific' views in 1412 is quite straightforward: in accordance with the customs of the nobility (and particularly justified in her case), the 'child of benediction' was destined to religious life. Joan was to be a Clare. It was the only life for a person of her rank who had to hide. Even after her adoption by the d'Arc family and her integration into this new milieu, the Maid's lineage excluded all other possibility. Marriage even to a nobleman was out of the question, as it would involve revealing the secret truth of her origins.

As for 'mysterious' views, there were some all right—after the Treaty of Troyes in 1420; after the defeat of Verneuil in 1424; and finally, after the siege of Orleans, in 1428. It is clear that the timing of the 'voices' coincided with these events. This is because, pushed by circumstances, Yolanda of Anjou, Colette of Corbie and Charles of Orleans slowly evolved a programme of national liberation, under the aegis of the Franciscan Third Order. Instead of dedicating Joan to a life of prayer, it would now be necessary to prepare 'God's emissary' for a public mission.

The year 1425 indeed corresponds both to numerous official visits of St Colette to Domrémy, and to frequent manifestations of the 'voices'.

Once the character of the mission had been determined, a broadly-based education would enable the Maid to bring about the predictions attributed to Merlin the magician, the Venerable Bede, and Hermine of Rheims: that the kingdom of France, lost by a woman (Queen Isabeau) would be saved by another woman (Joan); that a virgin from the marches of Lorraine would come to deliver Orleans; and the kingdom would be restored to its real master, Charles of France.

There followed three years of work, of secret meetings, of mysteries, and of voices real or from within—the latter brought on by the first.

Too many supporters of the legend have hastily concluded from Joan's remark, 'I know neither A nor B,' that she was illiterate. For them, her knowledge was gradually transmitted to her by divine intervention. Others however have adopted the more rational point of view that, like her childhood companions, she went to the small school at Maxey, in Lorraine, a short distance from Domrémy.

At home, Isabelle Romée used all her ability as a Tertiary to form Joan's noble character, and brought about in this daughter of a fallen woman the exceptional spirituality that marked her for life. That is why Joan, as a child, was little attracted by the games and dances enjoyed by her village companions. She often went off alone, to meditate, pray or receive some teaching at the *Bois-Chenu*, by the 'Fairies' Tree', though she also occasionally played with her brothers and the children of the lords of Bourlemont, who were related to the Joinvilles.

Although she categorically denied having kept the flocks owned by Jacques d'Arc, it would be a mistake to deny that Louis of Orleans' child took part in the daily work of the household. With her generous nature, which had evolved through education, Joan could hardly fail to participate in the work of the community which had adopted her. In any case, during her early years, she was in complete ignorance of her origins: for reasons of security, it was imperative that she should not be the object of obviously privileged treatment, though she was of course given a lot of attention.

7

CHARLES VII'S FIRST CORONATION

> Contrary to general opinion, deep religious faith does not sever family ties, or cause them to be forgotten.
>
> (Bessonet-Favre, *op. cit.*)

However nobody has ever asked objectively why Joan the Maid showed such indifference towards the d'Arc family, but such affection for the House of Orleans.

Give or take a few days, 21 years went by between her arrival at Domrémy and her departure from Vaucouleurs for the royal castle at Chinon. During these two decades, the Valois dynasty was in mortal danger of being excluded from power for good, while the kingdom of France slid irresistibly into the shadow of the English crown.

After the murder of Louis of Orleans by his cousin's retainers, the country sank deeper into a mire of unrest and merciless rivalries, while each of the opposing parties, the Armagnacs and the Burgundians, rapidly consolidated itself.

Completely disorientated, the Queen felt it politic to form an alliance with her lover's murderer. With the Duke's position strengthened in this way, Burgundy became a real 'state within the state'.

While the King fluctuated between madness and torpor, it was inevitable that the leaderless people should passively accept the idea of war with England.

Henry IV was too busy with civil strife on his own territory to take any interest in the claims that Edward III had put forward and was in any case a Lancastrian.

Despite these considerations, his son Henry V, who was ambitious and energetic, had no sooner succeeded to the throne than he changed policy and landed in France at the head of a powerful, well organized army. He started by taking Harfleur, in 1415, then two months later, crushed the élite of French knights in a frightful slaughter at Agincourt. The field of battle was strewn with over 10,000 dead. Charles Duke of Orleans was taken prisoner to London, where he was to stay for 25 years.

On the Burgundian side, John the Fearless seized the opportunity to march on Paris and take it. Supported by the corporation of butchers led by Jacques Caboche, he reigned there as absolute ruler for several years. In fact, from then on he administered the kingdom more or less alone, having exiled the Queen to Troyes, thereby keeping her and the unfortunate Charles VI under his control. French policy became no more than Burgundian policy.

Meanwhile, Henry also pursued his dream of domination, undisturbed, and little by little infiltrated the whole west, north-west and north of the country. Burgundy has so often been accused for allowing this that it is important to consider the facts objectively. John the Fearless certainly dreamed of dominating France, perhaps even of taking the crown. Nevertheless England's progress worried him enormously for a number of reasons, first and foremost economic.* Without being an Orleanist, he nonetheless favoured his own country. Also, the lawfulness of Lancastrian rule was strongly contested at the court of Burgundy. This veering of opinion in favour of the Valois is reflected in the following exchange:

Henry V: 'I would have you know that we shall have the daughter of your King, with France as a dowry and apanage.'

'By my faith, it is easy for you to talk,' John the Fearless promptly replied. 'Before you succeed in driving my Lord the King and myself out of the kingdom, you could well find it difficult to remain on your island.'

However, this improvement in Franco-Burgundian relations was nipped in the bud by the most unfortunate, dramatic turn of events, which reshuffled the cards yet again. In the course of an interview with the Dauphin Charles at the bridge of Montereau, John of Burgundy was in turn murdered by a faction of Orleanists led by Tanneguy-du-Châtel. Whether this was delayed revenge for the murder of Duke Louis, or political intrigue no one knew exactly. But either way the affair was particularly untimely as John had just confirmed his political leanings:

'By my faith, I know that I risk my life. But, if I return safe and sound, I shall take the people of My Lord the Dauphin with me, and together we will fight. Then, we will see who wins, Hannotin of Flanders,† or Henry of Lancaster.'

The result was that Burgundy now rushed into England's arms. The incident was so fraught with consequences that its genuine motives are still debated. It seems true to say that, while the murder was hardly to Charles VII's advantage, it was very much so to Henry's;

* Author's note: The Duke owned Flanders. If the English settled permanently in France, trade between Burgundy and Flanders would be jeopardized. He wanted to avoid this at all costs.

† Author's note: Nickname of the Duke of Burgundy.

indeed nothing could better serve his plans. In order to find the criminal, one must find out who profits by the crime.

Philip the Good succeeded to the title and a few months later Burgundy formed an alliance with England which was to last 15 years. It started auspiciously in May 1420 with the Treaty of Troyes, which Charles VI, who had laid all blame for the Montereau incident on the Dauphin, signed in his blind madness. It was the most damaging treaty in the whole of French history.

It is only fair to add, however, that even had he wanted to resist, he would have been unable to do so. A coalition had been formed between Henry V, Philip the Good and Isabeau—with Pierre Cauchon who was her secretary for several years, and whose intrigues already stretched as far afield as to Rome.

By the stroke of a pen, the status quo so laboriously maintained since the death of Charles V was upset. The act had such considerable political significance that repercussions went on till the Maid's Trial of Rehabilitation in 1456.

Indeed, the treaty's terms brought about a complete reversal of the situation and seemed to prove the future Charles VII's illegitimacy. On the one hand, the heir to the throne, henceforth known as 'the so-called Dauphin', was officially disowned and disinherited. On the other, Henry V, who had no legitimate right to the crown, was adopted then designated as 'the King of France's beloved son'. Precisely as he had announced to John the Fearless, he obtained, as a matter of course, the hand of the pretty Catherine, the legitimate daughter of Charles VI and Isabeau. Inheriting France, as he would on the death of the King, Henry, thanks to his wife, had overcome his handicap and re-established for his descendants the legitimacy which Edward III had claimed.

As to his territorial ambitions, Henry acted without delay in anticipation of his expected inheritance. Named regent of France, he first made a triumphal entry into Paris, then lawfully occupied the regions he coveted.

Faced with a situation which was going from bad to worse, excluded from his family, penniless and lacking regular troops, the 'so-called Dauphin' had but one resort. He sought refuge south of the Loire, in Berri, and became the 'little king of Bourges', supported only by the Armagnac party and by his mother-in-law, Yolanda of Anjou, the 'Queen of the Four Kingdoms'.

Fortunately for the safekeeping of the French crown, Henry V was the first to die, in 1422; Charles VI followed him shortly afterwards. In England, Henry VI, still in his cradle, succeeded to the throne, while his uncle John of Bedford was named Regent of France.

Bedford was a just and humane prince, and an excellent administrator. The source of much of this wisdom was probably his wife,

Anne of Burgundy, Philip the Good's sister, whom he married in 1423. It is of more than passing interest to know that Anne was a Tertiary of St Francis and that she had been trained by Colette of Corbie, all-powerful with the Burgundians. With this in mind, it is not surprising that the Duchess of Bedford showed such solicitude, even affection, for her cousin Joan at the time of her trial.

The Armagnacs, meanwhile, had suffered defeat after defeat since the Treaty of Troyes. Although Charles had had himself crowned King of France at Poitiers on his father's death, in 1422, doubts persisted more than ever about his legitimacy, so much so that he ended by having serious doubts himself.

It made Yolanda react, though she was in fact far less anxious to save the crown of a son-in-law she despised than to protect the possessions of her son Louis III of Anjou. With the help of her faithful followers and the support of Charles of Orleans in London, she devised a political operation with a religious base which would restore unity to the Kingdom of France and thereby protect Maine and Anjou.

8

EDUCATION

> Truth and honesty are but one. It is to be hoped that no one will claim, forgetting this axiom, that the legend is better than history!
>
> (Edouard Schneider, a Catholic writer, in *Jeanne d'Arc et ses Lys*)

> This young girl is of perfect elegance. She has a manly bearing and speaks little, showing admirable prudence in all her words . . . She is endowed with a soft woman's voice, eats little, and drinks wine even more moderately.
>
> She takes pleasure in fine horses and arms, holds men-at-arms and noblemen in great esteem.
>
> She detests social intercourse, and gatherings, readily sheds copious tears, and has a lively face. She shows both in the bearing and handling of arms so much endurance and strength that she can remain fully armed for six days and nights, without respite.[14]

There exists no better description of Joan the Maid as she marched on Orleans. This standard of perfection was the result of the concerted efforts of all those who had a hand in her education. The ground was admittedly exceptionally fertile—only one of the élite 'chosen by birth' could have acquired the necessary attributes so readily, forming a synthesis between the traditional qualities of her background and the simple humanity of those who brought her up. She understood, and assimilated perfectly, everything from the teaching of her voices, of her 'counsel', to the lessons in weaponry and horsemanship.

In another field, so excellent a Tertiary as Isabelle d'Arc was eminently capable of preserving her adopted daughter's sensibility and developing in her a balanced and moderate mysticism, despite the enormity of the task and its pitfalls.

Only masters such as Bertrand de Poulengy and Jehan de Novelompont were capable of imparting the essentials to her and making her into the brilliant horsewoman, the 'knight' described by Boulainvilliers.

What then is the significance of this portrait? Was Joan a humble shepherdess miraculously transformed in a matter of weeks into a knight of the Grail? It seems an unbelievable hypothesis.

Joan reveals her identity by the sum of ancestral qualities she had inherited; also by her education, the prerogative of the well-born; finally, because she received from her voices, or advisers, the political and religious data indispensable for the accomplishment of her mission.

She spoke about this superior and secret 'counsel' at the Trial, when mentioning the candles she used to place by the image of St Catherine. There was nothing very mysterious about it: 'I do it in honour of God, of Our Lady and of St Catherine who is in heaven. And I make no distinction between St Catherine who is in heaven . . . and the one who reveals herself to me!'[15]

Does this not clearly signify that there are two St Catherines, one in heaven, the other very much on earth?

As far as St Michael is concerned, there is no possible disagreement, because of a statement made by Joan. The 'Archangel' was the first voice she heard, when she was thirteen. The fact is of paramount importance, verifiable as much from religious sources as from the dates of important events which led to his appearance.

Joan: 'When I was thirteen years old, I had a voice from God to help me govern my conduct . . . I think it came on behalf of God!* The first time, I was very fearful. The voice came at the hour of noon. It was summertime . . . in my father's garden. After I had heard it, I understood that it was the voice of an angel . . . But, for today, you will not get out of me the form in which the voice appeared to me . . .'

Joan revealed later on in the trial that the 'angel' Michael, true to tradition, was fully armed like a knight. Providing further confirmation of her date of birth, their first meeting when she was thirteen took place soon after the Treaty of Troyes: the political motivation of an emissary *de par le roi du ciel*, the motto of the Franciscan Order which was inscribed on most of its banners, then becomes obvious.

Thereafter, so the legend says, 'visions and voices' continued to manifest themselves. Joan often left her playmates to go to pray and meditate by the Fairies' Tree or in the *Bois-Chenu*—the oak wood. In the fifteenth century, the Fairies' Tree retained its symbolism and importance as a meeting place. It was *Abre Dominarum*, the 'Abre' of the 'Mistresses' or 'Ladies' of the Third Order.

Just as St Louis reputedly rendered justice under an oak tree, these meetings of Druidic inspiration took place near symbolic oaks. Hence the misunderstanding of the word 'Abre', usually translated as 'tree', as though it came from the Latin *arbor*. The confusion arises of course from the place of these meetings. The truth is that Abre forms part of the Celtic tradition. One of the four cosmogonic circles representing the Universe, Abre or Abred corresponds to

* Author's note: Does she sound so sure? Is this answer not ambiguous?

destiny or *knowledge*—a meaning which has apparently been found as far away as Rumania, among the Celtic tribe of the Dacians.[16]

So, when Joan went to the *Abre Dominarum*, it was to receive the traditional teaching corresponding to the circle of knowledge, or 'third stage in the initiation of Ladies'. Politically, it signifies a great deal.

As at the Oak Wood, the voices that Joan the Maid heard here were perfectly terrestrial. In the course of secret meetings, the Celtic movement,* supported by the Third Order, worked on a plan of regeneration, not only of France, but of the whole of the West.

I am not trying to prove the non-existence of 'mystical dreams or talking apparitions', especially as in the light of modern research, their reality to the individual—depending on his emotional state—takes the discussion onto scientific ground. But I consider it imprudent to attribute to the supernatural an unbelievable accumulation of interventions in the life of the heroine.

New evidence, now of considerable proportions, is continually being discovered confirming the role of co-ordination played by Colette of Corbie in the social questions raised at this time by the Celtic and Franciscan movements. Joan was highly emotional as evidenced by her frequent tears, and in this she took after her father Louis of Orleans who was well-known for his gifts of foresight. However, apart from this, she had a sound and well-balanced personality, quite unlike most victims of uncontrolled extra-sensory perceptions. If she was mystical, her mysticism was enlightened and not in the slightest pathological.

Who then could do such an excellent impersonation of St Michael?

A terrestrial figure like the other 'saints' in their religious functions, Brother Michael was simply a knight belonging to the movement of liberation. Was not to come 'on behalf of God' or 'in the name of the King of Heaven', to use the Franciscan motto, one and the same thing?

Brother Michael was a first-rate psychologist and arrived at noon: in the brilliant sunshine, his armour was blinding—sufficient to impress the least impressionable of little girls!

A quick look at the terminology currently used in the fraternities of St Francis immediately replaces Michael, Colette, Catherine and Margaret, in the normal order of things. As in most religious orders and Third Orders, the affiliated were called, not by their surname, but by a Christian name accepted at the time of their profession of faith. Franciscan tradition furthermore ruled, particularly in the Middle Ages, that this name should be preceded by the word 'saint'.

* Author's note: See part V for the links between the orders of knighthood, the Order of St Francis and the Celtic tradition, which had considerable influence in the Middle Ages. It is indeed still very much alive, both in France and England.

So, instead of Sister Margaret or Brother Michael, it was St Margaret and St Michael. Joan, who detested lying, naturally conformed to this practice.

'Joan of Arc used these expressions, then currently used in Franciscan fraternities, to designate living personalities.'[17]

On the other hand, all that was rational in this child endowed with acute sensibility was the result of instruction. Her humanitarian education prepared the ground for the intense mental turmoil triggered off in her by the revelation of her true birth, the misfortunes still afflicting her family and the suffering of 'her kingdom' lacerated by war.

But from the first, contemplative grief gave way to enthusiasm and gradually the sense of a sacred, irrevocable duty, emerged as the voices relayed the urgency of the situation.

Have we not all, to a lesser degree, felt that fire within, and surpassed ourselves on occasion, such as on a battlefield or in the Resistance?

However, to envisage in 1420 the idea of a mission at some point in the future did nothing to counteract the disasters which continued to strike the country. In any case, the 'counsel' did not know what form the mission would take and probably thought in terms of a manifestation of a religious character.

The year 1424 saw another, serious defeat at Verneuil, where the French Army was crushed by John of Bedford. The kingdom was more than ever in the hands of the occupiers.

Shortly after this, in September 1425, Yolanda of Anjou officially met St Colette at Puy-en-Velay, on the occasion of a big pilgrimage. A political plan with a religious framework was formulated. Joan was no longer to be a Clare, but would instead be entrusted with the task of galvanizing the movement of liberation.

From this date, St Colette travelled more frequently to Barrois and Lorraine. The legend notes at this point that the 'voices' became more regular. Although Mother Nicolette's headquarters were in Besançon, she was often in Toul, Neufchâteau, and Domrémy.

The 'child of benediction' was instructed and trained for riding and the handling of weapons. It is likely that she already knew how to write, but it was not a matter of importance: most lords had secretaries, and signed more easily with their seal than their pen.

What we do know for sure is that she had a perfect knowledge of the secrets and of the agreed signs: like Colette, she would draw a cross as a rallying sign on her letters.

Three years were sufficient to complete the necessary preparations. The Maid was then admitted as a novice to the convent of

Neufchâteau, then received as a Tertiary in that of Vaucouleurs. She arrived dressed all in red, with her hair long. She left the small town for her mission dressed in grey, her hair cropped.

While the liberation of the kingdom was secretly taking shape, England felt weary, even though within an ace of victory. It was the price to pay for a hundred years of fighting. Conscious of France's exhaustion, the English command decided to bring the war to a quick close. Despite opposition from Bedford who would have preferred Angers, the English armies invested Orleans in the late summer of 1428, with Burgundy's full consent. It was a tactical error, as was soon obvious. The English had previously undertaken to keep their hands off the Duchy of Orleans. Their attack on the town provoked a reaction in both France and England, where, of course, Charles of Orleans was in captivity.

Immediately informed by her friends, Joan rushed to Vaucouleurs. In a first attempt with Robert de Baudricourt, she demanded to be escorted to Chinon. But the Captain, having received no orders, showed her the door and even threatened to have her exorcized.

Unflustered, she tried again, this time with the support of the Third Order. Baudricourt now hesitated, pending the arrival of the royal messenger.

Meanwhile, Charles II Duke of Lorraine expressed a wish to meet the future heroine and invited her to his castle at Nancy. If he had not been informed of the project by Yolanda of Anjou* it is tempting to ask why he should be interested in a little peasant girl, considered half mad by Baudricourt.

For her first official reception, she expressed such wisdom in her answers and showed herself such a brilliant horsewoman, that the Duke did not have a moment's hesitation. Won over by her qualities he spontaneously offered her a splendid black horse and four golden francs, surprising when one considers that the humble shepherdess had as yet accomplished nothing.

Shortly after her return to Vaucouleurs, Collet de Vienne, the royal messenger, arrived. A surprising fact is that on the very day he had left Chinon for Barrois, Dunois, the Bastard of Orleans, announced to the townspeople that a Maid was coming to deliver them, as the prophets had predicted.

Between 15th and 23rd February—current authors are not in agreement on this point—the clandestine journey began. Under the leadership of Novelompont, Poulengy and Collet de Vienne, the small cavalcade crept through Burgundian and English lines. To

* Translator's note: His daughter Isabelle of Lorraine had married Yolanda's son, René of Anjou, who inherited Lorraine at the Duke's death in 1431. The Duke's wife, Marguerite of Bavaria, was a cousin of Queen Isabeau.

(*left*) Dress given to Joan by Charles of Orleans—vermilion velvet knight's gown embroidered with gold nettles and trimmed with beaver. Joan was about 5 feet 2 inches tall.

(*right*) Dark green velvet *huque* with gold nettles and trimmed with marten, crimson velvet jacket. The wristbands are chequered black and silver.
(Sketches by Jacqueline de Sermoise based on illustrations in Adrian Harmand's *Jeanne d'Arc, ses costumes, son armure*)

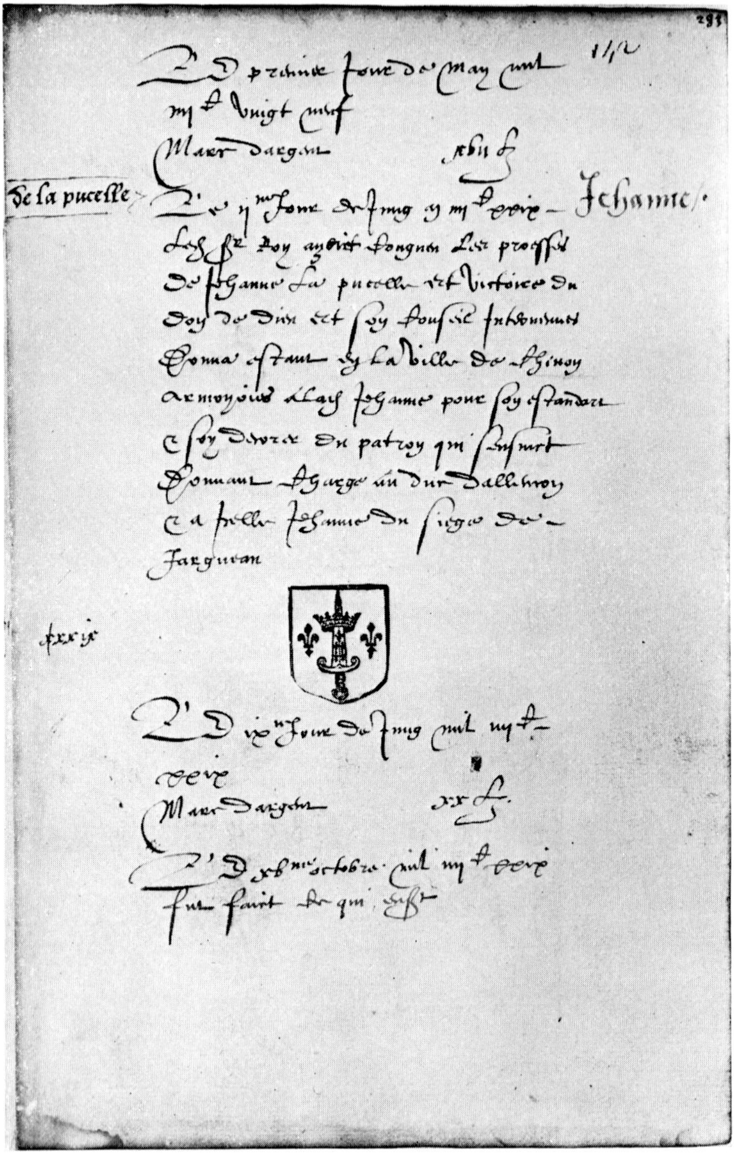

Royal grant of arms to 'The Maid . . . Jehanne', made on 2nd June 1429. The d'Arc family is not mentioned in the document. (Bibliothèque Nationale)

avoid coming face to face with the enemy, they marched by night and slept in the daytime in Franciscan missions.

Once the Loire had been crossed without incident, the party penetrated into French territory, and halted at Fierbois where Joan awaited final orders before leaving for the King's residence.

NOTES TO PART I

1 '*Quoniam, si mentiri non liceat, licite tamen veritas occultatur, loco et tempore, fictione bona, aut verborum circumlocutione . . .*' Latin text taken from *Procès de Jeanne d'Arc*, Jules Quicherat

2 *Editions H. Herluison*, Orleans 1894

3 In *La Guerre de Cent Ans*

4 *Histoires d'Amour de l'Histoire de France*, Guy Breton. Press Pocket, Paris 1965

5 From *Yolande d'Anjou, reine des Quatre Royaumes* (1933)

6 In *Jeanne d'Arc était-elle la soeur de Charles VII?* (1962)

7 Prediction by Engélide, daughter of the king of Hungary, attributed to Jehan Bréhal at the time of the Trial of Rehabilitation. Quoted by

8 Jean Bosler, *op. cit.*
Jeanne d'Arc à Domrémy by Siméon Luce; also, Boucher de Molandon

9 *Journal du Bourgeois de Paris* (Bibliothèque Nationale) an anonymous fifteenth-century chronicle. A recent English translation is available, published by Oxford University Press as *A Parisian Journal, 1405–49*

10 *Chroniques de Enguerrand de Monstrelet*

11 *Histoire de Bourgogne*, eighteenth century (Bibliothèque Nationale)

12 See *La Famille de Jeanne d'Arc était-elle originaire d'Arc-en-Barrois*, by the Chanoine de Longueville. Also the chapter on Burgundy in *L'Etat de la France* (see bibliography)

13 Bessonet-Favre, in *Jeanne d'Arc Tertiaire de Saint-François*

14 Letter of Boulainvilliers, quoted by E. Schneider, *op. cit.*

15 *Les Procès de Jeanne d'Arc*, Raymond Oursel, a recent translation of the proceedings of both Trials into modern French. It is quoted extensively throughout this book

16 *Cf.* Gérard Serbanesco, *Les Celtes et les Druides*

17 Bessonet-Favre, *op. cit.*; also writing under the pseudonym Francis Andrée in *La Verité sur Jeanne d'Arc*

II

THE BEGINNING OF THE SAGA

9

THE RECEPTION AT CHINON

From the very first days of the Maid's arrival, there were secrets . . .

(Jehan Bréhal, Grand Inquisitor of France, at the Trial of Rehabilitation)

It was because of these 'secrets' that the legend had to claim Joan had been sent by God to raise the siege of Orleans and crown Charles VII at Rheims. And, according to eighteenth-century historians, those were the only two points of her mission.

It is not generally known that the Dauphin had already been crowned officially at Poitiers in 1422. Joan was nevertheless adamant that a second ceremony should take place at Rheims because of its long-standing significance. Rheims had been the ancient spiritual capital of the kingdom of the Franks. As a result of the pacts made under Clovis, the anointing in the cathedral was not only of religious but also of political importance.*

The idea had been given to Joan by perfectly terrestrial advisers, as soon as the purpose of her mission had been specified. In these times of deep faith, the direct intervention of the divine in human affairs would, moreover, allow the most important State secrets to be hushed up for a very long time.

While Joan was being prepared for her mission, it was sufficient for the 'voices' to stress this two-fold necessity for her to persevere until she had reached her goal: Rheims, the only place of consecration for the kings of France—*Gesta Dei per Francos*, in other words, the will of God accomplished by the Franks.

Sunday 6th March 1429 is the date generally proposed by tradition† when the small cavalcade, guided by Collet de Vienne, arrived

* Translator's note: Clovis was a Catholic convert and was baptized in Rheims in 496 by the bishop St Rémi.

† Author's note: 23rd February is advanced by some authors, with more justification.

In any case, in the Middle Ages, the year began at Easter, which means that 6th March 1429 was in reality 6th March 1428. In the same way, the arrival at Domrémy on the night of Epiphany was still in 1407, and not yet 1408. However, I have used the modern system of dating throughout, and for convenience's sake have made the necessary adjustment of medieval dates.

in Chinon towards noon. The official reception in the castle was not to take place then, and Joan had to be patient for three days before being presented to the King, in front of the whole court assembled for the occasion. However, the wait was in all likelihood organized by Yolanda of Anjou. The Maid was decently housed in the *hostel* of a 'most honourable lady', who was the widow of Gustave de Coigny.

In the early afternoon, as soon as they had finished eating, Poulengy and Novelompont went off to see Gérard Machet, the King's confessor. The significance of this visit hardly needs to be stressed. As well as being chaplain to Charles VII, the Bishop of Carcassonne was one of the promoters of the movement started by the Third Order. A friend of Gerson and Gélu,* he was a very influential figure: the confidant of Queen Yolanda. That is why, at the end of the meeting, His Grace lost no time in taking his visitors to see the King. 'The King asked for the gentlemen who had come in the company of Jehanne, and had them questioned in his presence,' narrates the *Chronique de la Pucelle*.

The tenor of this conversation has nevertheless always remained a mystery. But Robert de Baudricourt was certainly mentioned by Novelompont:

> Sire, here is a letter that the said lord sends to you. There are secret things about her that no-one must see other than you.[1]

Thus, according to Novelompont, there were 'secret things' for the King's ears only. He thereby revealed that the Captain of Vaucouleurs was completely involved in the affair. He was again involved seven years later as he was a cousin by marriage of Robert des Armoises.

At the end of the conversation, Charles VII seemed so satisfied that he made immediate arrangements for the two messengers, as well as their companions, to be lodged during their stay in Chinon at the Treasury's expense, until such time as they left for Orleans.†

Alone with his confessor, Charles then considered the first item on the agenda: his sister Joan's reception at Court.

While this wait proved exasperating to the Maid, in her impatience,

* Author's note: Jean Gerson, Chancellor of the University, was a prominent figure at the Council of Basle and a promoter of the Maid's saga. He was a friend of Jacques Gélu, Archbishop of Embrun. Another promoter of the saga, Gélu wrote a memoir entirely in Joan's favour, which was read out at the Poitiers interrogatories.

† Author's note: The following is a receipt dated 21st April 1429, signed by Guillaume Charrier and Ragnier (accounts of the receiver-general of Finances and of the treasurer of War):

'To Jean de Metz, the sum of 120 livres for expenses incurred by him and by others accompanying "The Maid" [who, it is to be noted, is not called "d'Arc"] . . . granted by letter of the said King . . .'

we now have proof that these moments of inaction were spent on apparently secondary, but equally important, matters.

The first was that she went over to the castle to see Marie of Anjou, the King's wife and Yolanda's daughter[2]—this before any official meeting. It was certainly on this occasion in the Queen's apartments that she met Charles VII for the first time: the fact was confirmed at the trial: 'The voice had promised me that the King would receive me on my arrival . . . I went into the King's presence at the castle.' (Oursel) It certainly explains her miraculous recognition of the King two days later.

At the same time, the delay made it possible to condition opinion. For while the people usually accept the supernatural, the lords of this world, through pride, often resist any new or unusual ideas as a matter of principle. There were moreover at court some very sensitive feelings, unsatisfied hopes and mere rules of protocol which needed careful handling. To present Joan in public without any preliminaries would have been most risky and would have begged numerous questions. What, for instance, was a peasant girl doing in the midst of some of the most noble families?

Joan's mission started at this point so that it was imperative for her to win over the Court and those who would have to follow her. It would otherwise fail even before it had begun. For its part, the King's Council was far from favourably disposed for a number of sound reasons. But Charles was cunning and pretended to have his hand forced, agreeing that a Master of Petitions, Simon Charles, should go to find out from Joan what she intended doing.

She was furious at first and tried to throw him out. But he was a clever man. She calmed down, and finally revealed the aims of the mission.

After he had returned to the Council, opinion was still divided. But after Machet had deployed all the resources of his eloquence, the Orleans faction won: God's emissary would be received by the King, in front of the Court.

On the morning of the reception, the Maid was advised by her 'counsel' to keep on her simple travelling clothes. In this attire, she could not fail to create a sensation and inspire the sympathy which would instantly consolidate the foundations of the legendary version of the story.

It was already late in the day when the Grand Master of the King's Household, accompanied by lords of the Royal House, came to fetch her. It was a real delegation led by Louis of Bourbon, Count of Vendôme and prince of the blood: an escort usually reserved for the most illustrious personages.

The castle of Chinon at this time had all the appearances of a formidable fortress. The three main buildings were isolated by internal moats. The most important was the King's and the court's *logis*. Further west, the famous Tower of Coudray stood in the front of the castle of Bousset, which included a chapel dedicated to St George, and built by the Plantagenets of the Angevin period.

The large state room used for the ceremony was adjacent to the royal apartments. Seven steps gave access to this great hall measuring 90 feet by 50, consisting of three cradle-vaulted sections. The walls were covered with superb tapestries depicting mythological, Biblical and hunting scenes, all the work of the best artists in the kingdom.

Everything was done on a grand scale that day to receive the humble, inspired peasant-girl from Barrois, unknown three days previously. The room, with its panelling and tapestries, was lit by fifty torches, while the assembly of 300 people shimmered in their velvets and brocades. Ladies wearing *hennins* vied with lords in the splendour of their richest robes and in the costliness and brilliance of their jewels.

Charles of France, in all this, concealed himself in the crowd of courtiers. There was nothing to distinguish him other than his sullen expression and his unpleasing physique. He was very simply dressed, as always, in a tunic of green velvet belted at the waist. Standing at a short distance from the throne, he leaned languidly against the great mantelpiece, and chatted with his favourites: La Trémoille, the Count of Clermont, the Lord of Gaucourt, his chamberlain, and of course, Gérard Machet.

The door opened, and the two heralds sounded a trumpet call. The assembly fell back and crowded together at the back of the room.

Joan entered with Bourbon-Vendôme at her side, then advanced alone, 'proud and of noble bearing'. She wore a short dark grey tunic over her black doublet. Her black hair was covered with a hood.* A murmur of stupefaction went round the room.

'But . . . it's a boy!'

She then threw back her hood and made the obeisance demanded by etiquette, like a page of good birth. 'She made all the bows customarily made to kings, as if she had been nurtured at court,' says the chronicle.

At the sight of this unusual-looking young girl, dressed all in black, and like a page, the colourful crowd whispered. As Jeanne d'Orliac writes,

> One must imagine this court as being like any social set, with its members used to conventional rites they think of as immutable. Complicated, absurd rites, regulating the way of greeting, of walking, of

* Author's note: The colour of Joan's hair provides additional proof of her parentage: Isabeau of Bavaria had jet-black hair.

> being silent . . . a sort of intransigent and inflexible freemasonry, which excludes anyone who does not bear its signs.

Where did she learn these signs. these complicated rites, who taught her them? The second miracle was that she was accepted instantly.

While Charles remained in the midst of his courtiers, Joan the Maid walked up to him without a moment's hesitation.

'May God give you a good life, Gentle Dauphin,' she enunciated in the best French as she bowed.

Utter amazement greeted her words. This shepherdess had not even granted the King his title. And how did she know the language of the court when she should be talking a Meuse dialect, a peasant patois?

As though wanting to mislead her, Charles pointed to the Count of Clermont and said: 'There is the King.' Without so much as a look at Clermont, Joan turned to face her brother and genuflected in front of him.

Joan: 'Gentle Dauphin, you are the King, and none other.'

Charles: 'Who are you? What do you want?'

Joan: 'Joan the Maid is my name and God sends you word by me that you will be sacred and crowned in the town of Rheims, and will be Lieutenant of the King of Heaven who is King of France.'

Seemingly surprised, and tongue-tied, the Dauphin decided nevertheless to pursue the conversation alone with his sister. He took her over to a window recess where the rest of their talk remained muffled by the hangings. In silence, the courtiers studied from afar the sovereign's changes of expression.

First, the Maid seemed to ask a favour and obtain it. She then launched forth into a lengthy narrative, to which the Dauphin paid only polite attention. But then, slowly, his features expressed surprise. He asked a question to which Joan gave an animated answer. Charles smiled, amused and sceptical.

The exchange continued for all of two hours. Then, after a short silence, the tone changed. Her words became stressed with so much conviction that the King's normally expressionless face flooded with tears. He spoke in turn, questioned her, and then seemed so happy that he gave her the royal embrace in front of the amazed audience. The transformation in this introverted and indifferent man was completely unexpected.

Numerous questions have remained unanswered on the well-worn subject of the secrets, the revelation of which brought about this change. The only explanation is to be found in Charles' personality. The key to this was lack of self-confidence. But in less than two hours, Joan had turned the tables and made of his questionable legitimacy an indefeasible truth, 'in the name of God'. And, inspired by the Christian ideal which motivated her, she did not shirk any sacrifice:

to save the dynasty, she took upon herself the burden of their mother's adulterous lovemaking.

The first secret to be revealed was the ring taken off Louis of Orleans' hand on 23rd November 1407. 'Gripping Baudricourt's message to her bosom, she hid other more precious and more secret missives,' wrote the Franciscan Bessonet-Favre.[3] She showed her brother Charles this proof which he had never seen, nor owned, but which asserted that he was truly the son of Charles VI.

A second revelation then swept away all remaining doubts. 'The Virgin liberator of the Orchard of lilies and of the mystical gardens of the Church of God'[3] now announced to her newly-found half-brother the Third Order's spiritual and financial support.

The proof of this lay in the second ring brought by Joan, which Colette of Corbie had deposited in her cot in 1412. It was engraved with the conventional signs of affiliation to the fraternity—Jhesus Maria and three crosses.

It was at this point she had become emphatic and stressed the financial help that the Dauphin, now King 'in the name of the King of Heaven', would have to return, at least by his attitude towards his people.

Self-confidence and money were indeed the two driving forces capable of causing this sudden change in the 'little King of Bourges'. He who did not have a penny to his name would now be able to raise fresh troops.

The two of them then left the window-recess and Joan faced, with complete composure, the stares of the courtiers who crowded round. She spoke to the King once again, in a loud enough voice so that her words of victory were heard by all.

'I tell you, on behalf of *Messire* (the King of Heaven), that you are the true King of France, and son of a King.'

The reception was over and the game won. Charles gave orders to Gaucourt for the Maid to be installed immediately in the castle. The Tower of Coudray, the Templars' Tower, was to be her residence.

10

HONOURS

For a proud Prince . . ., not for a simple shepherdess . . .
(Martin Le Franc, a fifteenth-century poet)

As soon as she was settled in the Tower of Coudray, Joan became the object of special attention. Gaucourt, the King's chamberlain, started to select a few essential people to serve her; Gaucourt was also Charles of Orleans' confidant and often went to London for this reason.

As first lady, he chose Anne de Bellier, born 'de Maillé', of a high noble family. Her husband, Guillaume Bellier, had recently accompanied Gaucourt to London and there paid a visit to Charles of Orleans. Gaucourt then nominated Louis de Coutes, a page of high birth, for whose education he had once been responsible, after the death of Louis' father. In his lifetime the latter had belonged to the Orleans faction, being Duke Charles's chamberlain, captain of Châteaudun, and a former governor of the counties of Blois and Dunois.

In short, the 'Maid's household' consisted right from the start of a completely trustworthy guard. In a similar way, the same people appeared and disappeared throughout her whole life, depending on circumstances.

At a time when the rules of heredity retained their full force, the respect that was shown her, the caprices that were tolerated, are inexplicable if the eminent people around her had neither knowledge nor awareness of her origins.

The following day, after an invitation to the King's mass, which was a signal honour, she was invited to the private apartments. Thereafter something happened every day which cannot be explained in the legendary version.

Two days after the reception, in the middle of a colloquy with Charles VII, an elegant and handsome young man entered unannounced. The King introduced him as 'My cousin d'Alençon'. Without any further preliminaries, Joan, suddenly radiant, spoke to the young duke in words fraught with meaning:

'You are most welcome. *The more of us there are*, *of the blood royal of France*, *together*, the better it will be.'*

Though this will disappoint supporters of the legend, the warmth of Joan's welcome caused no surprise. Like herself, d'Alençon was of royal blood. Not only was he a descendant of Saint Louis, but he had married a daughter of Charles of Orleans.

It was the first time that Joan had met her nephew. Their kinship explains the affectionate terms she lavished on him after that—'my gentle Duke', 'my handsome Duke', etc.

Apart from its various strange features, this first stay at Chinon was marked by a scene so fantastic that its authenticity seems questionable. But the Franciscan Bessonet-Favre, one of those who described it, received the approval of the Bishop of Saint-Dié, in Lorraine, Mgr Alphonse Gabriel, such approval being tantamount to an *imprimatur*.[4] It took place one day when Joan walked into the Council chamber, where Charles VII, Jean of Alençon and La Trémoille were assembled. Interrupting the conversation, she strongly pleaded with the King to resign his kingdom in her favour.

Alarmed and embarrassed, Charles did not know how to answer. He finally assented and summoned notaries. 'Oh, have no fear,' she said, 'I will not make bad use of it.'

'Take note, Gentlemen, in good and proper form, of the donation that Charles of Valois makes to me, Joan the Maid, of the Kingdom of France.'

The deed was drawn up on the spot and read out in the presence of the flabbergasted d'Alençon and La Trémoille. Joan then designated the Dauphin with one hand and exclaimed:

> There, My Lords, is the poorest knight of the kingdom. But far be it from me to keep for myself such a fine gift.
>
> I am but a mandatory of Messire the King of Heaven. Most willingly, I hand over the Kingdom into the hands of the Almighty, King of Kings, Lord of Lords . . .
>
> Write on, Gentlemen.

* Author's note: A translation of *Plus on sera ensemble du sang du roi de France, mieux cela vaudra*, which is in turn a translation of the Latin text of the Trial of Rehabilitation, *Quanto pluris erunt insimul* . . .

This is usually rendered into English literally as 'the more they shall be together'. But the Latin text itself is a translation of what Joan said in French. It seems inconceivable that she said '*Plus ils seront*' . . .; it sounds like an off-stage exclamation in an edifying play.

There are two other possibilities, *Plus nous serons* and *Plus on sera*, which mean the same. They would both have been transcribed as *erunt*, the first because it was usual to write records in Latin in indirect speech (*dixit quod* . . .), the second because the French indefinite pronoun *on* is always translated into Latin by the third person.

See Quicherat & Goelzer's *Dictionnaire français-latin*.

A new clause was written. Joan kneeled to pray, then rose:

> In the name of God Most High, of Messire the King of Heaven, my Judge and Sovereign Lord of whom I am the humble messenger, I, Joan the Maid, invest Charles of Valois, son of Charles, sixth of the name, with the Kingdom of France, to keep him in command as the usufructuary and good lieutenant of the King of Heaven, only master and sovereign owner of the said Kingdom.
>
> Write, Gentlemen, and append the signatures of the Dauphin and of My Lords who are witnesses, before I sign myself.

The scene had a devastating effect for its symbolism was obvious to all. The power of the Franciscan movement was suddenly apparent, with all its latent forces. The potency of the motto 'in the name of the King of Heaven' annihilated any kind of claim from the English or Burgundians. Divine intervention had now entrusted the kingdom to the Dauphin, recognized as legitimate by an act authenticated by notaries and in front of witnesses.

Once the deal with Heaven had been completed, time-honoured tradition of the kingdom of France prevailed and an intimate dinner took place. There were four guests: Charles VII, Joan the Maid, d'Alençon and La Trémoille.

The likes of it had never been seen before and many courtiers were intensely annoyed. An intruder to the court, a country girl, a nobody, having a tête-à-tête supper with the King, and speaking to him in a familiar way in the presence of a prince of the blood and of one of the favourites? Few of them had ever dreamed of such an honour.

On her side, Joan was immediately conscious of her exact status. Contrary to what is generally thought, she only wore her page's outfit to go out, especially for riding which she adored as her father Louis of Orleans had done.

A horsewoman of high calibre, she vied in skill with her nephew, the 'gentle Duke'; their greatest pleasure was to run a-tilt, together, at manikins. At the first engagement, d'Alençon was amazed by her skill and grace and could not resist giving her on the spot his charger as a gift.

Anxious to keep up proprieties, Charles had asked her to stop wearing her travelling attire in the castle. To make up for this, magnificent dresses were tailored for her, mostly in masculine fashion, in the finest cloths. It is known that she loved them. But of course these court dresses were only known to her entourage.[5] The people had always remembered her as being dressed in dazzling armour or in the austere clothing subsequently perpetuated by the *Imagerie d'Epinal.**

Meanwhile, a number of people were trying, secretly, to divide the

* Translator's note: Broadsheets produced at Epinal from the end of the eighteenth century.

court. They could not tolerate the King's and his favourites' attitude. What right had this 'peasant-girl', who looked like a hermaphrodite, to be lodged like a princess of the blood and served by ladies of illustrious name?

For the courtiers who were jealous of Joan, these questions remained unanswered. But the man who had voiced them was completely in the know: it was her worst enemy, Georges de La Trémoille, conceited, venal, and a hypocrite. It inspired no confidence in him to know that a kinsman of his was Philip of Burgundy's adviser.

With her intuition, Joan doubtless sensed the duplicity of her brother's favourite. Each time she brought up the subject of liberating Orleans, a secret force thwarted her plans. As always, there were interests at stake. For history informs us[6] that during the siege of the town, the English army received arms and supplies from France, through the agency of Burgundy and the connivance of the two La Trémoilles. It was imperative to make money, by whatever means. So, until the delivery of supplies had been effected, the King's favourite did all he could to delay the plan of liberation. He did so well that Charles VII decided to make Joan appear before a commission of enquiry to judge whether the enterprise was opportune, and the heroine capable of bringing it to success.

It was to the King's advantage, for if the Maid passed the test, both their positions would be the stronger. The town of Poitiers was chosen, and summonses were sent out to learned doctors in theology.

Meanwhile, as it was all taking time, Joan accepted an invitation to stay a few leagues away from Chinon, with some 'ladies of the blood royal'. There is no obvious reason for it other than the fact that they were relations of hers. Jean d'Alençon's mother and wife treated her as an equal—in fact the intimacy which was instantly established between them soon evolved into affectionate respect on their part, an indication of Joan's higher birth.

The young Duchess went so far as to plead with the Maid to guard over her husband's life in the course of battle.

'Have no fear,' replied her cousin, 'I shall bring him back safe and sound, as he is, or in a better state than he is.'

11

THE BOOK OF POITIERS

This creature who was in the form of a woman, whom they called the Maid. Who was it? God only knows!
(*Journal du Bourgeois de Paris*)

The Lord Archbishop of Rheims, Regnault de Chartres, Grand Chancellor of France, was nominated to preside over the special commission convened at Poitiers. The highest Church authorities loyal to the King were to pronounce judgment 'in all good faith' on the operation's chances of success, and on the Maid's qualities. Thus the conference consisted partly of a super aptitude test and partly of the checking out of a promotional campaign at state level. There was also the mystical aspect which would make it possible to affirm to the world that, under God's direction, an authentic virgin was carrying out his plans.

This did not prevent the maximum effort being made on a terrestrial level, and 'God's emissary' arrived in Poitiers accompanied by the King and the élite of the court: Yolanda of Anjou, of course; d'Alençon and numerous lords, including Joan's instructors in knighthood from Domrémy, Novelompont and Poulengy.

On this occasion, the Maid stayed at the Hostel de la Rose, a very fine private residence rented by Jehan Rabateau, advocate-general of the King. It was not a fortuitous choice, for, while the lord of Gaucourt was the Duke of Orleans' confidant, Rabateau was his adviser. And it has been suggested, though without categorical proof, that he too belonged to the Third Order.

One would have expected the questioning to take place in one of the state rooms, of which there must have been a number. Yet preference was given to the Hostel de la Rose, no doubt because the 'secrets' would be better kept there. So, every morning, the numerous participants, including d'Alençon, went round to Rabateau's. In this connection people have wondered why Jehan d'Alençon should have listened so assiduously and without flinching to the answers of a 'village-girl of sixteen'!

It was certainly worth his while. It is known that from the start Joan was in turn proud, subtle and mocking, with a sense of humour which was less appreciated at Rouen two years later.

At Chinon, questioned on her age, she had answered the King: 'My age adds up to three times seven.' At Poitiers, questioned on her knowledge, she said: 'I know neither A nor B, but I know how to work and pray.' This was an esoteric answer the symbolism of which is discussed in IV, §32.

It was at Poitiers that Joan's arrogance revealed itself for the first time. Doctors in theology were in no way spared her insolence.

'What language did your voices speak?' asked Brother Seguin, who had a harsh voice.

'Ah! Sire, better than yours!'

'Do you believe in God?'

'More than you!'

These are baffling replies from a so-called humble and gentle shepherdess. And how is it she could express herself in the best French, in a Meuse patois, and apparently also in the ancient Celtic language, the *idioma gallica*?[7]

It is usually said that in the course of the Poitiers session, two minor brothers were sent to Domrémy, to hold an enquiry. There is in fact no proof whatsoever of this, but what is verifiable is that as soon as they returned, the members of the commission changed their attitude towards Joan. This fact was indeed confirmed by Joan herself: 'Then, they ceased worrying me,' she said at the Trial of Condemnation.

The answer to this further enigma is provided by Bessonet-Favre. The two monks had been to consult one of the most eminent Franciscan theologians of the time, Jean Gerson. Former Chancellor of the University of Paris, Gerson had taken refuge in Lyon and was preparing the Council of Basle. He was in constant touch with his friend Jacques Gélu who had considerable influence at the French court. The two monks hastened back to Poitiers to communicate Jean Gerson's advice to the assembly and thereby to sanction the start of the operation: for Joan, he said, was God's agent; and she fulfilled the prophecies.

But the eminent doctor added for the benefit of his colleagues:

> It must finally be appreciated that this Maid and the men-at-arms who rally to Her *should not abandon the ways of human prudence.* It behoves them to do whatever the situation necessitates, and it is important that *they should not rely on God more than is necessary.*

These words show that, like all truly great prelates, Gerson had, along with his faith, a sense of realism. They also invalidate the usual modern conception of men in the Middle Ages as being the naive victims of superstitious beliefs.

After reading out his report, the two monks handed over four documents.[8] The first concerned the King and the princes of the blood royal. The second, the King's and the country's military force. The third was about the religious aspect and the people. And the last concerned the Maid.

'What did these ancillary documents actually say?' asks Bessonet-Favre, 'for they are unfortunately lost.' There is however no need to look very far. Together with the 1429 interrogatories they form part of the famous *Book of Poitiers*, about which I shall give some important information in Part V. Meanwhile, if it is wondered why there was no trace of the *Book of Poitiers* at the trial of 1431, any more than at the Rehabilitation, 25 years later, the answer is that it disappeared immediately after Charles VII's coronation because it was a state secret. It was learnt with amazement at Poitiers that Joan was the King's sister, a fact liable to cast doubts on his legitimacy, and so to be forgotten at all costs. The slightest scandal could compromise the whole Valois dynasty and their succession to the throne.

Despite the importance of Gerson's report, the inquiry was not yet over. There remained the matter of the Maid's virginity which formed the keystone of the mystical edifice. The medieval belief maintained that witches were never virgins, so that a woman's virginity proved her lack of commerce with demons. If Joan was found to be a virgin, she could only be inspired by God. She therefore had to submit to this intimate examination, but her rank created a serious problem. An ordinary girl, even one sent by God, could have been examined by doctors or midwives. This was out of the question for the King's sister. And so the honour fell to the highest lady of the realm, Queen Yolanda, the King's mother-in-law. She presided over the examination, assisted by the wife of Raoul de Gaucourt, governor of Orleans.

In his statement at the Trial of Rehabilitation, Jean d'Aulon narrated that,

> The Maid was seen, visited and secretly regarded and examined in the secret parts of her body.
>
> After they had seen and looked at all there was to look at in this case, the Lady [Yolanda] said and related to the King that she and her ladies considered her to be a true and intact virgin in whom there was manifest no corruption or violence.

And for a very good reason. In 1431, Doctor Delachambre, who attended Joan during the Trial, gave more precise medical details. His diagnosis was confirmed by Abbé Villaret's description of Joan in his preamble to the saga, which provides further proof of his knowledge of secret documents:

> Rustic life had fortified her naturally robust body even more. She had only the exterior of her sex, without suffering from any of the infirmities which are characteristic of its weakness.

This disposition of the organs would necessarily have made her imagination more active.[9]

This unquestionably establishes that Joan was *gynandromorphous*,* was called 'The Maid', and that she necessarily remained a virgin all her life, even after her marriage. That is why there was no possibility of any error when she was canonized as a virgin.

Once the feasibility of the mission had been established and Joan had satisfied all the questioners, the Assembly of Poitiers consummated its wish for military operations to commence by the provision of the necessary finance.

Sufficient consideration has never been given to the question of how Charles VII found the necessary funds. It has been suggested that the Queen of the Four Kingdoms paid for the Orleans épopée. This is true enough, but where did she get the money from? The simple answer is that it came out of the collections of the Franciscan *clerks minor*. 'There was the favourable decision of the bankers of . . . the Third Order, amongst others, who agreed to lend the money needed for the resumption of fighting.'[10]

* Author's note: *Gynandromorphism* is partial pseudo-hermaphroditism in a woman with secondary male sexual characteristics, such as a join of the *labia majora* (*Dictionnaire des termes techniques de médecine*, Garnier et Delamare, Ed. Maloise, Paris 1955). Joan's malformation, which is described with astonishing precision by the Abbé Villaret, must not be confused with *androgyny*, a very different case by definition.

12

THE SWORD OF LOUIS OF ORLEANS

I also give you
These golden spurs
In order of knighthood . . .
(Words of Charles VII in the *Mystère du Siège d'Orléans*)

Joan had won her first, moral, victory and all would now follow her.

Usually close-fisted through lack of money, Charles VII became quite liberal for a time and gave orders for the 'military household' of the 'Most Noble Maid'[11] to be formed immediately.

La Trémoille selected the best equerry for her. Jehan d'Aulon, who was devoted body and soul to the King and to the House of Anjou, was the confidant both of Yolanda and of the Bastard of Orleans. He became Joan's most judicious adviser.

D'Aulon came from a long line of Languedoc nobility going back to the seventh century. In 1416, he had been nominated head of Charles the Mad's bodyguard, and a few years later had married the daughter of the Provost of Paris, Juvénal des Ursins. By this time, therefore, he was already a mature man, and was considered to be a most wise, honest and capable knight. His experience in battle was invaluable to Joan, providing a continuation of the military education given her by Poulengy and Novelompont at Domrémy.

On leaving Poitiers, a general meeting was fixed for Blois: 'There, the King summoned a great number of men-at-arms to take some supplies to the said town of Orleans.' As we know, Charles VII had no money and the convoy was in fact financed by the Queen of Anjou, who was in turn subsidized by the Third Order.

During the journey, Joan stopped off in Tours, where she visited the wife of one of Yolanda's private advisers. It was here she obtained the last of her equipment, and received at the royal Treasury's expense the most splendid gifts that a captain could hope for.

First of all, Yolanda gave her a luxurious suit of armour. Made to measure in tempered steel, it weighed no less than 25 kilos and cost

100 *livres tournois.** This was exorbitant compared to Charles of Orleans' armour which had cost 83 *livres*. It seems hardly justified for a 'shepherd-lass' sent by the party of the poor; apart from some sort of protection, armour was the luxury of lords. At that time it was conspicuous evidence of both wealth and power.

Armour was the product of skilled craftsmanship, each part being designed and constructed by an armourer specializing in that field and who might be living anywhere in Europe. After that, the different parts would be assembled by a local arms merchant.

But Joan's armour was an exception, for it was made by a local armourer specializing in brigandines, and not, as would have been normal for this type of armour, in Milan by a maker of side-arms. In price and luxury, her armour was comparable to the Rolls-Royces in gold or silver given to some maharajahs in the era of British rule.

In similar style, Joan was given twelve superb horses. To form an idea of what this represented, nowadays one must think in terms of the same number of luxury cars.

The day after her arrival in Tours, Joan was visited by Pierre d'Arc, accompanied by an Augustinian monk, Jean Pasquerel.

'Jehanne,' her foster brother said to her, 'we bring you here a good Father. When you know him, you will love him well.'

'I am pleased to receive Master Pasquerel, for I have already heard much about him.'

This visit was not fortuitous. The chaplain had come straight from Puy where there was that year a pilgrimage attended by all Franciscan authorities.

So, when she had acquired armour, twelve horses and the best equerry, Joan's military household was completed by the addition of a chaplain—as for a prince of the blood. The Maid of Orleans now lacked only the symbolic attributes of her military status: a banner, a sword, a hatchet and spurs.

The symbolism of her various banners was complex. According to the legend she had four of them. The first was of white wool embroidered with silk. Painted by the Scottish artist Hamish Power, its field was silver, spangled with golden fleurs-de-lis:

'On one side, the shield of France, held by two angels. On the other, the inscription *Jhesus-Maria*, with three crosses, and a picture of God holding the world in his hand.'

Writing about the various inscriptions on her banners, the Reverend Father de Grèzes revealed in 1895 that the abbreviation I.H.S. was

* Translator's note: This was money struck at Tours which was worth 1/5 less than Paris money, the *livre parisis*. Cotgrave's Dictionary of 1611 gives the exchange rate as 2 shillings sterling for the *livre tournois* and 2½ shillings for the *livre parisis*.

one of the esoteric symbols used by early Christians as a means of recognition. It signified both Jesus and *Ichthus*—the Greek for fish* —thereby indicating the start of the 'era of the Fishes' linked with the coming of the Saviour.[12]

The power of these symbols made the political and other opposition encountered at first melt away, as will be seen.

A number of incredible tales have circulated on the subject of her first sword; for instance, that it had been the sword used by Charles Martel† at Poitiers, which, preserved by some miracle, was concealed behind the altar of the little church of St Catherine of Fierbois. The 'voices', as usual, disclosed the hiding-place to Joan and on her orders it was immediately unearthed.

The truth is much simpler, but much more revealing. 'The sword was under the earth, all rusty. There were five crosses engraved on it,' said Joan at her trial (fourth public audience).

The point is that five crosses were one of the esoteric signs of the Celtic clan opposed to the policy of the English monarchy, in particular following the conquest of Wales by Edward I.‡

The sword had belonged to Du Guesclin and been left by him to Louis of Orleans. In 1407, after the Duke's assassination, Clignet de Bréban, one of his captains, took care of it. At his death, Bréban insisted that the sword should be placed on his tomb in the church of Fierbois.

Told of this by someone in her entourage—by Gaucourt perhaps —the Maid was impatient to retrieve the symbolic sword used by her father.

At the same time as orders were issued for the companies to regroup at Blois, the royal chancery disseminated a news-letter, as a means of propaganda, all over the country. We have a good idea of its tenor because there are extant 16 lines of Latin, to be found in Dauphiné, Alsace, Brittany, at Cambrai and even at Mayence.

> A virgin whose feminine limbs are attired in masculine fashion, proposes *on the orders of God* to rescue the King of the fleurs-de-lis who has been prostrated, then to destroy his baleful and impious enemies, in particular those who are at the present hour in front of the town of Orleans, crushing it under their siege. And if men have enough heart to join the war and follow the armies that the *white Maid* is now preparing,

* Translator's notes: The fish was used as a symbol of Christ because *ichthus* is made up of the initial letters of *Iesous Christos Theou Uios Soter* (Jesus Christ, Son of God, Saviour).

† Charles-Martel crushed the Saracens at Poitiers in 732, thereby saving Western Europe from Muslim conquest.

‡ Author's note: See part V, last chapter, on the Franciscans and the movement of Celtic inspiration.

have faith that the perfidious English will succumb to death . . . for the French will overwhelm them *with this feminine Mars.*[13]

The last few lines of this manifesto, which was inspired by Machet and Yolanda of Anjou, are typical of the Third Order's style:

> . . . Then the war shall end. Then *shall the ancient alliances be reborn.* All shall rally to the King who will administer justice to them and grant them a fine peace. In this way, none of the *English enemies bearing the leopard* will dare to call himself king of France . . .

Why were those who 'bear the leopard' mentioned specifically? There were at that time in England two sides: those who bore the leopard and those who did not.

At Blois the Maid was in the midst of eminent war-lords making ready to lead the troops—men such as Marshal Boussac, the Lord of Culant, admiral of the fleet, Etienne de Vignolles, known as La Hire, Ambroise de Loré, future provost of Paris, all of whom were to play a large part in the saga. In particular, there was Gilles de Rais, the richest lord of the time, who owned numerous castles. He arrived with men-at-arms from le Mans and Anjou and with a dazzling suite of pages, musicians and singers. His ostentatious luxury already provoked jealousy, perhaps even the King's.

Deep friendship blossomed between Joan and Gilles, born of their mutual admiration. It has never been known whether it was simple affection or secret love. But several years later, immediately after her liberation, the Maid of France rushed to see her great friend, who was then already on the road to ruin because of his prodigality.

Finally, just before leaving Blois, Charles VII made Joan another gift as a token of his gratitude for what she had already done for the crown.

> I also give you
> These golden spurs
> In order of knighthood
> As though you were a good knight
> Ordained in battle.
>
> (*Mystère d'Orléans*)

To know what these golden spurs represented, and to whom they were always given, go to the *Galerie d'Apollon* in the Louvre, where similar spurs are exhibited.*

* Translator's note: They were the exclusive privilege of the high nobility.

13

FIRST MIRACLE AT ORLEANS

In view of the sudden change in the wind, it seems to me that Jehanne and her military exploits were of God rather than of men.

(Dunois, at the Trial of Rehabilitation. Oursel.)

On the morning of 26th April 1429, riding her black charger, Joan the Maid led away the King's troops. Her armour, golden spurs, and hatchet bearing a crowned 'J', glinted with golden and silver rays in the brilliant morning light. Beside her, Louis de Coutes proudly carried the deeply symbolic banner. Behind them rode Gilles de Rais, La Hire, the Admiral de Culant and also Baudricourt 'who had just arrived from Vaucouleurs'.

At Orleans, after the recent defection of Burgundian troops, the odds against the English were three to one. There were 30,000 people besieged in the town. Dunois, the Bastard of Orleans, had been governor since the Count of Clermont's defeat at Rouvray.*

Three days later, the army of 7,000 men with the Maid at their head, arrived about six in the evening on the south bank, with supply convoys.

On the opposite bank, in the British camp, there were 5,000 men who had been on a war footing for many months already. They consisted of both mobile troops and troops defending the forts.

Until shortly before the arrival of Joan's army of liberation, the English had been supported by a Burgundian contingent, and the morale of the besieged had been at rock-bottom. But Philip the Good had suddenly decided to withdraw his troops from the siege 'after which the power of the English was much enfeebled'. His decision certainly came about as a result of the breakdown of negotiations with Bedford; and it was possibly also the dawn of an agreement with France.

It was a momentous decision for which the Duke had ample motivation. For, pushed by his Council, the Regent had announced his intention, in the event of victory, which indeed seemed assured, of joining the Duchy of Orleans onto the English crown. Worried by

* Author's note: This was the famous battle 'of the herrings'. The French had wanted to intercept an English convoy of provisions.

this possibility of annexation, the Duke of Burgundy decided that the best course was to remain neutral and thereby to a certain extent aid the French cause.

There is a completely objective description of the situation in a chronicle of the siege written by Antonio Morosini, a Venetian Councillor. He was merely an observer, and as a tradesman was anxious for the return of peace. Here is a summary.

The town was situated as today on the north bank of the Loire. On the Sologne bank there were several English forts controlling the river as well as all southern approaches. The west and north sides of the town were ringed by a close chain of forts extending perhaps to a quarter of the circumference of the town. This left a large space open on the Montargis side. To the east, the forts of Saint-Loup and of Saint-Jean-le-Blanc guarded each bank of the Loire.

There were therefore only two possible ways of access: the river, were the wind favourable, and the Montargis road, which, until shortly before, had been used to send supplies into the town.

We know that Joan took to military excursions straightaway; that at the head of her troops, she was brave, indefatigable, sometimes foolhardy. But, as a result of her upbringing, she also revealed herself to be far more human than this and more noble in her ideals. The broad outline is suggested in a Franciscan text:

> The treasuries of all the fraternities of France had received orders to distribute to the tertiaries . . . money to enable them to cross, without receiving any wages and without looting, all those parts of the sacred kingdom that strategy demanded should be fields of battle.[14]

Together with the description of a few engagements, this text reduces the liberation of the town to more rational proportions. Victory was assured by essentially psychological conditions. At Orleans, there was no holding to ransom or pillaging, and it in no way resembled any of the traditional massacres such as Agincourt.

The military command, in its wisdom, therefore took no notice of the still inexperienced Joan who with knightly enthusiasm wanted to attack the English directly on the north bank. Respecting Gerson's advice, Dunois decided that it would be best to approach by the south bank, and arrive opposite Chécy. From there, the safest way of entering the town would be by the Loire which at this point filled a moat under the drawbridge of the Bourgogne Gate. The nearest enemy forts were about two kilometres away.

This plan had in fact been prepared some time, for Yolanda of Anjou had warned the besieged: '. . . That they should make preparations to send as many boats as possible to the bank, before the island of Chécy, so as to receive all manner of provisions which would be brought to them.'

On the evening of Joan's arrival, the watch towers proclaimed that she and her army had settled in their quarters on the Sologne bank, opposite the *Isle aux Bourdons*.

Unfortunately, a contrary wind made it impossible for boats from Orleans to go upstream at that moment. However, a rowing boat finally managed to leave the quay, and made its way with difficulty. When it had finally moored by the liberators, Dunois, the Bastard, disembarked, went towards Joan and said, bowing low:

'How does my Noble Lady?'

A surprising way to greet her for this was a form of address only used between eminent personages. After the battle of Agincourt, for instance, Henry V addressed Charles of Orleans, who had been defeated and taken prisoner, in this way: 'How does my handsome cousin?'

Used to address the Maid of Orleans,* by an illustrious member of the royal house, 'Noble Lady' assumes its full meaning. With a degree of haughtiness, which indicated her superior birth, she called peremptorily to her half-brother:

'Are you the Bastard of Orleans?'

'I am he, and I rejoice at your coming!'

There is no better description of their first meeting than that given by Dunois in 1456:

> She then replied to me: 'Did you counsel that I should come by this bank and not go straight to where Talbot and the English are?' I answered her that it was I, and others wiser than I, who had given this counsel, thinking to do best for the success of the operation. Then Jehanne spoke these words:
>
> 'In God's name, the counsel of the Lord our God is safer and wiser than yours. You thought to deceive me but it is yourself you have deceived, for I bring you the best succour that captain or town ever had: succour from the King of Heaven . . . Not out of love for me but because God himself, in answer to the prayers of St Louis and of St Charlemagne, has taken pity on the town of Orleans and will not suffer that the enemies have the body of the lord of Orleans [Duke Charles] and his town.' (*Trial of Rehabilitation*, *op. cit.*)

The problem of the liberation of Orleans is clarified in the following quotation from a book which nevertheless supports the legend:

> It appears that Franciscan complicity in the ranks of the English army favoured a number of Joan of Arc's victories, such as Orleans, Beaugency, Patay, victories that were militarily incomprehensible, miraculous.[15]

* Author's note: She is indeed entitled to this appellation. There is in any case a bronze statuette of her, which is prior to 1440 and bears the engraved inscription *La Pucelle Dorliene* (or *Dorliens*).

I shall establish this in the following chapters.

> In an instant [continued Dunois] the wind which was contrary, and had prevented the boats laden with supplies from going upstream, suddenly changed and became favourable. The sails were hoisted forthwith, and I sent off the boats . . . From that moment, I placed great hope in the Maid, more so than before. I implored her to consent to cross the Loire and enter Orleans where she was awaited with impatience.
>
> She made a few objections, arguing that she did not want to abandon her people . . .
>
> Then Jehanne joined me, holding her standard in her hand . . . La Hire crossed the Loire with us, and together we entered Orleans.

D'Aulon also gave his account:

> At once the Maid embarked with the witness [himself] on the said boat. And the rest of her people went back towards Blois [to return only on 4th May]. And, with my said Lord of Dunois and his people, they entered into the city, safely and without injury. (Oursel)

The wise and honest Jehan d'Aulon made no mention whatsoever of the miraculous changing of the wind, because, in all likelihood, he knew about some of Nature's laws.

It seems incredible that the supernatural has invariably been called to explain an event which favoured the French and went against the English, yet such is the case.

The explanation, which is simplicity itself, can be found in any primary school textbook: namely, a climatic law whereby at certain times of the year, in certain regions usually near the sea, the wind can, at dawn and at dusk, change very suddenly—morning and evening breeze.

As at the time of embarkation it was after six o'clock, on this spring evening of 1429, the wind merely conformed to a law of nature.

14

FAITHFUL FRIENDS OF ORLEANS

They welcomed Jehanne the Maid as though honouring Duke Charles himself.

(A fifteenth-century Chronicle)

When dealing with facts it is not enough simply to describe them; they must be compared in meticulous detail and their political causes elucidated.

Dunois was commander-in-chief at Orleans, whereas Joan hardly ever had any say in the matter. His statement at the Trial of Rehabilitation was incompatible with the common sense consistent with a reliable professional soldier. He stressed the miraculous side of events to a far greater extent than the priests themselves. His motive at this time, when he was King Charles's confidant, was his imperative desire to ensure the security of the dynasty from which he had so far obtained the grestest honours.

The meeting had just taken place on the left bank of the Loire when, at dusk, for purely climatic reasons, the wind changed in a favourable direction. The vessels sailed up the river with ease, and moored upstream and downstream of the port of Boucher. A first consignment was then loaded.

> Fully laden, the boats set off again for Orleans, and let themselves be carried by the current up to the quay of the Bourgogne Gate . . . from there, the corn and other provisions were transported to Gilet Guéret's granary. (G. Pesme, *op. cit.*)

Putting an end to all debate on the subject, there are two receipts which add to the extensive evidence that 'the water-way was the only route taken to enter the town that day'.

The first mentions the consignments of 29th April and 4th May: 'Paid to Gilet Guéret, for the rent of his granary where part of the corn brought from Blois *on both occasions* has been stored and distributed . . .' The other mentions the second delivery only: 'Paid to Jehan de la Rue for expense incurred at his residence by the boatmen who delivered the corn brought from Blois, on the fourth day of May'.[16]

Once the convoys had been safely despatched, the Bastard was at last successful in convincing Joan that it was imperative to enter the town. Meanwhile, the royal army would return to Blois.

There then occurred something which seems surprising considering the customs of the time and the heroine's piety. Just as she was about to embark, she separated from her chaplain for several days. 'On the orders of Jehanne, I returned with the priests and the banner to near Blois,' said Brother Pasquerel in his statement at the Trial of Rehabilitation.

The fact that Joan should abandon her director of conscience on the eve of battle would be an enormity had it not hidden a major secret of the saga and thus proved that everything had been organized well in advance.

While the Maid kept her personal standard, decorated with fleurs-de-lis, the priests were charged with escorting the banner, the emblem which would rally both French and English affiliates of the Third Order.

Towards eight o'clock, by which time it was dark, the boat at last drew up by the Bourgogne Gate on the north bank. Mounts were saddled—for Joan, a white horse; it was the only white horse she rode in her life.

The cavalcade then crossed the drawbridge, and entered the town, into the midst of a crowd ecstatic with hope and faith, and fascinated by the gleaming armour in the glimmer of torches. Head bare, with her hair short cropped,* the Maid pranced in the lead, flanked by Dunois, who had lifted the visor of his plumed helmet.

Behind them came the rest of the escort: Louis de Coutes, carrying the standard, Novelompont, Poulengy and Baudricourt; Pierre and Jehan d'Arc brought up the rear.

> There was marvellous press to touch her, as well as the horse which she rode; so much so that one of those who carried the torches came so near to her standard that the pennon took fire.

It was Joan herself who put out the fire by squeezing the cloth in her hands,

> which the men-at-arms and the burghers of Orleans held to be a great marvel. They accompanied her the whole length of their town and city, giving her a festive welcome, and with great honour all led her . . . to the *hostel* of Jacques Boucher, who was then Treasurer to the Duke of Orleans, and there she was received with great joy.

* Author's note: Franciscan style. But it was moreover essential for wearing a helmet. Some portraits of Philip the Good give an excellent idea of it.

From this moment, Joan was adored by the people of Orleans for the rest of her life. And when in 1439 she returned under the name of Jehanne des Armoises, again dressed in a suit of armour and accompanied by Pierre d'Arc, they could not fail to recognize her. And they would have rejected indignantly any adventuress who dared pass herself off as the Maid, while being unable to show her wounds or her unique skills in horsemanship . . .[17]

Jacques Boucher, like his brother-in-law Jean Luillier, was one of the town notables—as Jean Jacoby has said, a bourgeois 'who included armorial bearings in his seal and liked to be deferred to as to a lord'. Owning 14 houses which he rented out, his coffers were full of gold; and through him passed all the pensions, including the thousand *livres* a year granted to the Lord Bastard.

It is most doubtful whether Duke Charles would have instructed his treasurer to provide lodgings for Joan, and then reimbursed his expenses, if she had not been a relation. The King himself stayed at Jacques Boucher's house every time he passed through Orleans.[17]

The torch-lit cavalcade arrived at the *Annonciade*, and helped by d'Aulon, the Maid dismounted. By the entrance, Boucher, his wife Jeanne Luillier, and their daughter Charlotte, all bowed low: 'Noble Princess, how does our Lady Jehanne. Be you most welcome . . .' Once Dunois had taken leave in order to return to his own residence, they all entered the house.

In the great room lit by a comforting log fire, a long table was drawn up facing the hearth. Joan sat in the place of honour; but tired after a day spent in 50-pound armour, she was unable to do justice to the meal: a little bread and wine was sufficient for her. As a cup-bearer prepared to serve her, Boucher suggested that she might like some Paris wine.

'We are in Orleans, I shall drink the Orleans wine.'

'Take care, my Lady, our wine is the headiest in France,' warned Jeanne Luillier.

'Have no fear, I take it only with water.' And she filled half the silver goblet with water, 'and put five or six pieces of bread in it, which she ate, and took nothing else to eat or drink'.[18]

Once they had all eaten (without forks, for the King alone used this 'refined' object!), most of the escort left the *Annonciade* for the house of Thévenon de Bourges. Only Joan's equerry and page remained. Joan went to her room, and slept in the double bed beside the ten-year-old Charlotte Boucher, for it was customary to sleep, naked, with a companion.

The next day, the first problems materialized. Joan rose early, attended mass, then later in the day went to see Dunois. In her impatience to fight and 'drive out' the English, she fully intended assuming control of operations. But the Bastard, who bore full responsibility for the military command, refused categorically. He wanted to wait till the army of Gilles de Rais arrived.

Disappointed by this unexpected setback, Joan flew into such a rage that in the end she extracted permission from her half-brother to address letters of summons to the enemy. The last one she sent was threatening:

> You, men of England, who have no right in this Kingdom of France, the King of Heaven commands you and sends you word by me, Jehanne the Maid, to leave your forts and retire to your own country; if not I shall give you such a harrying that no one will ever forget it.
>
> That is what I write to you for the third and last time, and I shall write no more . . . for *such is my good pleasure.*
>
> Jhesus-Maria signed: Jehanne.

Sent over by an arrow into the English camp, the note provoked immediate, ribald response:

'It is news from the Armagnacs' whore!'

The concluding words of the letter are revealing. 'For such is my good pleasure' is of course the royal formula. She certainly did not learn it by tending her flocks, and in any case would have had no right to use it.

Several days of inaction until the reinforcements arrived seemed intolerable to Joan. She spent the whole day on horseback, visiting every part of the town, 'and the people could not weary of seeing her. They all acclaimed her as though honouring Duke Charles himself.' Here the chronicle bordered on indiscretion, very nearly disclosing in unambiguous terms the kinship between the Duke and the Maid.

In the almost idolatrous enthusiasm generated by the presence of the closest relation of their 'beloved lord', although she had accomplished nothing yet, the twelve procurators or notables of the town held an official reception in Joan's honour, a token of respect and loyalty to the House of Orleans. Amongst these notabilities, some names are familiar: Jacques Boucher, called Largentier, Jean Luillier, Thévenon de Bourges. Another should be remembered: Jacquet Leprestre.

The corollary of this last fact should be revealed at this stage: ten years later, this same Council, including the four people just mentioned, organized six receptions and dinners in honour of Joan the Maid of France, by then Lady of Armoises.[19]

15

THE LIBERATION OF ORLEANS

One would have said they [the English] had all had their hands tied.

(Alain Chartier, a contemporary poet)

She was most pious towards God and the *Holy Virgin* . . . She would say to me, when we were in a place where there was a convent of Mendicants, that she should be reminded of the day on which the *clerks minor of the Begging Friars** received Communion, so that she could receive it with them, according to her habit . . . Indeed she received the sacrament of the Eucharist with the clerks minor of the Begging Friars . . . (Statement of Pasquerel at the Rehabilitation)

Thus, Joan's 'host' consisted almost entirely of affiliates. Furthermore, so Bessonet-Favre informs us, even lords left off wearing their family armorial bearings and had embroidered, painted or engraved, similar ones to the Maid's.

Of course, these 'similar armorial bearings' were not Joan's personal ones but those of the Third Order. It is known that she never officially bore her coat of arms, and moreover, according to Quicherat, the document of the royal grant of arms could not be found for a whole century.

As can readily be verified, the surrender of the English was largely explained by the full use of signs and symbols.

For example, between Orleans and the coronation, lead medals symbolic of the mission's double purpose were distributed on a large scale among the tertiaries and sympathisers. On one side was engraved 'the King of Heaven holding the world in his hand', the sign of the brotherhood of peace which united the Celtic movement and the Franciscan fraternities. On the other, was engraved Joan's coat of arms. This provides further proof that it belonged to the Maid of Orleans alone, and was not granted to the d'Arc family. As will be seen in the next chapter, it represented her mission as well as her royal birth.

* Author's note: The Franciscan friars minor.

These medals were soon caused to disappear, being either thrown into the Seine or destroyed: for some people, they were far too eloquent; for others, they were tantamount to treason.

The advance of the 'talismans of victory' had been very easy. Doubtless influenced by his wife Anne, who was a former disciple of St Colette, John of Bedford had granted freedom of movement to pilgrims who wished to go to the Great Jubilee at Notre-Dame-du-Puy-en-Velay, on 25th March. That year, Good Friday fell on the same day, and most affiliates must have attended. On this occasion, by the two symbols of the Incarnation of the Word and of the Redemption, the pilgrimage stood for 'the death of a world and the birth of another'. This last part was one of the secret objectives of the religious movement. It was enough to ensure a well-patronized pilgrimage and in particular a good hearing for the announcement of Joan's mission.

That is why she had exclaimed fervently: 'The men-at-arms will battle, and God will give them victory.' It indeed came to pass: with the minimum of bloodshed, the extraordinary mystical élan worked as well at Orleans as it did later on the road to Rheims.

On the eve of arrival of the reinforcements and the Maid's 'host', there was a great procession through the town in which she took part.

Patently, no angle was overlooked: a complete arsenal of psychological weapons was brought into play, to boost the military advantage given by an effective force double that of the enemy.

The battle of Orleans has frequently been described and is of little interest in itself, apart from a small number of significant incidents, which alone are worthy of mention.

The first incident occurred at the arrival of Falstaff, a rather enigmatic figure, and revealed the Maid's authoritarian temperament, once again indicating her rank.

On 4th May, after the second food convoy had been unloaded, the Lord Bastard met his half-sister and told her that the English leader was about to arrive with supplies for the besiegers and was then near Janville. It is incomprehensible that the following words, which are a part of history, should have been attributed to a simple country girl speaking to the first captain of the kingdom:

> Bastard! Bastard! In God's name, I command thee that as soon as thou knowest of the arrival of the said Falstaff, thou shalt make it known to me. For, if he pass without my knowing of it, I promise thee I will have thy head taken off.

Where is the gentle inspired girl, eyes turned heavenwards, of nineteenth-century iconography?

Nevertheless, history confirms that the 'child of benediction' only took a modest part in the command of operations in 1429. This does not detract from her fantastic personality, or her courage: on the contrary, it was outside Orleans, on the last day of battle, that she was seriously wounded by an arrow beneath the shoulder.

As for the battles themselves, the almoner Pasquerel stressed the mystical nature of the means used sufficiently for the truth to become obvious.

> . . . I returned to Orleans, through Beauce, in company of a strong army, and *always with the priests and the banner*! We did not suffer any hindrance.
>
> When Jehanne learnt of our arrival, she came out to meet us, and *together, we entered Orleans without impediment*, bringing in provisions under the nose of the English . . .
>
> It was truly a wonder, for all the English, with their great might and number, their arms and their training, could see the King's people, passing in weak numbers, under their eyes.
>
> They could see and *hear the priests singing*, and *me with them*, carrying the banner . . . And yet, nobody from their side budged. They attacked neither the King's people *nor the priests* . . . (Oursel)

The standard and the banner were therefore a decisive factor in the outcome of each battle, preparing the ground for the retreat of the normally strong and well disciplined English army. Indeed, very little was sufficient to bring about the raising of the siege and withdrawal: for an apparently insignificant incident suddenly disrupted English cohesion.

The French had attacked a redoubt of the powerful fort of the Tourelles, and towards the end of the day William Glasdale—or 'Classidas' as the French, including Joan, called him—was obliged to leave his command post, to direct in person the defence operations. He crossed the drawbridge, joined his men and found himself without cover and in danger of being surrounded.

At that moment, the Frenchman Jean Poitevin guided a barge full of resins and burning material under the drawbridge, then jumped into the water. The bulwark caught fire, burned through and collapsed.

As night had fallen by then, Glasdale decided to return and galloped off, not knowing of the disappearance of the bridge. His horse splashed down into the river which washed against the fortress. Riveted to his mount and dragged down by his weighty armour, Glasdale drowned.

That same evening, informed of the death of their leader, the English called a council of war and decided to surrender. The troops would lift the siege the following day and take the direction of Meung-sur-Loire.

In Orleans the people were almost delirious with joy, and the herald Fleur-de-Lys was immediately dispatched to Chinon to inform the King of the victory.

It was hardly a coincidence that in 1436, again at the expense of Duke Charles of Orleans, Fleur de Lys (or de Lilz) was sent to Arlon. His mission there was to verify the identity and armorial bearings of the Maid, who was then staying with the Duchess of Luxemburg. As a royal messenger, his word was sacred, and his recognition of Joan caused the people of Orleans to give her a warm reception in 1439.

16

THE HERALDIC PROOF

> In excessive outrage and presumption, she asked to be given and allowed to bear the most noble and excellent arms of France, which she obtained in part, and bore in several expeditions and assaults, as well as *her brothers . . . as it is said.*
>
> (Monstrelet, *Chroniques*)

These were the bitter accusations of the English, formulated by Henry VI in a letter to Philip the Good, the text of which is given at the end of the Trial proceedings and is also reproduced by Monstrelet.

Here was merely another political argument which contained statements true and false. It was false that Joan had ever asked for anything of the sort from Charles VII at this time, and that she ever bore these arms on the battlefield.

What was true on the other hand was that the 'most noble arms of France' had been 'granted in part', a fact which infuriated the English: too many people bore the lis as it was, and there was no need to bring others out into the open. The second truth lies in the doubting tone of 'as well as her brothers . . . as it is said', hardly the acceptance of the relationship. Were there no conclusive evidence to the effect that Joan the Maid was of royal blood, it would be hard to understand why the King gave her a coat of arms. The grant was made after the liberation of Orleans and before the Loire campaign, and thus before the coronation. Charles VII deliberately conferred on her, and on her alone, irrefutable armorial bearings. There was nothing missing: heraldic tinctures (gold, azure, argent) and charges: fleurs-de-lis gold, sword argent with five crosses—or fleurs-de-lis—engraved on the blade. And in particular, the ensign of her dignity: *a royal crown.* The grant read as follows:

> On the second day of June 1429, the said Lord King, knowing the prowess of Jehanne the Maid and the victories which came of God's gift and counsel, and being in the town of Chinon, granted arms to the said Jehanne, to decorate her standard *and herself*, according to the ensuing pattern, and gave to the Duke of Alençon and to the said Jehanne charge of the siege of Jargeau.

Under the text, is depicted a coat of arms the blazon of which reads: *Azure between two fleurs-de-lis Or, a sword argent hilted of the second, the blade charged with five fleurs-de-lis enfiled by a royal crown of the same.**

This grant only mentioned Joan the Maid, without a surname. The d'Arc family was neither mentioned nor in any way involved, contrary to what has been claimed.

Edouard Schneider, a Catholic writer and personal friend of Popes Pius XI and Pius XII, as well as of many eminent figures of the Church, has stressed this point insistently. 'We must remember,' he wrote, 'that in the royal letters dated from Chinon, the name of Joan the Maid was mentioned alone, without there being any question of her family.'[20]

Far too much ink has already been spilt on the subject, and it is high time the question was settled once and for all. Any conscientious researcher, working with reliable books on heraldry, will soon find out the following facts. The king sometimes gave his colours and the lis to subjects who were not of royal blood; it constituted an exceptional reward for loyal services. Therefore, at first sight, a coat of arms such as Joan's could have been granted to some valiant captain. Throughout history burghers were permitted to have a coat of arms, but it did not confer nobility. Armorial bearings that were not registered were of pure fantasy and nearly always 'canting', alluding to the name or profession of the bearer.

Some modern historians claim that in the fifteenth century the coat of arms did not possess the importance it later acquired. But this was surely not the case.

Joan's coat of arms was completely different and does not fit into these categories. A saga is not an everyday event, and most authors, supporters of the legend or not, have glossed over the true heraldic meaning, in a bid to make their point of view triumph at all costs.

Not only the tinctures in this coat of arms are significant. First of all the sword: that of Louis of Orleans had five crosses engraved on its blade. It is likely that Charles VII had these crosses changed into fleurs-de-lis, so as to conceal more effectively an already very obvious fact.

Following Jean Jacoby, a 'non-orthodox' writer, a number of authors have far too readily affirmed that the sword of Joan's coat of arms was a 'bar of bastardy' which provided proof of her royal descent. This is erroneous: the sword in this case is a heraldic charge

* Author's note: This document was found in the nineteenth century. See illustrations.

and could in no event constitute a mark of illegitimacy. The supporters of the legend have gleefully jumped on this mistake—and made a mistake themselves by denying the royal birth.

The truth is that the sword could either be a modification of the

Fig. 3

Official coat of arms of Joan the Maid.

third fleur-de-lis of the royal arms, a symbol of the campaign led by the Maid, or an indication, by its colour, of the link with the House of Orleans.

But in any case, it must be realized that Joan was not a bastard. She could not be since she was the love-child of the Queen. It was a very delicate position to define, especially as her brother Charles VII was exceedingly worried about his own legitimacy, for reasons of divine right. The father of Isabeau's last two children was legally Charles VI, since, as the Roman adage says, the legal father is the husband of the marriage. In reality, it was another affair, and gossip was rife about the identity of the King's father, at least until Joan's arrival in Chinon.

All this considered, the crown of the coat of arms is the only element which categorically authenticates the Maid's origins. In heraldry, the crown is an ensign of dignity, and the crown given to Joan was that of the Dauphins of France . . . At a time when armorial bearings constituted a real identity card at court, it was unthinkable to hand out such a symbolic element lightly.

Secondly, to give a crown without a title is absurd. Why would Charles VII spontaneously grant a royal crown to a shepherdess who had neither title nor name, other than that of 'the Maid'?

The secret of it was of such importance that the King's heraldists took the exceptional precaution of incorporating the crown into the coat of arms instead of placing it in the normal position above, which would have made the secret of the birth too obvious. This way the crown, pierced by the sword, would be irremovable.*

It is for these reasons that official historians are careful not to elaborate on its meaning.

* Author's note: Indeed, placed above a coat of arms, a crown can easily disappear for one reason or another. This is impossible if the crown is pierced by a sword. Similar royal crowns can be seen at the Louvre, on the ceiling of the *Salle de la Colonnade* (no. 2).

17

THE CORONATION

Gentle King, now is done God's pleasure . . .

(Joan)

On the morrow of the liberation of Orleans, the army council decided to return to the royal residence, without attempting to pursue the English who were falling back to Meung-sur-Loire. 'And all went before the King to confirm the good news of the noble task.' The Maid was certainly disappointed, for she would have preferred to continue fighting until final victory. But her wishes were not taken into account.

The journey however brought its compensations. Joan rode beside Gilles de Rais, and the confidences they exchanged for hours on end cemented the friendship which had started in Blois. It has been suggested it was during this journey that Rais conceived the idea of the famous *Mystère du Siège d'Orléans*, a play recounting in 20,500 lines and with fantastic pageantry, the marvellous adventure they had just lived through.*

The army arrived in Loches on 11th May, and Charles VII came out to meet them. Dunois, the effective commander-in-chief, was in the lead. Joan, who was further back,

> took her banner in her hand and rode towards the King, and they met. Then the young girl bowed her head before the King as low as she could and the King at once bade her raise it. And it seemed that he would readily have kissed her for the joy he felt.[21]

Other sources say that the King, having removed his hat, gave Joan the accolade.

However, in the months to come, despite these patent marks of affection, and the prerogatives which were bestowed upon her, the Maid was soon exasperated by Charles VII's behaviour. Whatever

* Author's note: The *Mystère du Siège d'Orléans* was commissioned by Gilles de Rais towards 1435. In it, Joan the Maid is invariably addressed in unambiguous terms: 'Most High and Most Powerful Lady', Most Excellent Princess', etc. In the fifteenth century it was unthinkable to address as 'Lady' or 'Princess' someone who was not of that rank. Also, each series of performances of the play cost a fortune, and this contributed to Gilles de Rais' financial ruin.

decision had to be taken, as though her advice was of no account, she never formed part of the royal Council. This annoyed her intensely and she let it be known:

'Gentle Dauphin, do not assemble so many and such long Councils, but come to Rheims to receive your fitting coronation.'

But the King failed to react, having soon relapsed into his natural apathy. He was once more dominated by his councillors, especially by his favourite of the moment, the two-faced Georges de La Trémoille.

It is possible that it was to curb Joan's impatience that Charles made her the grant of armorial bearings on 2nd June. With anyone but Joan, this implicit recognition of her birth would have been a sound move in default of action. But for her, it was trivial and left her indifferent. Her purpose remained to fight for her ideal, in conformity with the Christian spirit of her upbringing. The life of a princess she was obliged to lead was contrary to her principles, and with her integrity of character she could not tolerate the hypocrisy of courtiers.

She created envy in them from the start; it was inevitable. The lodging expenses of this intruder, her clothing, personal maintenance, as well as that of her household, were entirely defrayed by Charles of Orleans. No reasons were given. The likes of it had never been seen before.

And then, 'she wore knight's gowns, doublets and close-fitting breeches, laced shoes, small hat . . .',[22] an outfit which created such a scandal that the King had to request her to wear dresses. She complied, but only in part, for the dresses she wore were men's dresses. Only occasionally did she wear a woman's dress.

So, the 'peasant-girl from Barrois' was suddenly transformed into the most elegant and richly dressed woman in the kingdom.

From London, her half-brother the Duke had already given orders to Jacques Boucher to cover her expenses in his name. 'For payment to her made of thirteen *couronnes d'or* to the draper and to the tailor for the making of a dress in deep green adorned with nettle-leaves . . .'* Nothing was too fine: 'shimmering cloths, silk velvet; men's dresses trimmed with the rarest furs'. A cloth supplied by Jean Luillier reached the fantastic price of 170 *francs-or* a metre.

This was not all: her apparel was completed by the *huque*, a wide and floating surcoat worn over armour, the luxury of a lord or

* Author's note: 'The burghers of the town, wishing to honour Joan, presented her with half an ell of cloth in two shades of green, for nettle-leaves with which to decorate her dresses. It was a discreet allusion to her links with the House of Orleans for nettle-leaves had been the emblem of Louis of Orleans, and were still that of Duke Charles. *Vert-perdu*, which was the colour of the *huque* given Joan by him, had been adopted as a sign of mourning after his capture.' (Jean Jacoby in *Scènes de la Vie de Jeanne d'Arc*)

captain. Joan adored them and had them in all colours—cloth of gold lined with white satin, deep green, vermilion, and so on. Finally, as a mark of extreme elegance, and also of femininity, even on a man's dress, her hats and hoods had long bands of cloth with pinked edges. (See illustrations.)

Meanwhile, despite this sudden and unexpected passion for fashion, she was oppressed by her inactivity, and affected by it to the extent of being unable to control her ancestral arrogance. 'At the slightest vexation, her throat would constrict and she would stamp her foot, seize people by the collar . . . and would even lose her appetite.'[23]

During this period, when she resided for the most part in Tours, she made three journeys: two to Orleans and the third to Selles-en-Berri. From here she wrote to her good friends of Orleans. This letter is of the greatest interest for it bears her seal, and her signature: it means that the town council would be able to recognize them at a future date.

On the Loire there was then a series of victories which opened the road to Rheims. The nomination of Jehan Duke of Alençon to the post of commander-in-chief for the siege of Jargeau, brought Joan closer to her nephew; their mutual affection soon evolved into a deep and lasting relationship.

Joan: 'Ah, gentle Duke, art thou afeared? . . . Knowest thou not that I promised thy wife to bring thee back safe and sound? . . . Step back for here is a machine which will kill thee!'

It was a timely warning, for the 'machine' was a cannon.

The Duke had little experience as a military commander, but, fortunately, d'Aulon was there to compensate for his deficiencies. And the Maid continued to catalyse the enthusiasm of the men-at-arms and the people in the pursuit of her mission.

In 1456, d'Alençon's statement, in which he betrayed his relationship of familiarity and equality with Joan, was to stir up secrets contrary to the interests of the crown. This testimony so out of tune with the others was little appreciated.

Jargeau surrendered, then Beaugency, then Patay, where Joan, coming from the rearguard with Gilles de Rais, appeared at the end of the fighting.

Having returned on 19th June to Jacques Boucher's house, she now awaited the rendezvous at Châteauneuf-sur-Loire fixed by Charles VII for the 24th. There, after several days of meetings and councils, Dunois and La Trémoille declared themselves in favour of the march to Rheims, and this finally decided it.

The resistance of Troyes was unexpected. The inhabitants hesitated to abjure their oaths of loyalty to Philip the Good and Bedford.

Nevertheless, after the intervention of a Franciscan preacher, the keys of the city were brought to the King. 'The entry was effected because of the enticement of the bishop and of the dean of the said Troyes by a cordelier named Brother Richard,' said the chronicler.

The monk was indeed a first-rate actor, and his exit from the town by a secret passage and his arrival at the camp border on farce. He approached the Maid, making numerous gestures which expressed his fear of being in the presence of a witch, and she exclaimed: 'Approach without fear, I shall not fly away.' The monk then joined his hands and threw himself at her feet. Joan, annoyed by this exhibition, mockingly did the same, and the meeting took place with them kneeling opposite each other, hands joined.

When they had risen to their feet, she wrote a letter which she handed to Richard. The note was not well received in Troyes, and the town's eventual surrender was only brought about by the thundering eloquence of the Franciscan friar, an expert demagogue.

After Châlons had surrendered too, they arrived in Rheims on 16th July. The army had not even reached the town when a delegation of burghers, led by a bishop wearing his mitre, suggested a triumphal entry. When the gates opened, Joan, the King, the army and Brother Richard who had rallied the cause, were welcomed by the ecstatic crowd, shouting 'Noel! Noel!'

Problems immediately arose. Tradition decreed that the coronation of the King should take place on a Sunday, so there was only one night left to make all the preparations for the ceremony. Everything was arranged with great haste.

The crown of solid gold had not yet arrived, and a substitute was found in the cathedral treasury. Nearly all the twelve peers of France were absent and needed replacements. D'Alençon was chosen as first lay peer. The others included five illustrious names: Clermont, Vendôme, Laval, Beaumanoir and . . . La Trémoille.

Regnault de Chartres led the Church dignitaries, that day taking up his duties as Archbishop of Rheims after having waited to do so for many years. Then came the four prelates of Châlons, Laon, Sées and Orleans, the latter of Scottish origin.[24]

There was a bishop missing, Pierre Cauchon, but a replacement was easily found. Indeed, the diocese of Beauvais was suffragan to Rheims, so that the Lord Bishop Cauchon should have been present. Doubtless embarrassed by his political leanings he had thought it politic to disappear several days previously—and leave behind a number of his followers or secret agents.

The fact is little known, but credit for its revelation is due to a thesis presented in 1892 at the *École des Chartes* by M. Jadart.[25] In this thorough study, the real power of the Bishop of Beauvais is revealed, and a startling number of questions materialize. Why did Cauchon resign himself so easily? Why did he allow the town to open to Charles VII, and passively accept the idea of a coronation which was contrary not only to his own policy but also to the interests of his friends? It would have been simple for him to obstruct the movement of the Holy Ampulla, and perhaps even gain possession of it, with a little bit of complicity somewhere along the line. The only solution to the problem lies in his deep motivation.

Whatever the case may be, on 17th July 1429, an abbot bearing the Holy Ampulla returned from the abbey of Saint-Rémi. Towards nine o'clock, escorted by four great lords of the kingdom—Gilles de Rais, Boussac, Culant and Graville—he entered by the great portal of the cathedral.

In the nave, under the multicoloured banners, the congregation formed two lines of honour. At the foot of the high altar, the Dauphin stood, dressed in red velvet, with d'Albret, Count of Dreux, to his left, bearing the royal sword. To his right, the Maid of Orleans 'in most noble vestments of cloth of gold and silk well lined with fur', stood next to two unfurled standards. One was the standard of France, to which all others had to yield. Yet it was next to the emblem of the poor and the low clergy, symbol of the Mendicant Friars.

'Was it given precedence over those of the other captains in the Church of Rheims, at the coronation?' To this question, which expressed the political anxiety of a judge paid by the English, Joan made a sharp retort:

'It had been treated badly, it was meet that it receive the honour.'

Indeed, for the minor brothers and their affiliates, trials and tribulations went back nearly a century, what with war, the plague, devastation and extortion. In 1402, because Richard II had been their protector, Henry of Lancaster had scores of Franciscans hanged, and their heads posted up on London bridge. With this in mind it is hardly surprising that at Orleans English soldiers had defected simply at the sight of the banner.

Joan confirmed that this standard was indeed in the cathedral. 'I believe it was quite near the altar, but I do not know if Brother Richard was holding it.'

Why mention the Franciscan, unless she had a particular reason?

Some authors claim that the standard in question was *Baucéant*, that of the Templars which was argent and sable*. This idea is exceedingly attractive, especially if one feels, as I do, sympathy for the Order of the Temple. But it is highly unlikely. Its appearance that day would have been meaningless and seemingly difficult to justify.

The ceremony started with d'Alençon going to the King and putting gold spurs on him. With the flat of his sword, he then touched

* Author's note: Heraldic term for black.

him on each shoulder and finally gave him the accolade: Charles VII was dubbed knight. Then, holding the Holy Ampulla in one hand, the archbishop performed the rite and pronounced: 'In the name of the Father, and of the Son and of the Holy Ghost, I anoint thee with this holy oil.'

The twelve peers immediately surrounded the sovereign. His Lordship Regnault de Chartres seized the crown between his outstretched hands, then turned and placed it on the King's head. Charles was presented to the congregation who then intoned the *Te Deum.*

At this moment the Maid's voice rose in the nave: 'Gentle King, now is done the will of God who wanted me to lift the siege of Orleans and to bring you to this city of Rheims to receive your holy sacring, showing that you are truly King and he to whom the kingdom of the Franks should belong.' She then broke down, embraced her brother round the legs and cried, overcome with emotion.

Five hours had passed. The ceremony was about to end when Joan transmitted a rather unexpected request. For some time, a lord who had come specially from Lorraine had been talking to her earnestly.

'It would be,' he had said, 'the most marvellous day of my life if the King agreed to dub me knight, with his own hand.'

Peace in Lorraine interested France, and Charles unhesitatingly agreed to the demand. 'And at the said sacre, forthwith was the Lord Nicoles Louve made knight.'

The King's move was sound. Louve was indeed a powerful figure. Head municipal magistrate of Metz since 1408, he reigned truly on the 13 sworn aldermen of the town. He had been a councillor of the Emperor of Germany, and a chamberlain-councillor of the Duke of Burgundy. He only lacked in fact official acknowledgement of a worthy career. By intervening on his behalf, Joan brought it to him: Louve later became chamberlain of the king of France.[26]

Two points, which seemed insignificant in 1429, should be noted at this stage. First of all, Louve's family had been one of the few to be chosen to receive gifts offered to the Franciscan convent of Metz. This was to prevent any repetition of the frequent misappropriations.[27]

Secondly, Nicolas Louve had as 'dear and great friend', the knight Robert des Armoises, who owned property in the city of Metz.

Joan, Nicolas Louve, Robert, the Franciscans, were all to meet again.

18

THE TRAP

Children and dear friends, I tell you that I have been betrayed . . .

(Joan to the inhabitants of Compiègne)

As soon as the security of the throne was assured, latent forces in the King's entourage worked towards a rapid demotion of Joan as an active figure. She should have no more say in affairs of war and politics. Nevertheless she would still receive the honours due to her rank.

The military household of the Maid of Orleans was maintained for the time being, with Jehan d'Aulon at its head and in command of her faithful followers—Poulengy, Jean de Metz (Jean de Novelompont, or Nouillompont) Pierre and Jean d'Arc, and the page Louis de Coutes. This was why 'The Maid always rode dressed in war attire, as were the other people of her company, and spoke as wisely of war as any captain'.

Before the coronation, she had sent a carefully worded invitation to her cousin Philip of Burgundy. The Duke did not reply but sent along a few retainers. Henceforth, there were suspect intrigues, followed by negotiations with the court of Dijon, with all the appearances of a plot of which Joan would bear the consequences. Between Charles and Philip the Good, stood two men of questionable motives: La Trémoille and his kinsman, Guillaume de Flavy.

To start with, the prolonged rejoicing in Rheims, maintaining the euphoria created by the coronation, was an opportunity to receive the Burgundian delegation led by David de Brimeu.

Joan took advantage of the lull to visit her adoptive parents. Staying for a whole month at the Auberge de l'Ane Rayé, Jacques and Isabelle d'Arc seemed to have come for some other reason than the coronation ceremonies.*

* Author's note: In his book *Le Dossier de Jehanne*, Maurice David-Darnac makes the following pertinent remarks:

'The Maid never mentioned the fact that she met her so-called parents at Rheims. What is one to think of the filial devotion of this child of benediction?

'It was strange that Jacques d'Arc stayed so long in Rheims. He was probably waiting for the royal decree granting a tax exemption to the inhabitants of

On 21st July, the royal army set off in the direction of Compiègne, the gateway to Flanders. Paris was named as the objective of the new campaign. As it was indispensable to control the towns near the capital, the itinerary included lengthy zigzags—Soissons, Château-Thierry, Compiègne—which would otherwise seem surprising.

On the first day, the King's escort stopped at Corbény, which was a good hour's ride from the village of Liesse (or Liance), near Laon.

The Reverend Father Ayroles was one of several authors who have wondered whether Joan went to Notre-Dame de Liesse.[28] Their conclusion was that it was likely. To my mind this supposition is almost a certainty. The evidence for it can be readily established: it is sufficient to compare the average distance ridden with the date of arrival at each meeting-place. It shows that Charles VII and Joan had time to go to Liesse, before arriving at Vailly on 22nd July, and Soissons, on the 23rd.

There must in any case have been a good reason for them to pass by Corbény when there was a direct road which was open; the round-about route taken is incomprehensible without deep motivation.

The chapel of Liesse had been built in the twelfth century by Hospitallers who had later brought a 'Black Virgin' there. A decision of Pope Clement VII, in 1386, made it so important a place of pilgrimage that it was the object of a royal letter of 1412. The text was transcribed in the seventeenth century:

> . . . The confraternity of Notre-Dame de Liesse had been founded in the Church of the Holy Ghost by King Charles VI and Isabeau of Bavaria who joined, with their son King Charles VII, the number of brothers and sisters of the said confraternity, following letters patent of the months of April and May 1412, with their successors, princes and princesses of same devotion . . .[28]

These lines seem sufficient for us to accept that Notre-Dame de Liesse was a place frequented by the Royal House. Charles VI, Isabeau, Charles VII, all met there regularly, as well as the 'Most Excellent Princess' Joan the Maid who, as we know, was especially devoted to the Black Virgin.

It is all the more certain in that 1412 was a symbolic date for the saga: for, according to the Barrois legend, St Colette decided precisely that year which spiritual path the 'child of benediction' was to take.

They stayed in Compiègne on 17th August, and there followed a

---

Domrémy-Greux. Dated 31st July, the decree read: "On the wish of our well loved *Joan the Maid* . . ." It is surprising that a fiscal concession concerning Domrémy did not bear the surname d'Arc—if this name had indeed been hers; it would have been an obvious occasion to use it.'

week's rest which was marked by two critical events. The King named La Trémoille governor of the town, and the favourite who, it must be remembered, had ties with Burgundy, hastened to choose Guillaume de Flavy as his deputy.

At this point, the second Burgundian delegation arrived, led on this occasion by John of Luxemburg.

Finally, on orders from the King, d'Alençon and Joan set out on 26th August with an advance-guard. They settled in Saint-Denis. Contrary to what is generally thought, they did not leave Compiègne of their own accord. At the Trial, the Maid confirmed 'that it was at the request of the men of war that we undertook an action in front of Paris. And it was also at the request of the King that I went before La Charité. It was neither against nor at the command of my voices.'

Therefore, d'Alençon was only obeying orders he had been given to attempt to reach an agreement. After a few insignificant skirmishes, he wrote to the Parisians, inviting the Provost to submit to the King 'with salutations and fine words'. The letter was taken amiss by the Council of Paris, and the affair deteriorated into an exchange of insults. 'The Provost replied that in writing to him thus, the Duke fouled his paper.'[29]

Meanwhile, Charles VII and the army had arrived, and it was decided to launch an attack the same day.

'It was she (the voice) who had told me to stay at Saint-Denis, in France. As for me, I wanted to stay. But the leaders led me away against my will,' Joan recounted.

And so, accompanied by Gilles de Rais and Graville, she went to the Saint-Honoré Gate. Using the 'knightly' approach which came naturally to her and which had previously been so successful, she cantered forward, holding her banner in her hand, and threatened: 'Render the town to the King of France. Otherwise we shall enter by force before it is night, whether you will or no, and you will all be put to death without mercy.'

This was underestimating the Parisians. 'Nay, whore . . .' From the top of the battlements, an archer instantly sent down an arrow. It pierced her thigh—her second wound. She was forced to lie down on the battlefield for the whole day.

In the evening, the assault troops folded back, abandoning considerable equipment, and reassembled at La Chapelle. Here the defeat was confirmed, and the King decided to give up a fight that was unequal and beyond France's strength. The Council decided that the only viable strategy for many months would be patience helped by diplomacy.

As a result, so as not to jeopardize what had been achieved, Joan would have to stop fighting. Any failure on her part could well dissipate at one fell stroke the emotional charge accumulated in the people since the announcement of the mission.

Disappointed, but facing the facts, the Maid decided to go to the basilica of Saint-Denis to offer her armour as an *ex-voto*. The following day, despite the pain caused by her wound, she put her armour on again and broke in two the sword with five crosses.

On 21st September, at Gien, Charles VII dispersed his army. Joan went on to Bourges, where she was expected at the residence of one of the King's financial counsellors, Régnier of Bouligny. There, a lodging fit for a princess was appointed for her by the assiduous and attentive Count of Dreux, lord of Albret, though her mission was at an end and there was practically no further need for her. And to crown it all, she found herself living under the same roof, on an intimate footing, as her sister-in-law, Queen Marie of Anjou.

A few weeks later, the King was warned that attacks were being considered against Bourges, coming from Saint-Pierre-le-Moûtier and La Charité. He immediately recalled the army. But this time he did not have the advantage of the Third Order's support.

As Joan was not recalled, Gilles de Rais interceded, at her request. Charles gave in, and the Maid joined Gilles and the troops. Saint-Pierre-le-Moûtier surrendered after a very short siege. This victory was so heartening that it was decided to invest La Charité-sur-Loire.

Meanwhile, Joan had gone to Moulins where, on 9th November, she wrote to the inhabitants of Riom, asking them to send her arms and equipment. Contrary to her habit, she did not inscribe on her letter any of the Franciscan signs, though, according to Siméon Luce, 'at the time of Joan's visit to Moulins, the reformer of the Clares (St Colette) lived in the convent which she had just founded in this town'.

There was in fact a convent of Clares at La Charité also, and Mother Nicolette, anxious for the peace of mind of her nuns, was fearful of military brutality in all its forms. The town's resistance was therefore boosted by this religious factor, and the assailants had to withdraw after a month's siege.

What could have been said at Moulins during the interview between Colette of Corbie and her former disciple? Joan was no doubt asked in what ways, as 'God's emissary', she was following the humility and simplicity prescribed by the order, and why she had agreed to act without the consent of the 'voices'.

In the course of her Trial, when questioned by minor brothers, she was extremely embarrassed, and defended herself to the best of her ability.

'. . . Did you not have the counsel of your voices on that?'

'I wanted to go back to France,* but the men of war told me that it was better to go before La Charité first . . . it was neither against nor at the command of my voices . . .' (Oursel).

Insofar as Charles VII was concerned, the issue was more clearcut. After accepting help in March, the King, once he was victorious, showed reluctance to meet his obligations.

The following text by a Tertiary was approved in the nineteenth century by the Bishop of Saint-Dié:

> It is all the more certain that the people sent to Blois to Queen Yolanda were Franciscan treasurers in that later the subsidies stopped.
>
> They stopped because Charles VII, misled by the perfidious counsels of intriguers and traitors, decided on the disbanding of Joan's victorious Host, and on abandoning the celestial plan that the army of the Tertiaries and of the Begging monks were to bring about.
>
> The King was at that point rich enough to pay the courtiers who were dragging him into the abyss. The treasurers of the King of Heaven had other penury to succour.[30]

With the characteristic lucidity and realism of the religious of her stature, St Colette decided in the end to let the Maid manage on her own. And Charles VII, abandoned for good by the movement which had carried him to the throne, was obliged a few months later to disband his army completely and retrench himself south of the Loire, as before the mission.

After spending Christmas as Jargeau, Joan returned to Orleans, where she stayed as usual at Jacques Boucher's house. For five weeks, she was fêted by Luillier, Le Prestre, and all her friends.

On 4th March she went to stay at La Trémoille's superb castle of Sully-sur-Loire. With hunting and court pleasures she soon forgot her warlike ardour, especially as the King and Gilles de Rais were there too.

The lull was to be short-lived though. The balance was disrupted when John of Bedford, in a bid to consolidate an insecure alliance, offered Philip the Good the counties of Champagne and Brie 'in male succession'. It was vital for the Duchy of Burgundy that it should be linked with Flanders, and Philip was anxious to exploit his advantage without delay. It was incumbent upon him to conquer the lands granted him, and to provide some additional troops, their maintenance to be shared by the two allies. War threatened once again.

Around Compiègne, pivot of the whole operation in northern France, the situation worsened rapidly. Guillaume de Flavy's own brother had just sold Choisy-au-Bac to the invaders for three thousand *saluts d'or*, when there was news of another betrayal at Soissons.

* Translator's note: In the fifteenth century, this term still meant the Ile de France only.

Guiscard de Bournel, who had allowed entry to the Maid's escort, refused it to the royal troops and handed over the town for four thousand *saluts d'or*.

It was at this point that Charles VII decided to abandon the region, disband the whole of his army and take refuge south of the Loire.

In short, apart from Orleans and the coronation, the position was as before. But Joan would not accept the facts. Ignoring her brother's orders, she refused to obey, and led away, on her own account, a small company of men commanded by her faithful followers—d'Aulon, Xaintrailles, Poulengy, Jean de Metz and Pierre d'Arc. It is to be wondered where she found the money.

This serious disobedience violated the current negotiations. For the King and his Council, it was an intolerable transgression which would be exploited. In strong terms, His Grace Regnault de Chartres condemned the one he had previously praised, saying 'that the Maid had set herself up in pride, because of her rich clothes . . . and that she did everything according to her pleasure and not according to God's will'. On his side, La Trémoille intrigued to such good purpose that Joan was abandoned by her best friends—by the King, d'Alençon, Gilles de Rais and Richemont. As for Yolanda of Anjou, nothing more had been heard from her.

On 23rd May, Joan left Crépy-en-Valois for Compiègne where she incarcerated herself, believing the town to be threatened.

'But how could she succeed with a company of 300 men, when an army of 10,000 soldiers had failed?' remarks Gérard Pesme, who provides the key-text on the subject: 'Guillaume de Flavy had as yet been unable to hand over Compiègne, but he might be able to do it if the Maid were no longer there . . . This is what the lawyer Rapiout claimed in an action brought in 1444 against this same Flavy . . . who did not deny it!'

And so, at the end of a foolhardy sally against Margny, Joan fell into the trap which seemed to have been elaborately set up by her enemies—and by France?

Joan: 'I arrived secretly in the morning, so I believe; and the same day, towards evening, I made the sally in which I was taken.

A judge: 'For the sally, were the bells rung?'

Joan: 'If they were rung, it was not at my command, nor with my knowledge . . . I did not know that I would be taken. I had (from the voices) no other command than to go forth. But I had always been told it had to pass that I be made prisoner . . . by the bridge and by the boulevard* I went in the company of my men against the men of the Lord of Luxemburg. I drove them back twice to the Burgundians' camp, and the third time to half-way . . . and then, the English who

* Author's note: boulevard, a fortification which ended in a town exit.

were there cut the road between me and the boulevard. Our men retreated. And I, in retreating to the fields on the Picardy side near the boulevard, was taken . . .' (Oursel).

A comparison of facts provides proof of treachery. Dressed in her *huque* of cloth-of-gold, the Maid was the cynosure of all eyes. She had hardly left the town when the bells pealed out as a signal to the enemy. Although there were archers on the ramparts watching the operation, not one of them covered the retreat. And finally, the most glaring fact of all: just as Joan was about to re-enter the town, the drawbridge, which had until then been down, was promptly raised almost under her horse's hooves.

English and Burgundians then rushed towards her. Seized by the floating skirt of her *huque*, she fell from her horse.

'Surrender,' demanded Lionel of Wandonne.

'I have sworn and granted my faith to another, and I shall keep my oath to him!'

That same evening, at Margny, Wandonne received her very respectfully, pending the long and mysterious meeting she was to have with Philip the Good. Mysterious is the word, for Monstrelet, who was present at the interview, merely wrote:

> . . . the said Maid, whom the Duke went to see in the lodging where she was, and spoke some words to her which I do not remember well, although I was present.

In other words, the most eloquent chronicler of his time was struck with sudden and inexplicable loss of memory.

NOTES TO PART II

1 *Chronique de la Pucelle*, an anonymous fifteenth-century chronicle
2 *Bulletin de la Société des Lettres, Sciences et Arts de Bar-le-Duc*, July 1904
3 Bessonet-Favre, *op. cit.*
4 In *Jeanne d'Arc, Tertiaire de Saint François*
5 See *Jeanne d'Arc, ses costumes, son armure*, A. Harmand, after documents in the Vatican Library
6 See *Le secret de Jeanne d'Arc*, Jean Jacoby
7 Bessonet-Favre, *op. cit.*
8 *Ibid*, and other documents—see part V
9 *Histoire de France en 30 vol*, Velly, Villaret and Garnier
10 Bessonet-Favre
11 Expression taken from the *Mystère du Siège d'Orléans*
12 In *Jeanne d'Arc franciscaine*
13 Quoted by Bessonet-Favre and Gérard Pesme, *op. cit.*
14 See Bessonet-Favre, *op. cit.*
15 *Les Moines du Moyen Age*, G. Ambroise
16 Boucher de Molandon, Orleans, 1874
17 Gérard Pesme, *op. cit.*
18 Jean Jacoby, *op. cit.*
19 *Accounts of the Town of Orleans*—see part IV, § 38
20 In *Jeanne d'Arc et ses Lys*
21 Extract from a German chronicle, quoted by Régine Pernoud in *Jeanne d'Arc par elle-même et ses témoins*
22 Edouard Schneider, *op. cit.*
23 Quoted by Gérard Pesme, *op. cit.*
24 Siméon Luce, 'Jeanne d'Arc et les ordres mendiants' in *La Revue des Deux Mondes*, 1881
25 *Tableau du Chapitre de Reims et présence de Mgr Pierre Cauchon avant et pendant le sacre de Charles VII*
26 See *Metz Ancien*, by Baron Gérard d'Hannoncelles, first President of the royal Court of Metz, 1856
27 *Monastica Metensia*, E. de Bouteiller, 1869
28 *Histoire de N. D. de Liesse*, J. Macquart
29 Quoted by Gérard Pesme, *op. cit.*
30 See Bessonet-Favre, approved by Mgr A. Gabriel

III

THE TRIAL OF CONDEMNATION

19

PIERRE CAUCHON OF SOMMIEVRE, LORD COUNT-BISHOP OF BEAUVAIS

Ego Porcus sum: I am 'Pig' . . .
(*Jeanne au Bûcher*, Paul Claudel)

This pathetic pun on the Bishop's name* exemplifies the mediocrity of mind of some supporters of the outworn legend. The melodramatic official version in general is equally off-putting: Mgr Cauchon made his appearance at the time of the Trial, after having been the 'creature of the infamous Queen Isabeau. Liegeman of the King of England, he organized an odious Machiavellian scheme bringing about the iniquitous condemnation of Joan to be burnt at the stake.

I do not intend to whitewash the Lord Bishop of the many underhand dealings that an opportunist of his stature usually engages in. But it is high time the man was put in his rightful position.

'The Rouen Trial contains a mystery which has not yet been penetrated, probably because it is not yet the hour,' said the 'saint' Bessonet-Favre, in the nineteenth century, with the approval of her bishop.[1] There is indeed a mystery, though it is hardly ever admitted.

The future Bishop of Beauvais was born near Rheims, where his father Rémy Cauchon, a Bachelor of Law who was ennobled by Charles VI in 1393, owned the vineyards and manor of Sommièvre. After intensive studies, Cauchon obtained his degree in Canon Law, then became Rector of the University of Paris in 1403. A brilliant jurist, doctor of theology, and a distinguished orator, he was then nominated a member of a royal commission set up to reform the kingdom's institutions. But, after involving himself too deeply in Jacques Caboche's revolution, he was banished from the King's entourage and so became a follower of the Dukes of Burgundy. And the post of vidame† of the chapter of Rheims cathedral, obtained for

* Translator's note: Cauchon is a homophone of the French for pig, *cochon.*

† Author's note: In the Middle Ages, one who represented the bishop in temporal matters, and commanded his troops. Cauchon therefore represented the Armagnac archbishop, Regnault de Chartres.

him by John the Fearless, decided the direction of his whole career.

He found himself at the hub of all the big political and religious problems, and his influence gradually extended to all parties, and much of western Europe—Burgundy, England, the Holy See; even to the Armagnac party, through his superior in the hierarchy, Regnault de Chartres, Lord Archbishop of Rheims in 1413. As soon as Isabeau of Bavaria settled in Troyes, Cauchon himself appeared there to act as her secretary, and thereafter engaged in indefatigable diplomatic activity.

An observer at the Council of Constance, he intervened and intrigued to such good effect that, through him, Martin V succeeded to the throne of St Peter. The reward came before long, for the new Pope did not forget the service rendered and named Cauchon papal referendary.*

In the following decade, he obtained the highest posts. After taking part in the drawing up of the Treaty of Troyes in 1420, he became Count-Bishop of Beauvais. Through Burgundy, Grand Aumônier and Peer of France, he then obtained from Bedford, whose chaplain he was, a seat on the Great Council of England.

Jean Gerson, himself, 'though an impetuous Armagnac', showed him much consideration and even friendship.[2] This is a vital bit of information for Gerson was the main promoter of the Franciscan movement of liberation, and intervened forcefully in the Poitiers decision on the Maid.

Finally, to fit all the pieces together, it should be remembered that Anne of Bedford-Burgundy, the Regent's wife and Joan's cousin, was a *Dame Très Discrète* of the Third Order.

It is well known that the setting up of a big political trial is always more important than the trial itself. In 1431 it was indeed in the course of the trial preparations that its mysteries were formed, for Cauchon had to foresee all the implications. And it is only now that the motives are apparent.

What did Cauchon's visit to Beaurevoir in the middle of the summer mean? Why did he seem to have failed? For what reason did the Maid only arrive in Rouen in November, when she had been captured in May, and the first audience only open on 21st February 1431?

Of these nine months of shilly-shallying, three were spent by the Bishop setting up his politico-legal edifice: 'I shall produce a fine hearing for you,' he had promised the English.

But this delay was so excessive for those times and seemed so odd

* Translator's note: An official whose duty it was to examine and report on petitions and requests.

that in November 1430 His Lordship Pierre received a sharp reprimand from the University:

> We are surprised in the extreme, Reverend Father and Lord, at the great delay brought to the cause of this woman, commonly called the Maid . . . whilst she is, it is said, in the hands of the King our Lord . . . If Your Paternity had shown greater diligence in pursuance of this affair, the cause of the said woman would already have been tried before the ecclesiastical Tribunal . . . In order that the authority of the Church suffer not the more serious injury of a longer delay, deign that the zeal of Your Paternity work to the effect that the said woman be put into your power and into that of the Lord Inquisitor of heretical perversity . . . Pray bring about that she be surely led to this town of Paris where sit in great number scholars and erudite men . . .

More than simply a wish, it was a demand addressed to the Reverend Father in Christ. However despite his colleagues' dangerous power, Cauchon was unmoved. On the contrary, once the trial had been set up, he did not tolerate any interference whatsoever in his Machiavellian plan by which nearly everybody was deceived.

Continually playing upon appearances, he made illusive statements by which only a few of his associates were not deluded.

There is little doubt that if Joan had been captured before the coronation, Cauchon would have acted differently. But in the last year, despite some defeats, there had been a marked improvement in the fortunes of the French, and our brilliant political opportunist had weighed up the situation. It was so modified by the psychological success of the salvage operation that Cauchon, until then faithful to the Anglo-Burgundian coalition, astutely decided, if not to make overtures to the side in the ascendant, then at least to wait and see the turn of events.

The important thing was not to incur the displeasure of a possible master. In a few months the situation had reversed. For some time, public opinion, carefully moulded by the Third Order, had supported the 'virgin come on God's order', and the prophecies had come to pass. 'On behalf of the King of Heaven', France once again had a real, indefeasible king who had received the sacred unction, like the Frankish kings, Charlemagne and Saint Louis. To contest this principle legally in the fifteenth century would have been to risk undermining the whole Christian edifice, and plunging the west into social and religious chaos again. And that was the last thing that Cauchon wanted after all his endeavours to end the Great Schism.

Also, as soon as he left Rheims at the time of the coronation, he understood that the game was as good as lost for England, that sooner or later there would be a *rapprochement* between Burgundy and the Valois. Eighteen months later, when he opened the trial, he was already considering rallying the party soon to be in power, and the 'One and indivisible' Church he had consolidated would follow suit.

At Rouen, a summit conference opened secretly. Cauchon, acting as intermediary between the parties, could go ahead with his plan. Through Isabeau, he had knowledge of the 'mysteries' concerning the birth both of Charles VII in 1403 and of Joan in 1407—it is even possible that it was he who had coined the expression 'the so-called dauphin'.

It was many centuries before a similar accumulation of titles and functions were vested in one man—Talleyrand for instance—capable of adapting himself to every situation. Here again, the legend is so puerile that it is incomprehensible. To present the Bishop of Beauvais as a downright brute is an insult to anyone's intelligence. In his true light, he in no way resembles the traditional description of him in a 'teaching orientated for the good cause'. It required Cauchon's cleverness and universality as a diplomat to conduct so complex an intrigue involving all at once: the unity of Christendom, the demands of the University of Paris, the sanguinary instincts of a few *godons** rampaging round the country, and particularly, political and dynastic exigencies.

* Author's note: *Godons*: pejorative expression, probably derived from the swear-word 'goddam', used by Joan and her men to designate the English soldiers.

20

ENGLISH POLICY AND THE UNIVERSITY

> The English did not have the reasons that the Paris University doctors had to hate Joan to death . . . A life sentence would have been sufficient to bring about Joan's disqualification as an agent of the divine will and would have satisfied the English. . . . All they wanted was an annulment of the Rheims coronation.[3]

The various attitudes, when the trial started, can be explained by the political and religious circumstances.

The University of Paris consisted of the 'pick of the collaborators' of the time. It is indubitable that this assembly, composed largely of religious fanatics, was inspired by the outward concern of defending Christian orthodoxy against the manoeuvres of the 'Armagnac witch'. But the ideal of these people was more down-to-earth. They had personal interests, prerogatives and social positions conferred by the English to defend. Moreover, the University was under the control of the Dominican Order. Whereas St Francis of Assisi had gathered the people and the lower clergy, in other words the poor, the Order of St Dominic flattered the financial powers.

Opposing the social tide provoked by the banner 'Jhesus-Maria', the Dominicans had chosen to support the University, the Burgundian party and the incipient capitalism of the English. This is confirmed by André Maurois in his *Histoire d'Angleterre*:

> . . . Manoeuvres utterly contrary to the spirit of the Middle Ages which had believed in imposed prices, in limited profits, and held as a crime any scheme to make the price of commodities rise.
>
> But this spirit was dying, the king was under the domination of merchants; they became members of his Parliaments. They alone fed his Exchequer.
>
> It was for them that England's foreign policy was adopted.

Things have not changed since then, and armed conflict is more than ever conditioned by the economy.

And yet, in the fifteenth century, the English were divided amongst themselves. As we have seen, it was not only the French Third Order which had brought about the deliverance of Orleans and the revival of the ancient pacts made at Rheims between the spiritual and the temporal.

> French and English tertiaries of the 'King of Heaven' all rallied to the common sign of the fraternities: *the white dove* . . .
>
> . . . The English seemed struck with vertigo . . .
>
> . . . The baronial militias of the landlords openly separated themselves from Talbot's royal troops. But they were all united when it was a matter of lifting the siege . . .[4]

This is correct and every point is verifiable, if only by Brother Pasquerel's statement at the Trial of Rehabilitation.

Under the impulse of the Franciscan movement, latent forces had taken effect. They are still actively at work on the plan that the nations of the world should unite in order, social justice and peace. Did Joan not say that her sign would last a thousand years?

If the Rouen trial reveals that pressure was exercised by Cauchon on the other judges, an attentive reading of texts, together with an enquiry into motives, shows that secret forces first of all acted on the Bishop himself. This is the root of the problem.

It was the same in the case of the notorious witnesses at the time of the Rehabilitation.

In the English camp, Joan's death would only reassure people of little importance: superstitious old troopers, and a few captains worried by their men's morale. Politically the least sophisticated, they were the easiest to hoax.

Furthermore, it is by no means clear that Henry Beaufort, Cardinal of Winchester, really bore the Maid deadly hatred. What is certain on the other hand is that he was more powerful in London than in the rest of the country.

In their opposition to the financiers' power, the landlords often took an interest in the traditional movement of Christianized cults. For centuries they had fought to protect their liberties. At the time of King John, the Magna Carta had granted the barons a few prerogatives against the centralized power allied to capitalism. But the landowners were at the mercy of the continual variations in the price of wool, and their fear of ruin and resentment are understandable.

Everything is linked in that all the opposition parties took their inspiration from the cult of the Virgin Mary, whose dogma of the Immaculate Conception had been rejected by the Dominicans. A representation of the Mother-goddess, the Black Virgin was worshipped in all the religious centres of France: at Chartres, Puy-en-Velay, Notre-Dame de Bermont, Notre-Dame de Liesse. She inspired not only the Franciscans and the Armagnacs but the secret confraternity, which is still active in the twentieth century, directed by the celticizing group of Wales, and existing in Scotland, Ireland and Brittany.[5]

A highly significant element of this union is that St Bernard had engaged the knights of the Temple to take as guide, and to honour particularly, the one he considered as the Mother of humanity.

To return to John of Bedford, official history is once again full of contradictions. The Regent of France was a just man, moderate and loyal. If he had not been, historians would have criticized him. But there is nothing to fault about his administration.

The first contradiction is that this friend of Pierre Cauchon absented himself from a trial of which he was in fact one of the chief initiators.

Secondly, history specifies that Bedford bore his wife Anne, who returned it fully, a very deep and pure love, but then avoids saying that Anne was a tertiary. Brought up in Burgundy, she had followed the precepts of Colette of Corbie so well that in the nineteenth century, at the height of anglophobia, she was named 'patriotic and angelic duchess'. This is utterly incomprehensible. How can one reconcile the fact that the first Lady of England was 'patriotic and angelic' towards her cousin Joan and the Armagnac party, while she was the Duke of Burgundy's sister and the wife of an Englishman who reigned in occupied France?

Who were the traitors? Bedford and Anne of Burgundy? Who else then? To quote Jean Grimod, 'The one fact that Cauchon, contravening the instructions he had received from the University, acted in such a way that Joan was handed over to the English, is sufficient proof that he was not playing a straightforward game.'

21

FROM BEAUREVOIR TO ROUEN

It seems to me that it did not please God that I should escape *that time* . . . and that I had to see the King of the English, as my voices had told me.

(Trial of Condemnation)[6]

Immediately after her arrest, the Maid was taken by the Burgundians to the fortress of Beaulieu-en-Vermandois. She was allowed to have with her a few of her followers such as Jehan d'Aulon and Pierre d'Arc.

'Tell us about your attempt to escape from the castle of Beaulieu,' demanded her judges.

Joan: 'I have never been a prisoner in any place but that I sought to escape. At Beaulieu, I was about to lock up my keepers in the tower, but the porter saw me and surprised me . . .'

A judge: 'Have you leave from God or from your voices to depart from prison every time it pleases you?'

Joan: 'I have asked for it several times, but I do not have it yet . . . without leave, I shall not go away.'

Transferred to the castle of Beaurevoir, she then spent four months in the pleasant company of the Ladies of Luxemburg, the enormously rich owners of the place, before undertaking the long journey to Arras, Crotoy and Rouen.

It is difficult to understand what made Jeanne of Luxemburg, who was the aunt of John of Luxemburg, Count of Ligny, leave Beaurevoir with Joan for the grim coastal fortress of Crotoy. But it is to the point to emphasize that the Lady and her niece, John of Ligny's wife, always treated their prisoner with tender affection.

Just before her departure, the Lady of Luxemburg made her will, leaving the whole of her huge fortune to her nephew.* He was then hard put to reconcile conflicting loyalties.

How could Jeanne of Luxemburg, who was related to the Maid and who had protected her so well, then unconditionally accept her

* Translator's notes: On condition he did not hand over Joan to the English.

transfer to Crotoy, knowing what the issue of such a journey would be? Why did she not alter her will?

The knight Aimond de Macy's statement provides a partial explanation of the motives and gives some inkling of the outcome:

> I made acquaintance with Jehanne when I saw her for the first time at the castle of Beaurevoir . . . I saw her very often in that prison, and I talked several times with her.
>
> Several times also, I tried playfully to touch her breasts, by putting my hands on her chest. She would not suffer it and repulsed me with all her strength . . .[7]

His action is understandable, for it is well-known that Joan was very beautiful.

> It was there that I was taken with love for her [continued Aimond de Macy]. That is why I begged the Count of Ligny to put her to ransom. The *Dauphin was disposed to pay a good price for her* and to grant her me as a wife . . .[8]
>
> Then, she was taken to the castle of Rouen,* in a cell which looked out towards the fields. And while she was held there, the Count of Ligny also came to Rouen, and I with him.
>
> One day, the Count wished to see her and went to her, accompanied by the lord Earls of Warwick and Stauffort [Stafford], and in the presence of the Chancellor of England, Bishop of Thérouanne, who was the Count of Ligny's brother. I was there too.
>
> He addressed Jehanne, saying to her: 'Jehanne, I have come to liberate you against ransom, on condition that you promise me never to take up arms against us again' . . .

The transaction was therefore possible, although this has always been denied by history. This proposal is the first step towards the abjuration. The facts are clear.

> . . . She replied: 'In God's name, I know that you have neither the power, nor the wish to do so'.

Whereupon, according to the Trial of Rehabilitation, she refused vehemently.

What was the reason behind this attempt to buy her back? First of all, Luxemburg had a prior right to her, according to prisoner-of-war etiquette, and was entitled to do this. And it is possible he had a guilty conscience after the promises he had made to his aunt. Secondly it was vital to make the prisoner conform to the political views demanded by the English attitude towards France.

The journey from Beaurevoir to Crotoy had been interrupted by a six-week halt at Arras. Here the Maid had received a number of visits, such as one from Jean de Naviel, a clerk from Touraine, who brought her 22 gold crowns.

* By this time she had of course been handed over to the English.

'A particularly liberal regime,' emphasizes M. David-Darnac, 'since not only was she able to write to the nearest city supporting Charles VII, but she was allowed to keep the gift which was made to her.'[9]

Another of her visitors, and a more important one, was Jehan de Précy, Philip the Good's private secretary. In the course of their meeting, at which no one else was present, Précy handed her a message. It will never be known what exactly was said between them, nor what the tenor of the letter was. Numerous documents have likewise disappeared since the fifteenth century, but happily their existence is usually confirmed by other indisputable documents. And so there is little doubt as to the gist of their conversation. Philip, having reached an agreement with King Charles, assured Joan of her impunity on condition that she executed the established plan; which, in fact, she did. This is the only explanation of her sudden, unexpected and uncharacteristic resignation.

When questioned at the trial, she merely pointed out the part 'Saint' Catherine had played in her decision: 'Without fail, you must take everything in good part, the voice had announced to her. 'And you will not be delivered until you have seen the King of England.' (Oursel).

When the old Lady of Luxemburg died at Crotoy on 13th November, Pierre Cauchon decided to act swiftly, in the fear that the Maid of Orleans would be handed over to the blind University doctors, ignorant of the secret of her birth. As soon as he was in possession of the ransom paid by Bedford, he rushed to Crotoy on 15th November, so as to proceed with the exchange. The sum of ten thousand *livres* for an inspired shepherdess would have been exorbitant. But it was, as it happened, 'the ransom fixed for Princes'.[10]

Besides, compared with the enormous fortune he was about to inherit, the sum was paltry for John of Ligny-Luxemburg.

The date of the journey from Crotoy to Rouen is the subject of disagreement. Some authors maintain that it took place between 15th and 18th November; others feel the Maid made a senseless journey, accompanied by Cauchon. According to Régine Pernoud, Joan did not arrive at Bouvreuil before 21st December 1430. It does not matter either way. What is of vital interest is the account given by the Bishop to his masters, on 18th November.

'Now,' Cauchon said to Henry VI, 'the bastard of Louis of Orleans will be confounded and the terrible scandal he has caused will be undone . . .' Then, addressing the Earl of Warwick, he added:

> . . . before the throne of God, the soul of this woman is of as great a value as yours or that of our young King; and my first duty is to save

(above)
Bishop Pierre Cauchon from the statue on his tomb in the chapel dedicated to the Virgin in Lisieux Cathedral.
(Bibliothèque Nationale, Collection Gaignières, Photo by Giraudon)

(above right)
Woman going to the stake with her face veiled, and wearing a mitre.
(Based on A. Harmand's illustrations)

(right)
Joan's coat of arms; above it the black face in the helmet symbolizes the Black Virgin.
(Fifteenth-century wood sculpture in the author's collection. Photo by Michel de Sermoise)

Bouvreuil Castle, from an old postcard. (Author's collection)

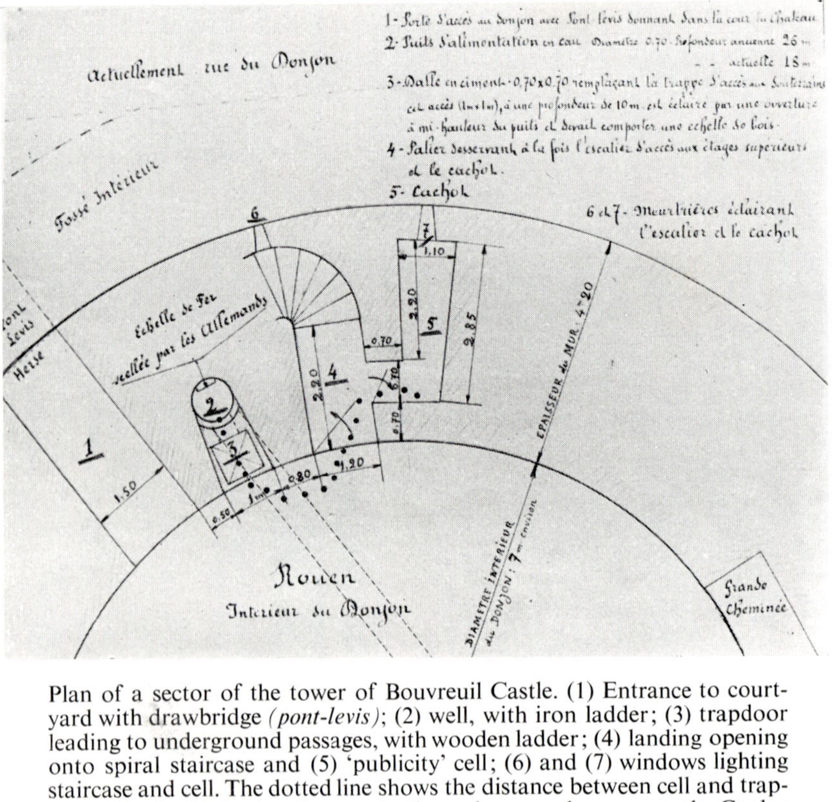

Plan of a sector of the tower of Bouvreuil Castle. (1) Entrance to courtyard with drawbridge *(pont-levis)*; (2) well, with iron ladder; (3) trapdoor leading to underground passages, with wooden ladder; (4) landing opening onto spiral staircase and (5) 'publicity' cell; (6) and (7) windows lighting staircase and cell. The dotted line shows the distance between cell and trapdoor. The double broken line marks the underground passage to the Gaalor aqueduct. (From a photo loaned by courtesy of M. Jean de Saint-Jean)

> her. I cannot allow that Your Lordship should smile thus at my words as though I uttered senseless ones or as though it had been agreed that I would hand over this woman to you by betrayal.
>
> 'I am not one of your political bishops. My faith is to me what your honour is to you . . .'[11]

Of course, seeing that the 'witch' was going to escape them, the University was furious and registered its protest in two letters. The first was written in courteous terms to Henry VI. The second, more vehement, was the sharp reprimand to the Bishop already quoted.

One is truly justified in querying the reasons which led Cauchon, who was Rector of the University, to use every possible means to withdraw the Maid from the jurisdiction of his colleagues. Immediately after the installation at Rouen, why did this specialist in canon law take liberties with the statutory regulations, acting as though they did not exist? Falsifications, alterations, suppression of documents, irregularities in procedure: all means were used by him to invalidate a trial which in reality did not raise any difficulties. Judging and executing a heretic was a simple matter in the fifteenth century.

Another liberty taken by the Lord Bishop was that he incarcerated the accused in the castle of Bouvreuil, under the fallacious pretext of having better control of her, while he himself lived in the archiepiscopal palace of Rouen.* This choice of a civil prison was a serious infringement of the law: for a crime smacking of heresy, an ecclesiastical prison was the rule.

There have been countless official descriptions of Joan's imprisonment, and for those who like their thrills while sitting cosily by the fireside, plenty of masochistic flights of fancy are available. One of these is Joseph Delteil's fictional description in which he speculates as was his wont.

> . . . In her cell there must have been a stench of urine, carbonic acid and putrefaction! The greasy, black ground must have teemed with huge bloated rats . . . and vermin. The Maid was certainly infested with vermin . . .[12]

Returning to reality, a comparison of various statements made at the Trial of Rehabilitation brings to light a number of contradictions. There is little doubt that Joan was chained, at least during the day, to a wooden post acting as a shackle. But although it did not appeal to her, the precaution served a two-fold purpose: first of all that of propaganda, to reassure the *houcepilleurs*, her bullying English jailers, so that they would tell their comrades that the witch was well chained. Secondly that of protection: the Maid had been the object of attempts of rape and had complained about it. Securely chained, she was in no such danger.

* Author's note: '*In domo habitationis episcopae Rothomagi.*'

22

PRISON

A Judge: 'The voice, was it in your chamber?'
Joan: 'I do not know, but certainly in the castle.'

Built in 1204 on the orders of Philip Augustus, the castle of Bouvreuil was demolished in 1809, in Napoleon's reign. In 1430, it was a huge, almost circular fortress consisting of seven main towers. Warwick was its governor.

Like most royal castles of this magnitude, it comprised, as well as the keep and the outbuildings, a central building which was the king's *logis*. It was a well appointed residence where the young Henry VI had lived for several months with his mother, Catherine of Valois.

At the same time as Joan arrived at Bouvreuil, Bedford and his wife also came to live there. Once again, then, there was a reunion of these eminent members of the 'medieval Gotha',* which is hardly surprising. It is possible that, on Jeanne of Luxemburg's death, responsibility for Joan had been passed by a Franciscan injunction to Anne of Bedford. But in any event it was no coincidence that Henry VI, Catherine of France, John of Bedford, Anne of Burgundy and the Maid of Orleans were all living under the same roof.

Opinions vary as to the precise location of Joan's cell. Yet it may be established by an attentive reading of the trial proceedings. According to the witnesses' statements as well as to her own, she was not 'lodged in the common prisons'. Several times she mentioned 'returning to her room', after the hearings. She had a room in which there was a bed, for she was sitting on it when one of her 'voices' visited her (Session of 24th February, *Trial of Condemnation*). This obvious comfort is a curious exception to the usual treatment of witches in prison. For it must be remembered that her jailers defined her as such, at least for public consumption.

The attempt to establish possible locations of this room shows up the contradictions in the statements but does nevertheless point to the probable place where she was locked up. The tower looking out

* Translator's note: The *Almanach de Gotha* was an annual survey, first published in 1764, of European royalty and nobility. It appeared in both French and German.

'towards the fields', in which she was put for a short while during an illness, could not have been a permanent prison. By Joan's own account, her room was close to the Great Hall, that is to say adjacent to the King's *logis* or else incorporated in it. This location would confirm the existence of those famous 'secret passages' which are a well-worn subject of debate.

Several statements tally to establish that the Maid's residence consisted of 'a room in the middle, having a room on either side'.[13]

According to Doctor Cerné's investigations, Joan's room, in the middle of this real suite, measured on its own at least 23 square metres.[14] This rules out the possibility of imprisonment in a tower, which could only have had one room as large as this on each floor.

As Pierre Cusquel said: 'I never saw her led into prison, but I saw her two or three times in a room of the castle of Rouen, towards the rear entrance.'[15]

Cusquel was a burgher of the town and not a member of the Tribunal. His visits, other than to the hearings, were therefore made in the company of the 'master of masonry works', Jehan Son, who knew the castle thoroughly. Through him, Pierre Cusquel was informed of the maze of underground passages, most of which were described in Doctor Cerné's plan.

This was why he was able to narrate that 'Jehanne had escaped and some other had been burnt in her place'.[16]

These secret passages, a feature of all large fortresses of the time, thus confirm the likelihood not only of the frequent manifestations of the 'voices in the castle', but also of John of Bedford's ungentlemanly indiscretion committed during the check on the Maid's virginity.*

As we have seen, a woman who was not 'recognized to be a virgin' could be accused of commerce with demons, therefore of witchcraft, so that this second examination is understandable—the first, presided over at Poitiers by Queen Yolanda in person, had validated the mission. At Rouen the second took place under the supervision and with the assistance of a very high lady, the King of England's aunt, Anne of Bedford. Joan was recognized to be a virgin and intact, said the usher Jean Massieu, 'after which, the Duchess had the guards and others forbidden to do her any violence'.[17] This was an affair far more momentous than that of a common witch and it was the only way of giving the Maid of Orleans a chance.

Ever since she had been held in captivity, the young Henry VI had shown a disturbing proclivity in the way he displayed a child-like logic together with his well-known tenderness. Then aged nine, the sovereign had expressed the desire to meet Joan, a natural enough sentiment on the part of a nephew.

The scene has been recounted by Raymond de Rigné.

* Translator's note: He witnessed it from 'a secret place'.

Henry: 'Tie her up, if you are frightened. But I would be unable to eat anything more if I knew she was always locked up in that cage, like a wild animal.' He continued in a low voice: 'She has a gentle face and she is so beautiful . . . you will make her die by leaving her thus, and that would not be to your advantage: you would no longer be able to do her trial.'

Struck by the logic of this, the Earl of Warwick gave immediate orders that Joan should be secretly released from her chains so that the soldiers would continue to believe her well chained.[18]

It is quite possible that for a short while the Maid was subjected to harsh treatment. Certainly her internment cannot be compared to Charles of Orleans' 'golden prison'. Nevertheless it gradually became less rigorous.

As the trial mentioned repeated changes of residence, it was sufficient to place her in an official jail during the day, but in her room the rest of the time.

President Cauchon actually took part in these conciliatory measures and one day sent her a carp for her dinner—or it may have been an allice-shad, there is some disagreement on the subject. It was a thoughtful gesture. But the fish cannot have been very fresh, for Joan fell seriously ill after the meal. Modern authors have jumped on the incident to accuse the 'wicked bishop' of trying to poison his unfortunate victim.

Would it really be possible to act in such an illogical manner and to enter to such a degree into contradiction with onself? If Cauchon had intended this, why did he take such precautions to protect Joan's life right until the end of her trial?

23
FRANCE AND BURGUNDY

> Philip the Good had had to continue his fight against the Countess Jacqueline, until the victory of August 1428 . . . The inevitable conclusion is that the stance taken by the Duke about Orleans, which was favourable to Charles VII, was the prelude to further negotiations.[19]

The Duke of Gloucester, Bedford's brother, had married Jacqueline of Bavaria, Countess of Hainaut, in 1422, and this alliance had led him to seek an extension of his power in the Low Countries, which was a prime market for English produce. On his side, Philip of Burgundy also coveted these regions, which were a natural extension of his Flemish possessions, and indispensable to his economy. This rivalry had engendered much diplomatic strife between the two allies. The English plan to annex the Duchy of Orleans was then sufficient to trigger off the inevitable abandonment of Burgundian support at the time of the siege.

As a result, although the Maid had been handed over to Cauchon by Jean de Ligny, Philip the Good was prudently non-committal, which enabled him to maintain his relations with Charles VII with complete equanimity.

For once, France, or what remained of it, gave the appearance of unity, the country retaining for its legitimized sovereign a loyalty that the Maid's disgrace could have been expected to jeopardize. As we have seen, the subsidies stopped because the 'treasurers of the King of Heaven had other penury to succour'.

But, quite apart from the general indifference to Joan, events were determined by two far deeper causes.

On the one hand, the King's volte-face made a breach of contract with the movement, causing the plan for the West's social regeneration to be abandoned for good.

On the other, there were cracks signifying a rift in the Franciscan Order between Observants and Conventuals.* A century later, the failure of the movement provoked the reaction; and even the Reformation assumed some of the fifteenth-century emblems or symbols—the white dove, the tongue of fire, and especially the Celtic cross; this

* Translator's note: The Observants were stricter Franciscans than the Conventuals who followed a mitigated rule.

was confirmed to me by pastors of the Reformed Church whom I questioned on their symbols.

The accusation generally levelled against Charles VII with regard to his sister is therefore a facile solution. He had in fact not hesitated to warn the Duke of Burgundy 'that he would inflict similar treatment on those of the other party whom he had in his hands'[20] should the handing over of the prisoner to Cauchon have a fatal issue.

In any case, the King's interests were not in avoiding a trial or even a condemnation. The power of such an emotive charge could only render him a political service: nations are in need of martyrs, even if they are invented, 'prefabricated'.

Furthermore, diplomacy had been more fruitful than military action, often disastrous in this naturally undisciplined country. And Joan's enemies, of whom the foremost was La Trémoille, were there to dispel any desire to openly settle accounts. Instead of an ostentatious show of force, which could end in failure, it was infinitely preferable, as is so often the case, to conduct discreet negotiations with Bedford and Cauchon.

This was why, although he had a prior right to buy her back, the King of France, Duke Philip's suzerain, did not pay the ransom. More surprising was the fact that no-one even suggested it—neither Joan's former friends in the Franciscan fraternities, nor Charles of Orleans, despite his well-known generosity towards his half-sister. The orders were to be silent on the subject. The only measure that was taken was to send some troops to the Rouen area towards the end of the trial, in order to impress the enemy should the agreement not be respected.

These points are not stressed by historians, but merely mentioned in a medley of contradictions, to reinforce the emotional factors of the legend, and to show up the Maid's most faithful companions in a bad light.

Why is it that La Hire, d'Alençon, or Gilles de Rais, never made the slightest protest?

For Yolanda of Anjou and 'Saint' Colette, the question is easier to settle. These Franciscan ladies were *Discrètes*, and manifested themselves accordingly: 'The voice was in the castle . . .' It has even been claimed that there were some Franciscans amongst the judges.[21] It is likely, but the secret was well kept.

The Hundred Years War, which had started as an affair over inheritance, became a 'family council' on a European scale. The role of notary was held at Rouen by His Lordship Cauchon of Sommièvre, president of an incredibly versatile Tribunal of which several members, when cited 25 years later, then showed themselves as ready to rehabilitate Joan as they had been to condemn her.

24

CAUCHON'S FORGERIES

> It is to be wondered whether the Bishop did not wish to see some embarrassing witnesses disappear . . .
>
> (Reverend Father Doncoeur)

It is a fact that a few witnesses soon disappeared, sometimes in mysterious circumstances. With all the authority of the cloth, Father Doncoeur continued:

> The fact that Cauchon should have taken five or six years to translate into Latin the questionings of Joan and assemble all the documents is disturbing . . .
>
> . . . what Joan did not know is that the official instrument drawn up by Cauchon to be the authentic one for history, would only enter the archives of England, France and Rouen after having been re-written by her hypocritical judges . . .
>
> . . . Precisely because it is official, the Latin text of the Trial only conveys a political and partisan version of the truth . . .[22]

It did indeed convey a political and partisan version of the truth, but with aspects which concerned all the powers involved—the two states, the Church and the parties.

The original documents of the Trial have not been found. We only have 're-writings' which were authenticated and established after the event. The most specific doubts can be expressed about their sincerity, if one assesses the problems involved objectively.

First, an official record of the execution, which would have been the one conclusive document, never existed and was never even mentioned in the text. Yet the execution was the crowning of the whole affair.

In the course of the preliminary investigation, Cauchon took all the factors into account, considered each party and provided against all eventualities, including a rehabilitation.

If a question was embarrassing, it was hurried over. Countless difficult ones were thus replaced by easy ones, pointed out Father Doncoeur after 25 years' research.

> The notes taken day by day by the clerks formed a record of the Trial. Cauchon translated it into Latin, taking five or six years to send

it to the University of Paris and to communicate it to the chanceries.

The chief clerk Guillaume Manchon had kept minutes of the questioning and he submitted them to the judges presiding over the Rehabilitation. They were accompanied by a text denouncing the articles falsified by the Bishop of Beauvais . . .

It was a copy of Manchon's minutes that Father Doncoeur found in the library of the chapter of Orleans.[23]

With this evidence, it is an easy matter to find proof of the fakes. It suffices to compare certain features in the French copy and in the Latin translation. Two points in particular need to be stressed. The first is that 'Cauchon had made the participants swear to keep silent about all that was said and all that was done'. But, emphasized Father Doncoeur, 'there is no trace of this oath in the Latin translation'.

By this astuteness on the part of the Bishop, the statements made at the Rehabilitation by some of the original judges of 1431 were automatically invalid. The judges would otherwise be perjuring themselves, something a good Christian would not contemplate.

The second is that the act of abjuration, so astonishing that it had always appeared suspect, was modified to such an extent that it became unrecognizable. So much so that the copyist of the notarial minutes, taken aback, added:

Then the tenor of the abjuration that the aforementioned Bishop of Beauvais and other judges said was made by the said Jehanne and signed by her hand . . . which I do not believe, and is not to be believed, in view of what shall be said hereafter.[24]

That the Lord of Sommièvre should have taken such liberties on his own authority was startling behaviour from so eminent a jurist—unless he had a number of things to hide. And at a time when the English cause appeared irrevocably lost, while the King of France kept on gaining ascendancy, it is inconceivable that the Bishop, being a good diplomat, should have drawn up the trial in a spirit contrary to his future interests. This is amply proved by the fact that, despite the official outcome of the trial, and despite the threats issued by Charles VII, the latter never took vengeance on anybody, not even on Cauchon who should have been the first victim.

From the second comparison exposed below, it is now apparent that the 're-writing' of the Trial of Condemnation constituted an excellent spring-board when it was a question of drawing up the first summonses of the Trial of Rehabilitation. On 15th December 1455, Master Guillaume Prévosteau, the attorney for Isabelle, Pierre and Jean d'Arc, after having presented the Rescript of Pope Calixtus III for the second time, exposed in twelve points the manifest defects of the first trial. This is what made it possible to invalidate the condemnation. The 'family councils' were therefore followed by the cleverest legal hoax of the Christian era.

The following points constituted the grounds for appeal at the first session of the Trial of Rehabilitation.[25]

1. *The accused did not reside and had not committed an offence in the diocese of Beauvais.*

2. *Pressure was exerted on the Inquisitor to adjudge the charges against Joan a matter of faith.*

Why did the University of Paris claim the prisoner, if the charges against her were not a matter of faith?

3. *Joan had several times impugned the competence of the Bishop of Beauvais to judge her because he was her mortal enemy.*

The article shows that the Maid was well educated and of keen intelligence, contrary to the opinions of witnesses who testified at both trials. For example, Brother Ladvenu's statement: 'She was very simple-minded. She barely knew the Paternoster.'

It is our turn to question Brother Ladvenu: 'When did you disguise the truth? When you voted for the condemnation at Rouen, or in your statement of 1456?'

4. *The accused had made an appeal to the Pope and the Council.*

Who gave Joan this idea? Ysembart de la Pierre, Martin Ladvenu? An appeal to the Pope was sufficient to send Joan straight to Paris.

The Bishop's great cleverness lay in saving her from the Inquisition, the terrible legal process of contemporary tribunals. It was another infringement of the rules of Canon Law.

5. *A trial that touched on secret revelations belonged only to the Apostolic See.*

6. *Such harsh prison treatment, together with duress amounting to torture, when applied to a minor, in a matter of faith, entail annulment.*

This clear indictment reveals the partisan spirit which pervaded the Rehabilitation, for the sole benefit of Charles VII.

7. *A lawyer's services should have been granted to the accused.*

This is an obvious charge to make. Cauchon of course did not want anyone putting a spoke in his wheel. A condemnation was essential, and he obtained it. Public opinion would be satisfied.

8. *The accused was a minor. A sentence cannot be passed on undefended minors under 25.*

This is an important point. It explains the perseverance shown in 1431 as in 1456 to establish unequivocally that Joan was a minor. If it had been known that she was nearly 25, it would have changed everything.

I shall not mention the last four extremely tendentious charges in which insincerity had the one purpose of facilitating the rehabilitation of the accused, and thereby proving *ad vitam aeternam* that the

King of France had not regained his throne by the intervention of a heretic.

Such were the accusations levelled at the 1431 proceedings, which had been conducted by one of the greatest specialists of Canon Law, the Bishop of Beauvais. Despite this, though I do not wish to lengthen the list of his deceits, it must be said that, as a result of his intrigues, Cauchon knowingly put himself in an extraordinary position. And this was before the trial had even opened, when he had only just received the letters granting him a 'concession of territory' which enabled him to preside over the Rouen tribunal. Yet no one in his entourage thought to call him to account—neither the assessors nor his conformist contemporaries.

By what manoeuvre was Cauchon able to persuade the Grand Inquisitor of France, Jean Graverend, to stay away from the trial, and to go off to his diocese of Coutances?

> That the general representative of the Inquisition should be absent in a cause bearing on faith was unprecedented! The trial could not open, and the whole procedure was paralysed . . .
>
> Graverend was guilty of dereliction of duty, without having received from Rome any precise instructions as to the course of action he should take . . .
>
> . . . It was extremely odd and the connivance of the two men is proved in that Graverend made no protest about the infringement of Canon Law perpetrated by Cauchon in having Joan detained in the royal castle of Rouen. Similarly he made no protest when the name of his local representative, Jean Le Maistre, was abused: for the Bishop had no hesitation in linking Le Maistre with the trial preliminaries, particularly as the latter was also absent from the opening session on 9th January 1431.[26]

For the Trial indeed opened, at long last.

25

IN NOMINE DOMINI . . . AMEN

Here begin the Proceedings in Matter of Faith, against the woman Jeanne, commonly called *The Maid*, 9th January 1431.

In other words, this 'Maid', who at this juncture was not called d'Arc, was suspected of heresy.

> The crime of heresy, considered in the Middle Ages to constitute an attempt upon the security of the State, was punishable by death.
>
> It attracted the sentence of the stake . . . but the ecclesiastical tribunals themselves never pronounced the death sentence.[27]

Since heresy constituted an attempt upon the security of the State, President Cauchon used all his skills in avoiding the pitfalls of unnecessarily indiscreet questions and dangerously revealing answers.

It is certain, not to say obvious, that there was an understanding between the Bishop and Joan. In the interests of her party, she did not blunder. Helped by her excellent memory, she was ever in control and never gave in.

His Lordship Pierre had chosen a secular prison, for at the royal castle he was free to come and go as he liked, without the danger of indiscreet comment by a blundering colleague.

This was why Joan was not granted a lawyer. Unreasonable gossip had to be avoided. The only person tolerated was Nicolas Loyseleur, the Bishop's loyal associate who has incurred so much odium. Entrenched in his inaccessible legal fortress, Cauchon could suggest and even dictate replies to his prisoner, as he wanted. The questioning was in any case under his control or that of his confederates:

'You would have done better to have kept silent,' was his sharp reproof to a judge who was uninitiated.

An analytical reading of the Trial proceedings shows that the questioning turned on the same problems, and was invariably superficial. If an inopportune revelation seemed imminent, they switched to some other topic.

As at Poitiers, Joan's replies showed both her subtlety and her arrogance. Whilst this assessment may well invite contradiction, the evidence is there, for all to read. The truth is that in every age, some supercilious intellectuals have judged their predecessors to be excessively puerile. It is a bad mistake. Our ancestors were no fools, and could in many ways teach us common sense.

A detailed commentary of the Trial is not the purpose of this book, and I shall merely list several categories of Joan's more significant replies, in an attempt to show their line of thought and thus recreate their spirit.

At the first public session, on Wednesday 21st February 1431, Joan categorically refused to reveal secrets of State and only took the oath with reservations.

> There may be questions to which I shall answer you according to the truth, others to which I shall not answer.
>
> . . . As for my revelations from God [from 'the King of Heaven', viz. coming from the Franciscan fraternities], I have never told or revealed them to anyone, but to Charles my King.
>
> . . . I have already told you: I am willing to swear to tell the truth on everything that I know touching the trial. But there are many things that I know that do not touch the trial. There is no need for me to tell you them . . .

When a question embarrassed her, her ancestral arrogance came to the fore.

'Pass over that.' (In other words, leave me alone.)

'I accept no restriction.'

Or else she would be threatening:

'Ha, if you were better informed about me, all of you, you would wish me to be out of your hands.'

She was more discreet about her age, her origins, and her condition: 'I am nineteen years old, or thereabouts, as far as I know.' 'I do not know my surname.' The medieval French *surnom*, in Latin *cognomen*, indeed corresponds to the modern surname, while *nomen* is the Christian name. She therefore refused to call herself *d'Arc*. This patronymic was first bestowed upon her by Pope Calixtus III, in his rescript authorizing the Trial of Rehabilitation.

When Joan declared 'My father was called Jacques d'Arc, and my mother Isabelle', she was not lying; she was merely implying the word 'adoptive'. In any case, Queen Isabeau herself signed 'Isabel'.

'. . . I had several other godmothers, so my mother said . . .'

'. . . I did not go to the fields with the flocks . . .'

'. . . After reaching the age of discretion, I did not usually tend the flocks, but helped to lead them to the fields and to a castle [the castle of l'Isle, that Jacques d'Arc had rented], when there was a scare about soldiers.'

On the other hand, she omitted no detail concerning the physical reality of the 'voices' (angels and saints), thereby designating living personalities, according to the Franciscan usage. This *discrète* terminology was confirmed by a tertiary, Bessonet-Favre, when she wrote about the court: '. . . It will be readily understood what the difference in scope was between the policy-making of *Saints and Angels, tertiaries and monks*, and that of courtiers, of wily diplomats and hypocritical favourites . . .' This text was approved by Mgr Alphonse Gabriel. So even angels and saints dabble in politics. . .

Joan: 'The voice had promised me that the King would receive me immediately on my arrival. Those of our party knew well that the voice had been 'sent by God' (the King of Heaven) to me. I went into the King's presence at the castle . . .'

This was the first meeting before the reception arranged by the promotional campaign—or the country's 'Public Relations Council' as it might be termed.

'. . . I recognized him (the King) amongst others, according to information given by my *voice* . . . That I do know, I am sure about it . . . The King, and many others with him, were able to *hear and see the voice* which was revealing itself to me. Charles of Bourbon was there, and two or three others.'

A judge: 'Jehanne, do you believe that St Michael and St Gabriel have human figures?'

Joan: 'I have seen them, seen them with my eyes. And I believe that it is them, as firmly as that God exists.

A detail about the sign given to the King's treasury:

'. . . It was an angel, from God and from nobody else, who gave the sign to the King. And I thanked Our Lord many times for it.'

Brother Jean de La Fontaine: 'Then the men of the Church saw the sign?'

Joan: 'When the King and those who were with him had seen the sign, and even the Angel who brought it, I asked the King if he was content. He answered that he was. So I departed and went to a small chapel hard by. And I heard tell that after my departure, over three hundred people saw the sign.'

Brother Jean Le Maistre: 'Did the Angel who brought it come from above, or from the ground?'

Joan: 'He came from above: I mean that he came by the command of Our Lord. He entered by the door of the chamber. When he arrived before the King, he made an obeisance before him, and pronounced the fine words that I have said concerning the sign . . .'

This seems curious behaviour from a being supposedly insubstantial!

'. . . He reminded him of the sweet patience he had shown in the great tribulations which had befallen him . . . Yes, from the door, he walked upon the ground, as he came to the King . . . When the

Angel came, *I accompanied him and went with him* by the stairs to the King's chamber. The Angel entered first. I said to the King: "Sire, here is your sign, take it" . . .'

Brother Jean Le Maistre: 'Did all those who were present see the Angel?'

Joan: 'I think that the Archbishop of Rheims, the Lords d'Alençon and La Trémoille and Charles de Bourbon saw him. As for the crown, several Churchmen and others saw it, who did not see the Angel. . . . St Catherine and St Margaret went with this Angel, and with the other angels too, right into the King's chamber . . . The King and the people who were with him believed that it was an angel because of the teaching of the Churchmen present at the ceremony, and the sign of the crown . . .'

Here she no longer hesitated, and implicated not only Charles VII and several supporters of his but also personal contacts of Cauchon—Regnault de Chartres, his superior of Rheims, and La Trémoille. However, she sidestepped any precise questions concerning the substance of the saints and angels.

A judge: 'The saints which appear to you, have they hair?'

She replied, with humour bordering on insolence: 'What a funny question! . . . They spoke very well, with distinction . . .'

The *Book of Poitiers* came to be mentioned.

Joan: 'To my King, I revealed all one day because it concerned him. But I have not had leave to reveal to you what St Michael said to me . . . You who question me, I would like you to have a copy of the Book which is at Poitiers, if it should please God.'

She was more reserved about the secrets concerning her family, and she spoke of the House of Orleans, and of the King:

Joan: 'I know that God loves the Duke of Orleans. About him, I have had more revelations than about any living man, excepting the King . . . I know well that God loves my King and the Duke of Orleans better than me, for the good of their bodies. I know it by revelation . . . I also have revelations touching upon the King, of which I shall not speak to you . . . Of my revelations to the King of France, I shall not tell you anything without leave of my "voices". . . . They were the voices of St Catherine and St Margaret. I have leave "from God" to say that. If you should doubt it, send to Poitiers where I was once questioned. At Poitiers, there are revelations which concern the King of France, of which I shall tell you nothing without leave of my "voices".'

Brother Jean de La Fontaine: 'Have you had no letters from St Michael or your voices?'

Joan: '. . . I have not leave to tell you. Eight days from now, I shall willingly tell you what I know.' (Oursel).

This was how the realm of secret politics was merely touched on. Confronted with such problems, why did the Rouen tribunal not attempt to find out about the conclusions reached at Poitiers? These would have revealed many things useful to the English cause. For instance, a revelation of the promotional campaign would have resulted in the immediate condemnation of Joan for essaying an attempt upon the security of the State, and especially in the conclusive discrediting of Charles VII.

It is moreover unbelievable that the extraordinary Areopagus of Rouen, composed of eminent prelates, and monks from every Order, should not be cognizant of the conventional terminology of 'saints and angels'.

These points alone prove the deliberate orientation and the faking of Cauchon's writings, as well as the tacit connivance of some assessors.

In any event, the secret plan was being realized, and for the time being, both questions and answers remained well within the limits that were never crossed.

This Inquisition tribunal really showed precious little curiosity. Nevertheless, the attitude of the accused was so wilfully obstructive that it was decided, in conformity with the custom of the Church in the Middle Ages, to 'pursue the questioning with the aid of torture'.

26

TORTURE

> . . . The accused was first reduced to a state of minimum resistance by preliminary detention on a diet of bread and water.
>
> Then damaging answers could be drawn out of him by clever and insidious interrogation.
>
> Finally he was put to the question* in all its different forms: the torture of water, of the pulley, of the boot, of the torches, of the rack . . .
>
> (*Les Moines du Moyen Age*, G. Ambroise, *op. cit.*)

Despite the Inquisition's recommendation not to endanger the limbs or life of the accused, the latter's experience of torture invariably left him horribly mutilated.

'With cases that were doubtful,' adds G. Ambroise, 'the main objective of Church procedure was to extort confessions and obtain repentance . . . by all means at their disposal.'

If there was a doubtful case in 1431, it was truly that of the Maid of Orleans. As those suspected of heresy were unfailingly submitted to the question, it is easy to imagine what would have befallen the unfortunate girl had she been tried before the ruthless University of Paris. Her frequently arrogant answers would undoubtedly have irritated the Tribunal, and no refinement of torture would have been spared her.

At the time of this episode, Joan had been in the Bishop's hands for six months. If she had been subjected to the usual treatment, so long a detention would have affected her state of health and lowered her morale. Yet, despite various statements to the contrary, this was not the case. Indeed, her answers remained sharp and caustic throughout the exhausting sessions, so that serious doubts about the severity of her treatment can be entertained. The fact that her morale was in no way impaired contradicts most of the statements.

On Wednesday 9th May, guards came to drag the accused from her bed, and led her promptly to the lower room of the great tower of the castle. At this level, the walls were as much as four or five

* Author's note: The question, the application of torture as part of a judicial examination, had already been abolished for some forms of interrogation, but its use had been rigorously kept in fifteenth-century Canonic procedure.

(*above*) Painting of knights in combat, with a background of red artemisias, on a beam in the Templars' oratory in Metz. (Bibliothèque Nationale)

Nicolas des Armoises ('The Bawler'), after a reproduction of his stele by Henri Vincent in his book on the Armoises family.

Joan the Maid holding a standard decorated with the cross of the Franciscan missions on a field of artemisias. Hispano-Peruvian art of the sixteenth century.
(Collection of Pedro de Osma. Photo by Giraudon)

metres thick, and no sound or scream of agony had ever come through them. Joan knew what awaited her.

Flanked by her guards, she beheld the torchlit scene of the executioner and his helpers busying themselves round the gruesome appliances made ready for her. There is no text describing the scene, which must have been a most traumatic one for her. But it is easy to imagine her horror at the glowing braziers, the rack, the instruments of torture.

The Tribunal had been reduced for the occasion, and there were only some ten assessors, including Jean Massieu, the usher whose memory was so faulty at the Trial of Rehabilitation, and in particular Nicolas Loyseleur. The French representatives of the Inquisition were both absent. And, equally illogically, President Cauchon was also missing.

The instruments of torture capable of extorting any confession were ready. However, cornered by wily interrogators and the threat of suffering, she held her ground.

Joan: 'Truly, though you were to break my limbs and send my soul out of my body, I would not tell you anything more . . . And if you should force me to talk, I would still say thereafter that you had made me talk by force.' Providing she was still capable of doing so . . .

'On Holy Cross day last,* I received comfort from St Gabriel . . . I knew [that it was he] from my voices . . . I asked my voices whether I would be burnt, and they answered me that I should trust in Our Lord, and that He would help me.'

A judge: 'About the sign of the crown which, you say, was granted to the Archbishop of Rheims [Regnault de Chartres]; are you willing to abide by what that Prelate says?'

Joan: 'Bring him here. Let me hear him speak, and then I shall answer you. He would not dare to say the opposite to what I have told you.'[28]

Thereupon, the questioning ended. As still happens nowadays, judges and assessors whispered in consultation, leaned towards each other and shrugged their shoulders. The Bishop had inscribed in the record of this session, at which he was not present:

> In view of the obdurate soul of the accused, and the nature of her answers, We, the aforementioned judges, fearing that the torments of torture would be of little profit to her, have decided to postpone their application until we have deliberated more fully on the question.[1]

And Joan returned unscathed to her cell.

Three days later, the Tribunal convened in the President's residence

* Translator's note: Feast of the Invention of the Cross, 3rd May.

to confirm that the question was unsuitable in this case. As appearance had to be kept up, two judges hypocritically pronounced in favour, as well as Loyseleur who was more conciliatory.

Therefore, contrary to the most deep-rooted customs, the Maid was not subjected to torture, despite that 'obduracy of soul' which ordinarily goaded interrogators into using torture—as witness the Gestapo.

What was the motive behind this exception to the rule? If, as some people may claim, it was all a plot, it was certainly not a diabolical one. Torture would undoubtedly have enabled the Tribunal to obtain the information required, but it was avoided. And it should be added that had His Lordship Pierre been the man usually portrayed, he would not have hesitated to use torture.

But there were other factors: he feared the revelation of facts virtually he alone knew, but more than anything he wished to keep unharmed this prisoner of the highest rank for whom he was responsible.

27

THE ABJURATION

> I believe that, by the Trial, the English were trying to defame the King of France for having involved himself with a witch. (Brother Martin Ladvenu)
> The English sought to have her deemed a heretic, to reach thereby the King of France, our Lord: yes, that was truly their most certain intention. (Brother Pierre Miget)
> (*Trial of Rehabilitation*)

Seven days later, on Saturday 19th May, the Tribunal convened in plenary session, in the chapel of the archiepiscopal palace of Rouen. Twelve articles drawn up by the University of Paris, the Faculty of Theology and the Faculty of Canon Law, were submitted to the assembly for their consideration.

No one seemed shocked by the flaws in procedure that day, and no remark was made about the extraordinary liberties taken. The reason is obvious: together with the specious contents of the twelve articles, they would make it possible to annul the trial in 1456.

The text of the articles was approved without reservation. It was then decided to exhort the accused for the last time. Before concluding the proceedings, they would help her to find the path of truth, her spiritual and corporeal salvation. Finally, a day was fixed for the sentence to be passed.

One of the objectives of the admonition of 24th May was incontestably to compel the so-called heretic to stop wearing men's clothes.

The supporters of the orthodox view have tried to prove Cauchon's forgeries with captious arguments and have always missed the real motives for them, which are indeed difficult to grasp at first sight.

This judicial rigmarole would have smacked of lunacy had it not been dictated by political exigencies. And His Lordship Cauchon, a man of many parts, and one of the most sensible of his time, disconcerts us by his cleverness. He kept up appearances, satisfied everybody, and finally achieved his purpose.

'Cauchon was a traitor, agreed, only to the University of Paris,' said Jean Grimod. To deny this merely confirms the crude popular conception of him.

The Church was considerably indebted to him. Because of his

negotiations which had brought about the election of Martin V, Christian unity had been restored, and the Great Schism had ended with the re-establishing of pontifical authority. In 1430, widespread and thorough activity on his part resulted in a reconciliation between the Count of Armagnac and Martin V, doubtless after meetings with the papal legate, the Cardinal Duke of Bar. His devotion to the Vatican cause did not stop there, and after 1431 he maintained cordial relations with Eugenius IV, the new Holy Father.

It seems hardly necessary to add that His Lordship Pierre, having become Bishop of Lisieux, ended his days peacefully, despite the threats issued by Charles VII after Compiègne against anybody who made an attempt upon the Maid's life. His two conflicting reputations are impossible to reconcile. In the legend, he is an odious character. But his other reputation was perpetuated by his faithful diocesans of Lisieux, by the chapters of Paris and Rheims: until 1789, masses commemorating his interment in a chapel of the Virgin were celebrated every 19th December 'for the repose of the soul of His Lordship Pierre Cauchon of good memory'.

The abjuration scene, outcome of the whole political machination, was the culminating point of the trial.

On 23rd May, a summary of the Twelve Articles condemned Joan for the secrets which she had refused to reveal, for the secret signs, and for her relations with the saints and the angels. Despite the terrible threat which hung over her, the Maid was unmoved: 'As for my deeds and sayings . . . I shall maintain what I said at the Trial, even unto death.'

It was in this state of mind that the following day she confronted her judges in the graveyard of the abbey of Saint-Ouen. A large crowd had gathered by the two platforms. On the first, sat the judges —the Very Reverend Father in Christ and Lord, Henry Beaufort, Cardinal of England, Bishop of Winchester, and at his side the Bishops of Thérouanne, Noyon and Norwich; then, under the presidency of the Bishop of Beauvais, the whole of the Tribunal. On the other platform, Joan was surrounded by ecclesiastics.

The accusations for which the Articles reproached her were repeated. Her statements were declared untenable, erroneous; but she held her ground. Guillaume Erard, doctor of theology, then said to her:

'Will you revoke your sayings and deeds?'

Joan: 'I appeal to God and Our Holy Father the Pope.'

Erard: 'That does not suffice. To fetch Our Holy Father from such a distance is impossible. The Ordinaries* are judges, each in his own diocese . . .'

* Translator's note: The diocesan bishops.

Three exhortations were then read to her, without obtaining any recantation. So Cauchon began to read the final sentence handing Joan over to the secular arm, while the executioner waited at the stake.

The rest of the scene is described in some of the statements of the Trial of Rehabilitation. It makes fascinating reading.

First, Guillaume de la Chambre, an assessor and the Maid's doctor, declared:

> I was present at the sermon preached by Master Guillaume Erard. I forget what he said, but I remember the abjuration . . . after much delay, it was Guillaume Erard who induced her to make it telling her that she should do what she was advised and that she would be freed from prison. It was on this sole condition that she did it . . .

The abjuration therefore did mean eventual freedom for Joan.

Guillaume Manchon, clerk and copyist, added to this:

> She was led onto a platform. Two judgments had been written, one of abjuration and the other of condemnation, and were in the Bishop's hand.
>
> He began to read the sentence of condemnation while Master Nicolas Loyseleur recommended Joan to do what he had told her and to accept woman's clothes.
>
> There was then a short pause. Then, one of the English who was there told the Bishop that he was a traitor.
>
> Meanwhile, Joan signified that she was ready to obey the Church. Then she was made to pronounce her abjuration by being told the formula:
>
> . . . *I, Jehanne, called the Maid, a miserable sinner, recognizing the snare of error in which I was held, and being by God's grace returned to our Holy Mother Church, so that it is apparent that I have returned to her not feignedly but with good heart and will, I do confess that I have most grievously sinned in falsely pretending that I had revelations from God and His Angels, St Catherine and St Margaret . . .*
>
> . . . *And all my words and deeds, which are contrary to the Church, I do revoke. And I wish to dwell in the unity of the Church, and nevermore depart from it. As witness my hand.*
>
> signed Jehanne, a CROSS[29]

Guillaume Manchon continued: 'I do not know whether she repeated it as it was read to her, or whether, when the reading of it was finished, she merely signified her acceptance of it. She was smiling . . . I did not see the letter of abjuration.'

It seems odd that the chief clerk should declare he had not seen the essential document of the trial, neither before nor afterwards—I refer to the short abjuration and not to the long one.

The second clerk-usher was not very communicative on the subject either: 'For a long time, she refused to sign. But finally, hard pressed to do it, and through fear, she signed by making a cross.'

But Haimond de Macy's statement threw light on one of the biggest secrets of the saga.

> . . . to avoid the danger, she said that she accepted to do what they wanted. Then the secretary of the King of England, Laurent Calot, drew from his sleeve a short written document, which he handed to Jehanne to sign. She said that she could neither read nor write.* Despite this, Laurent Calot gave her the document, and a pen to sign it. As if by derision, Jehanne drew a sort of circle. Then Laurent Calot took Jehanne's hand and made her do, with the pen, a sign which I do not remember.
>
> I believe that she is in paradise.[30]

The two abjurations are only known to history through the transcriptions of the Trial. The original documents are missing and the longer one officially handed over to the chanceries six years later was a political instrument.

The other, mentioned by the witnesses and quoted here, was extremely vague and committed Joan to precious little. It was merely a ratification of her submission to the Church. The important point, and the key to a secret, was the symbol drawn on the document: we will see it again. Cauchon actually insisted on it in the official translation:

> And in sign whereof, I have signed this *with my sign.*
>
> Signed Jehanne, a *CROSS.*

A superimposition of the marks made gives:

The cross inscribed in a circle is the quartered circle of Celtic tradition, taken up by the Knights of the Temple and a few initiatory orders.

At the end of this scene, some witnesses affirmed 'that she was smiling, that she laughed, even; that it was a derision.' How could the Maid laugh in such circumstances, a few steps away from a stake prepared for her?

On being questioned, the Bishop of Noyon seemed struck with amnesia. Speaking first of his participation in the trial, he said: 'I think I was present, yes. But I do not remember it well . . .'

About the abjuration scene he added:

* Author's note: What was the reason for this new disclaimer, when everyone knew that she read and signed her letters? Was it not symbolical?

There were some who said that it was not in earnest, that she did but laugh. Amongst them an Englishman, an ecclesiastic and doctor, who was of the House of the Lord Cardinal of England, said to the Bishop of Beauvais that he was too favourable to the accused in this trial . . .

The Bishop replied to him that he was lying. And then, the Cardinal of England prayed this doctor to hold his tongue. [Well, well, so Beaufort was in it too!]

Whereafter, there were several amongst the assistance who said that no heed was being taken of this abjuration . . . that it was not in earnest . . .

In my opinion, she herself was not concerned about it nor attached any importance to it. (Oursel)

This altercation with the Englishman made Cauchon, though chaplain of the Duke of Bedford and member of the Grand Council of England, lose his temper. After his interlocutor had said to him: 'Hurry, hurry, you are too favourable,' the Bishop, furious, threw down his papers, saying that he would do nothing more that day, for he was acting according to his conscience.

'You will render apologies to me . . . I reckon to favour nobody in this affair . . . Judge in matter of faith, I must seek her salvation rather than her death!' (the statement of Pierre Bouhier at the Trial of Rehabilitation).

And the scene at Saint-Ouen ended with the reading of a new 'mitigated' sentence, pronounced by the Bishop. The Maid was condemned to life imprisonment, to the bread of pain and water of affliction, so that she should be a witness to the mercy and moderation of the Tribunal.

With the official pronouncement in these circumstances of Joan's guilt, England could reckon herself satisfied with regard to public opinion, and it was in theory pointless to continue with the trial.

As Joan enquired about her future residence, the promoter Jean d'Estivet answered her: 'The castle of Rouen.'

28

THE JUDGMENT

> All has not been said on the lugubrious drama of Rouen. One has only seen what the judges and the English were willing to be seen.
>
> (Bessonet-Favre)

'Take her to where you found her,' was Pierre Cauchon's order as soon as the abjuration scene was over. Witnesses added that Joan returned to her prison dressed as a woman. It has never been asked where, between Saint-Ouen and Bouvreuil, she could have effected a change in clothing.

From this 24th May 1431 onwards, after she had been taken back to the castle under heavy escort, the Maid of Orleans—or if one prefers, the Maid of France, these two titles both designating someone of royal blood—lost all contact with society. Nearly all her judges were unaware even of her destination.

None of those let into the secret reacted when in 1436 the heroine reappeared under the name of 'Jehanne du Lys, the Maid of France'. The authenticated deed which designated her thus is irrefutable, established as it was in the presence of people whose integrity it is hard to challenge.

But history books relate that a day or two after the abjuration, Cauchon felt concern about the moral health of the one he had until then jealously protected from being 'prosecuted by the goddamns' —or rather, to my way of thinking, by the University.

'Wherefore the Lord Bishop of Beauvais, judge, sent Jean Beaupère and Nicolas Midy [two theologians, who were Joan's arch enemies] to induce and admonish her to persevere and continue in the good resolution she had had on the scaffold.'

On arriving there, the two monks were astonished to find the door of the prison locked and the gaoler gone. He was later discovered in a tavern of the town.

'But they [Beaupère and Midy] were unable to find the man who had the key of her prison. And, while they waited for the gaoler of the said prison, were inveighed against by some English soldiers,' who sought to chase them away by threatening words.[31]

So, as soon as Bedford and Winchester had obtained satisfaction, they relaxed their supervision of Joan. It was logical: by her abjuration, Charles VII's legitimacy was once again compromised.

Supporting this assertion, the consideration shown to the Maid by her English gaolers was violently criticized on the following 4th July in a Paris pulpit: indeed, Jean Graverend, Grand Inquisitor of France had now reappeared, and preached a sermon in which he attacked the future national heroine.[32] Summarized in the *Journal d'un Bourgeois de Paris*, it presents mind-boggling contradictions:

> A friar of the Order of St Dominic, who was Inquisitor and master of theology, preached a sermon. This preacher said also that she had recanted and that she had been sentenced to four years of prison on bread and water, as penitence, but that she did not serve a single day of it . . . She had been waited on like a Lady . . .

And the Bourgeois added that 'Brother Richard* had given communion to my Lady Jehanne the Maid'.

In other words, one month after being condemned as a heretic and being supposedly executed, Joan remained a 'Lady' even to her enemies. The reading of this text prompts one to praise the honesty of the Inquisitor who, floundering in the morass of this complicated subject, nevertheless permitted some of the truth to emerge.

On the other hand, no surprise should be felt at the attitude of the King of France, nor at the myth created by his 'public relations council' in an effort to establish the validity of his right to the throne. The principle of martyrdom rendered a disservice to England, and France reaped the benefit.

But the facts are confirmed by the account in Beaupère's statement, with its surprising conclusion: 'With regard to the final sentence, he is unable to say anything for on the Monday after the abjuration, he left Rouen to go to Basle [to the Council], on the orders of the University of Paris. Thus he knew nothing of the condemnation until he heard of it in Flanders.'[33]

This means that one of the most influential judges abandoned the tribunal at the decisive moment. For those who consider that Cauchon had prepared an inexorable sequence of events leading to the trial for relapse, *viz.* to a death sentence, is it not curious that at that very moment he allowed so reliable a confederate to leave? What difference did two or three days make at the Council, in comparison with the Trial?

On Sunday 27th, Joan, under constraint from her jailers, put on her man's clothes again. According to the legend, it was this very reason that enabled her to be handed over to the secular arm. For Cauchon, this resumption of man's clothes offered a two-fold advantage. First of all, the trial could be brought to a quick close.

* Author's note: The Franciscan who had facilitated the surrender of Troyes.

Secondly, they would be far more practical for the ride following the escape.

Once again, the statements about this exchange of clothing are conflicting. On the whole, those of 1456 contradict the account contained in the 1431 trial proceedings. According to this, on the Monday morning, His Lordship Pierre rushed to Bouvreuil, together with several assessors, to witness the offence. The names of two of their number should be remembered: Thomas de Courcelles and Ysembart de La Pierre.

Cauchon: 'What is this?'

Joan: 'Yes, I have left off woman's dress and resumed man's dress.'

'Why? Who compelled you to put it on again?'

'Myself alone, under no compulsion. I prefer man's dress.'

'Have you not made abjuration, and promised not to go back to wearing this dress?'

'I would rather die than be in irons [at any rate this was what the Bishop made the notaries inscribe]. But, if I am allowed to go to mass, and I am taken out of irons, put into a decent prison and have a woman with me, I shall be good and shall do what the Church wishes.' (Oursel).

But according to public opinion, she was forced to change clothes. The Lord Bishop of Noyon, the man with the faulty memory, declared 'Who it was, I no longer remember . . . but I have heard it said that man's clothing was thrown to her through the window, or between the bars of her prison.'

There are, therefore, two versions to choose from. I personally opt for that of Joan, in agreement with the Bishop, deliberately exchanging her clothing.

Thereupon, the questioning re-started on the usual themes—the voices, the sign, the crown, the promise not kept. 'If you wish it, I shall go back to woman's attire, but for the rest I shall not change,' said Joan. 'And we will draw our own conclusions,' replied Cauchon—conclusions which had doubtless long since been foreseen, if one recalls the sessions of 1st and 3rd March when Joan had hinted at her liberation within three months. That is why as soon as the damaging fact was established, the Bishop's behaviour changed entirely. Until then, he had taken his time, but he now precipitated events, wishing to avoid any indiscretion and escape the University's bitter recriminations. An example had to be made, and, as he had promised, he would give one 'in good form'.

The Tribunal assembled once again in the chapel of the archiepiscopal palace. On this occasion, there were two notable absentees: Jean Beaupère and the elusive Inquisitor Jean Graverend. Forty-two judges then reached the verdict that the Woman Joan, commonly called 'the Maid', had relapsed into several of her errors against orthodoxy. It was decided almost unanimously to

> summon the said Maid to appear, the following day, at eight of the clock, on the square of the Old Market Place of Rouen so as to be declared by Us relapsed, excommunicate, heretic, with the intimations customary in such cases.
>
> signed Manchon and Boisguillaume, clerks.[33]

It is thereby apparent that in order to please their current masters, the eminent theologians of Rouen were at one to formulate the condemnation required by Paris.

In the same way, at the Trial of Rehabilitation, the surviving judges who were summoned testified with equal unanimity to annul their own sentence, this time cravenly submitting to Charles VII who had proved to be the real master.

29
THE STAKE

> She was brought from the castle with her face covered [*le visage embronché*] to the said place where the fire was ready . . . according to the report of those who said they had witnessed it.
>
> (*Chronicle of Perceval de Cagny*)

Contrary to the fanciful definitions put forward to make it tally with the legend, the verb *embroncher* means quite precisely to cover, veil, tilt forward, with the purpose of shadowing or hiding. Turned down, a hood shadowed a face and concealed it. And this was how the Rouen victim was led to the Old Market Place—as can be seen in numerous illustrations of the legend.*

Those authors who sometimes impugn this text by Perceval de Cagny on the grounds that he was not present at the execution forget two things: first, that almost all the witnesses questioned were not present either; second, that Cagny emphasizes the phrase 'the report of those' who had witnessed the scene. As he was also the Duke of Alençon's aide-de-camp, he could hardly have been unaware of the difference between a report and idle talk. And the 'gentle Duke' would hardly have taken on a joker as his confidant.

The controversy can readily be settled by a quotation from Brother Pasquerel's statement. The Maid's former chaplain established precisely and unequivocally that Perceval de Cagny could only be very well informed by his own masters about the deeds of the heroine: 'The King our Lord and the Duke of Alençon know much about it. They know certain secrets that they could reveal, if they wished. I know no more about it.'

This discretion, rather than any loss of memory on his part, was a practical example of the aphorism formulated by Guillaume Prévosteau in his request for the opening of the Trial of Rehabilitation: 'If lying is forbidden, it is none the less licit to hide the truth.' This is tantamount to a licence to say anything.

* Author's note: In his book *Jeanne d'Arc, ses costumes, son armure*, for which he had access to Vatican archives, Adrien Harmand wrote:

'Hidden in the depths of the projecting hood, her face remained invisible . . . And it was thus that she appeared on the platform, for all to see, and heard the sermon before being handed over to the secular arm.' (See illustrations.)

Amongst those who saw the Maid between her relapse and departure from the Great Tower—*viz.* immediately before her disappearance—only four judges came to testify in 1456.

First, Ysembart de la Pierre, questioned on Joan's 'saintly' death, answered laconically: 'Everything that is in the article is true.' Brother Ysembart's statement was especially non-committal in that it was contradictory in several places, and merely repeated the utterances of an English soldier suddenly touched by grace,* and an anecdote describing the executioner's distress!

Testifying in his turn, Master Thomas de Courcelles seemed franker, but showed the same discretion: 'I was present at the last sermon preached in the Old Market on the day of Jehanne's death. However, I did not see HER burn. Immediately after the end of the sermon, and after the sentence had been pronounced, I retired.'

Otherwise, each time official history describes that morning in detail, it defies rational analysis, wallowing in exalted, pietistic preternaturalism—unless this be a form of symbolism, which would be preferable.

Early that morning, at the castle, despite her crimes of heresy, Joan was granted the sacraments of penance and of the Eucharist. This paradox has never been sufficiently underlined: she received communion just as if she had not been cut off from the Christian community by a greater excommunication that alone the Pope could lift.

After this, His Lordship Pierre Cauchon who, as president of the Tribunal, should normally have been waiting on the platform beside his legal colleagues, paid her a visit. One wonders why he did so, unless he had a very special reason, which in fact he never divulged to anybody.

Soldiers then came to fetch the victim from her cell—the cell of tradition. It has been suggested that just over 2·5 square metres was space enough for a bed, at least two English guards, and on occasion as many as ten judges. Was there room for Joan as well? It is possible, for she has frequently been portrayed in it, sitting on the wooden beam to which she was shackled . . . But there is no doubt that it was no more than an official cell for publicity purposes. Fortunately, Dr Cerné's study put the record straight.[34]

According to the witnesses the escort, now about 120 strong, advanced across the town bearing swords and lances. It was a real human screen which made it impossible for anyone to see or come near the future martyr who apparently 'uttered pious lamentations,

* Author's note: It was the soldier who is supposed to have seen 'a white dove flying up from the flames on the side towards France.' (*Trial*, op. cit.). This is typically Franciscan symbolism, and it seems likely that this soldier was a representative of English Tertiaries.

repeating again and again the name of Jesus, and pronouncing it up to six times in succession at the moment of expiring'.

Meanwhile her features remained completely concealed by the dark-coloured hood drawn down over her face. Yet this was contrary to custom, it being considered a salutary example for the condemned to have the face uncovered.

Once again, the Bishop of Beauvais was not to be deterred, for necessity has no law. The density of the escort and the anonymity conferred by the hood would prevent any embarrassing revelation. These precautions were in fact superfluous as few people in Rouen actually knew Joan the Maid.

Surprisingly, too, the escort arrived an hour late although it had only to come a few hundred yards from the castle.

According to the text of the trial, the meeting had been fixed for eight o'clock, but it was past nine when the procession came to the Old Market. The Tribunal had been waiting a long time already, and showed signs of impatience and intense irritation.

More than 800 men-at-arms deployed over the square, pushing the crowd back to its periphery. A small scaffold opposite the official platform welcomed this 'Jeanne'* who then heard two exhortations. The second admonition pronounced by Cauchon included the sentence: the condemned was to be handed over to secular justice. 'We pray the secular arm to moderate its judgment towards you on THIS SIDE of death and the mutilation of your limbs; and if signs of true penitence appear in you, to permit the sacrament of penance to be administered to you,' concluded the Bishop.

'On this side of death', 'the sacrament of penance': these were the subtly ambiguous expressions used by the Bishop of Beauvais who, with full knowledge of the facts, was in a position to add all necessary reservations.

Unfortunately for the legend, there was never any sentence from the 'secular arm'—in other words the lay judges.

The clergy then all retired, leaving only Ladvenu and Ysembart, who had been appointed to assist the condemned in her last moments. There were therefore only two witnesses.

And what did the crowd see of all this? Their attention was distracted by an inordinately long sentence daubed on a large panel which itself partly hid the stake:

> Jehanne who calls herself the Maid, liar, pernicious, deceiver of the people, sorceress, superstitious, blasphemeress of God, presumptuous, disbeliever of the Faith in Jesus-Christ, braggart, idolatress, cruel, wanton, invoker of the devil, apostate, schismatic and heretic.

* Author's note: One of the witches bearing the name of Jeanne, as will be seen in the next chapter.

In short all the sins; and the unusual length of the inscription justified the unusual dimensions of the placard.

Still according to the texts, the unfortunate woman was then dressed with the enormous mitre usually worn by heretics at the stake. This mitre has inspired impassioned discussions even quite recently, frequently being confused with the hood.* It is all quite simple however. Like the placard, the mitre also bore defamatory words and—this is the important part—it was put over the hood, and came down low over the forehead.

Immediately the sentence had been pronounced by the ecclesiastical Tribunal, the sheriff Raoul le Bouteiller, who had been sent by Bedford, ordered the guards to hurry.

She was then seized 'by the English soldiers in great fury without any sentence by the secular judge, although the sheriff of Rouen and the council of the lay court were present,' said Ladvenu.

Ysembart confirmed this in his statement, saying that he had seen well and clearly perceived, because he was present at both the summing up and conclusion of the trial, that the secular judge did not condemn her to death, nor to consumption by fire . . . Notwithstanding this, without any final sentence, she was delivered into the hands of the executioner.

This was another violation of legal procedure: it was the rule that a second sentence should be pronounced by the sheriff before the executioner was empowered to carry out his duty.

Whatever some modern authors may claim, this departure from traditional procedure shocked most of the judges so profoundly that they were to speak of it vehemently in 1456, 25 years later.

And because of this break with tradition, the only accounts of the way that morning ended are to be found in the ambiguous statements of the two preaching friars who, so they said, remained by the stake.

Questioned on Joan's holy death, Ladvenu cleverly equivocated: 'The article expresses the truth. The executioner—I saw and heard him myself—provided in my presence the evidence that she had undergone a terrible death.' In short, in order not to lie, the brave friar was first evasive, then took care not to testify directly by making the executioner speak in his stead.

As for his friend Ysembart, after referring too to the article's accuracy, he even added 'that on this occasion, the Bishop of Beauvais, who was one of the judges, wept!'

That really is too much to accept.

* Author's note: As, for example, by Maurice Garçon, in *Ecclesia*.

30

THE SUBSTITUTION

> In the town of Rouen, in Normandy, she was heated and burnt in a fire, so it has been claimed, but the contrary has since been proved.
>
> (*Chronicle of the Dean of Saint-Thibaud of Metz*)

'Serious doubt still prevails, especially in Lorraine, as to whether the Maid, who was led veiled to the stake, really was burnt.' This fresh confirmation was written in 1783 by Dom Nicolas Lelong, in his *Histoire Ecclésiastique et Civile du Diocèse de Laon.* He was a churchman who had no personal interest in the matter and he too emphasized that the victim's face was *embronché* until the last.

After Joan had been taken prisoner at Compiègne, the University had felt anxiety about the dealings between His Lordship Cauchon and his Burgundian friends, and in July 1430, had been moved to write to Philip the Good about it: '. . . We greatly fear that, by the falseness and the seduction of the evil enemy, by the malice and the subtlety of wicked people who so ardently wish to deliver this woman by exceptional means, she will be removed in some way from our control.'

Thus the University had sensed the plans which were afoot to 'place the accused beyond its jurisdiction'. The Bishop of Beauvais had successfully duped his Paris colleagues all along. And now, to maintain absolute plausibility, a real witch or some such person would be substituted for the Maid of Orleans to pass off as her.

This witch 'was one of five who were burnt in Rouen between 1430 and 1432, and whose names are inscribed in the *livres des comptes des Domaines*, as well as the price of wood and the wages of the executioner: Jeanne-la-Turquenne, Jeanne Vanneril, Jeanne-la-Guillorée, Alice-la-Rousse and Caroline-la-Ferté'.[35] This list alone gives three different Jeannes who were burnt. Why then was Joan the Maid's execution mentioned in neither the registers of the *Domaines* nor in the archives of the chapter of Rouen? Why was there no sentence by the sheriff, as custom demanded?

As the record of the execution has never come to light, there is no conclusive document proving the claimed martyrdom, apart from the famous Rehabilitation testimonies. The dates proposed for it do not even agree.*

These were not the only anomalies of this closing day of an essentially political trial. One of them was confirmed by the sheriff's lieutenant, Laurent Guesdon, a respectable burgher of Rouen.

> It does not seem to me that the procedure was regular. Shortly afterwards, a malefactor called Georges Folenfant was similarly handed over to the secular arm by ecclesiastical sentence. But he was then led to the sheriff's court, and condemned by the lay judges. He was not led to the stake so promptly. (Oursel)

It is strange that for the Maid of Orleans the conclusion should have been so hurried that no positive trace remained of it. Yet in order to preserve its full psychological impact, the staging of it should surely have been done according to the book.

It did not matter to Cauchon however, for the trial record was only handed over to the chanceries several years later. As for the episode of the stake, it was only publicly revealed 20 years later, for the glory of Charles VII, which makes it impossible to accept without reservations.

It is also surprising that the Bishop of Beauvais, who until the abjuration had spun out the proceedings over seven months, should suddenly be seized with frenzied haste. After he had said to Warwick: 'Farewell, it is done . . . be of good cheer' following the constat of relapse, Cauchon hastily completed his work, leaving to posterity the most illegal juridical act possible.

The woman executed on 30th May was literally hooded, and unrecognizable. What with the large number of soldiers, the placards, inscriptions, and the summary execution, it seems that extremely odd instructions were carried out that day.

For the edification of any doubters, the fire was even 'opened' after a while, exposing a half-charred body which was indeed a woman's.

> When she was dead, the English, fearing lest it be said that she had escaped, begged the executioner to push back the fire a little, so that the crowd might see she was dead, and that it might not be said she had escaped. (Deposition of J. Riquier at the Trial of Rehabilitation.)

Whereupon, these same English hastily gathered up the ashes, which were 'thrown into the Seine, because they greatly feared lest she escape or lest some believe she had escaped. I know no more.' (Pierre Cusquel.)

* Author's note: An *Abrégé Chronologique de l'Histoire de France*, published in Paris in 1749 with the royal privilege and seal of approval, mentions 14th June. According to several authors including Jean Grimod and M. David-Darnac, Hénault also gives the 14th June, and de Serre the 6th July. Caxton and Polydore Vergil suggest February 1432, after nine months' supplementary detention. It is a far cry from 30th May 1431.

Many people indeed believed this, and as it was becoming something of an obsession, the English were acutely embarrassed.

The executioner was in a good position to know more. The monks having withdrawn, he proceeded to the 'toilet' of the condemned, dressing her in a long tunic covered with sulphur and pitch. At the end of the execution, he was apparently greatly troubled. 'Then, on the same day, he came to the convent of the preaching friars and said to Brother Ladvenu and to me that he was in great fear of being damned, for he had burnt a saint.' (Brother Ysembart)

However it did not make him forgo his lunch. He apparently went to confession . . .

This executioner must certainly have had doubts, which would explain his agitated state. It is tempting to speculate on his amazement had the Bishop sanctioned the application of torture on 9th May. For he would then, on baring part of Joan's body, have noticed the marks of serious wounds she had received in battle. Suddenly, on 30th May, he would have been shocked to find that the woman he was preparing had no such marks, and appeared to be much older.

The first text which supports this course of events is to be found, curiously enough, in the British Museum.

'Finally, they had her publicly burnt, or some other woman like her. As to which many people have been and still are of diverse opinions.'[36]

A later document, the 1540 Breton Chronicle stated: 'The Maid was burnt at Rouen, or condemned to be.'[37]

A century later, Gabriel Naudé, a man of letters, and the librarian of Richelieu and Mazarin, went so far as to think that only an effigy of Joan had been burnt.

Finally, Abbé Cochon,* an apostolic notary from Rouen, who kept a detailed account of important events of the town after 1404, abruptly interrupted his *Journal* on the day after King Henry VI's arrival in 1430, and only resumed it after the political turmoil, in 1433. He therefore mentions neither the trial nor the execution.

All of this lends credence to the view that Joan was indeed liberated as she had forecast in her declarations during the early sessions. In the session of 1st March:

A judge: 'Did your voices tell you that you will be delivered within three months?'

Joan: 'That has nothing to do with your trial. In any case, I know not when I shall be delivered.'

Beaupère: 'Did your Counsel not tell your that you would be delivered from the prison that you occupy at present?'

* Author's note: A purely coincidental homonym of Bishop Pierre Cauchon of Sommievre.

Joan: 'Speak to me of it in three months' time . . . (suddenly smiling) . . . I am bound to be delivered one day. Do you want me to tell you what only concerns the King of France?' And in the session of 3rd March:

A judge: 'Have you learnt by revelation that you will escape?'

Joan: 'That has nothing to do with the trial . . . I trust in God. By my faith, I know neither the day nor the hour when I shall escape.'

The fact these exchanges took place on 1st and 3rd March is highly significant, for three months later to the day, the trial was over. One is hard put to regard this as one more coincidence or miraculous premonition, for both are already legion in the saga.

Even if the Maid of Orleans did not recover her total freedom on 30th May 1431, then at any rate she safely left the castle of Rouen that day.

While Ysembart de la Pierre acted as intermediary between the archbishopric and Bouvreuil, Martin Ladvenu arrived at the castle early, accompanied by Brother Jean Toutmouillé. He administered the sacraments to the condemned 'rather irreverently', as he said in 1456.

Cauchon then arrived on the scene. Why this visit? As we have seen, he was not supposed to be here. There is seemingly no logical reason for it. Understandably overcome with anxiety, Joan exclaimed: 'Bishop, I die because of you.'

'Ah! Joan, have patience, you die because . . . blah . . . blah . . . blah . . .,' continued the Bishop in solemn tones.

'That done, I went out and heard no more,' concluded Brother Toutmouillé.[38] What an escape clause!

For the general public, it was then that Joan the Maid disappeared, at least symbolically; and it was then that the substitution took place. This was the corner-stone of an entirely rigged trial.

A study of the castle itself not only allows one to follow the unfolding of the plan in all its various stages but also to verify its feasibility.

In the wall of the tower, at the same level as the 'publicity' cell, there were two almost contiguous passages, separated by a recess.* To the left, the entrance to the tower led on to a drawbridge which linked it to the interior court of the castle. To the right, a landing preceded by two steps led to the cell, which was immediately to the right, and to a spiral staircase which went up to the first floor.

Between the two, there was a dark recess, two yards long. In it, a square trapdoor gave access to underground passages; then, further back, was a well which was linked half-way down with these underground passages.†

* See photographic reproduction of the plan of the tower.

† Author's note: See Jean de Saint-Jean (*op. cit.*): 'The well supplied the keep with water and was linked to a similar well situated in the *tour de la Pucelle* by

While the monks waited outside, the Bishop of Beauvais remained alone with Joan and handed her a coat which had been brought in unobtrusively, in order to conceal her masculine clothing. It is possible that the Earl of Warwick was present, in which case the two men entirely obstructed the entrance to the cell.

It was now time for the designated escort officially to fetch Joan's substitute from the floor above. Dressed, and veiled, she had been brought there and chained fairly early. The escort came down the stairs, passed in front of the cell, joined the monks, and set off for the Old Market.

As soon as the commotion had died down, Cauchon moved away from the door of the small cell. With a few steps, the Maid crossed the two yards separating her from the square trapdoor, and disappeared beneath it. His Lordship hastened to the tribunal over which he presided solemnly.

Still trembling with emotion, Joan came to the bottom of the 30-foot ladder, where she found two knights waiting to lead her to the exit of the underground passage and act as her escort.

At the time, this exit apparently came out 'towards the fields'. Nowadays, it still exists, at the back of the courtyard of number 102 rue Jeanne-d'Arc—an ironic coincidence.

Three mounts were ready for the flight, which passed unnoticed in the general excitement which prevailed in Rouen that morning.

Thus, paradoxically, Joan's masculine attire, which had been the cause of the condemnation, facilitated her escape.

No defence of the traditional version stands up to the five blatant anomalies of this day:

1. Why did the President of the Tribunal, make that last visit to his captive alone and after everyone else?

It is hard to believe in unexpected crocodile-tears shed by men of his ilk.

2. Why were so many precautions taken to conceal the victim's face from the eyes of the public, whereas the fire was pushed back to show an unrecognizable body? What needed proving?

3. After the hour's delay, and although the judges had recommended moderation to the secular arm, the sheriff did not pronounce a final sentence, but on the contrary rushed this execution which none of the authorities witnessed.

4. Why was the stake so much taller than usual?

On his own admission, the executioner was unable to do his duty

---

the subterranean aqueduct of Gaalor. During the Second World War, the Germans made a shelter out of this keep and fixed an iron ladder in the well as a means of access to the underground passage.' The internal height of the aqueduct was great enough to allow a man to stand upright.

efficiently. Impeded by the high faggots, he was unable to strangle the condemned, as was the custom so as to curtail the agony.

5. Exhaustive research done in the registers of the Archbishopric of Rouen has never brought to light 'any mention of the burning of Joan the Maid'. This has recently been confirmed by the Archives Départementales de la Seine-Maritime.

Catherine de la Rochelle's prediction, uttered after the Maid's incarceration, that she would leave prison with the help of the devil, became clear, particularly in view of the fact that Catherine was incited by that well-known Franciscan intriguer, Brother Richard.

Obviously, in the eyes of the crowd, Pierre Cauchon was the devil personified, if only by reason of his intelligence. That is why historical exigencies have always conveniently depicted him in the blackest light.

Four lines by Georges Chastelain (1404–1475) provide a neat summary of the affair:

> Burnt to ashes at Rouen
> To the great detriment of the French,
> But since giving to understand
> That, in other times, she is reborn.

These words are particularly credible because Chastelain was both the chronicler of the House of Burgundy, and a councillor of Philip the Good and Charles the Bold. He could hardly have been in a better position to know the truth—that the Maid had survived the trial.

NOTES TO PART III

1 In *Jeanne d'Arc, tertiaire de saint François, op. cit.*
2 See David-Darnac, *Le Dossier de Jehanne, op. cit.*
3 Jean Grimod in *Jeanne d'Arc a-t-elle été brûlée?*
4 See Bessonet-Favre, *op. cit.*; and *La Vérité sur Jeanne d'Arc* by Francis Andrée
5 See part V on the modern manifestations of Druidic cults in Brittany
6 Quoted by Régine Pernoud in *Jeanne d'Arc par elle-même et ses Témoins, op. cit.*
7 *Trial of Rehabilitation, op. cit.*
8 *La vraye Histoire de la Pucelle*, R. de Rigné
9 *Le dossier de Jehanne, op. cit.*
10 Bessonet-Favre, *op. cit.*
11 R. de Rigné, *op. cit.*
12 Joseph Delteil. Quoted by Claude Pasteur in *Les Deux Jeanne d'Arc*. A translation of Delteil's book (*Joan of Arc*) by Malcolm Cowley was published by Allen & Unwin in 1926
13 *Trial, op. cit.*
14 See 'L'Enceinte et les Tours du Vieux Château de Rouen' in *Bulletin de la Société des Amis des Monuments rouennais* (1928 to 1931)
15 *Trial of Rehabilitation, op. cit.*
16 Marcel Hervieu in 'Jeanne d'Arc a-t-elle été brûlée à Rouen', *La France au combat*, 1947. Quoted by Jean Grimod
17 *Trial of Rehabilitation, op. cit.*
18 R. de Rigné, *op. cit.*
19 Jean de Saint-Jean, *op. cit.*
20 M. David-Darnac, *op. cit.*
21 Bessonet-Favre, *op. cit.*; Oursel
22 *Les Faux de Cauchon*, by Father Doncoeur. Quoted by Jean Grimod, *op. cit.*
23 Jean Grimod
24 *Ibid*
25 The eight charges quoted are taken from Raymond Oursel, *op. cit.*
26 See *Le dossier de Jehanne*, M. David-Darnac, *op. cit.*
27 See *Les Moines du Moyen Age*, G. Ambroise
28 Oursel, *op. cit.*
29 Official text taken from the Orleans Manuscript. Quoted by Jean Grimod
30 Trial, *op. cit.*
31 See Quicherat, *Procès*, tome 1
32 See Mélanges, by Charles de Beaurepaire
33 Oursel, *op. cit.*
34 *L'Enceinte et les Tours du Vieux Château de Rouen*, see above, part III, § 22

35 See *Jeanne d'Arc et la Normandie*, by A. Sarrazin, quoted by G. Pesme, *op. cit.* Also letter from the *Archives de la Seine-Maritime*
36 MSS 11542.
37 *Chronique Bretonne*, Bibliothèque Ste Geneviève, Paris
38 *Procès.* Quoted by Régine Pernoud, *op. cit.*

IV

THE END OF THE SAGA

31
EXILE

. . . The same year (1436) on the 20th day of May, the Maid Jehanne who had been in France . . . and was calling herself Claude . . .

(*Chronicle of the Dean of Saint-Thibaud of Metz*.[1]

Ruling out the stake hypothesis, the Dean of Saint Thibaud's Chronicle seemed until recently to be the sole testimony to Joan's survival. And it was not known what she had done between 1431 and 1436.

The mistake which has been made by most authors, for a variety of reasons, is to disregard her adherence to her religious ideals. It provides the link between the two phases of her life. Hagiographers have conveniently persisted in their denial of facts, clinging instead to their beliefs in a supernatural explanation, whilst dissidents have indulged in guess-work. Thus it has been suggested that Joan was incarcerated in Crotoy, protected by her cousin Anne of Bedford. It is an irrational theory: for a start, Anne died on 14th November 1432. But the Maid was in any case too well known in this castle and town held by the English.

Another suggestion is that she spent the time in a Burgundian jail. This is closer to the truth but no more satisfactory.

The only valid historical method is to fit the characters to the actual events by what can be logically substantiated by the detail and by what is psychologically in context. It is inadequate merely to align the facts with data said to be irrefutable because of conformity to preconceived politico-religious views.

The name 'Claude' mentioned in the Dean of Saint-Thibaud's text, never the subject of serious discussion, was the focal point of my research. It is indeed the key to this whole period of exile with the events following in perfectly logical sequence. Joan the Maid cannot be divorced from her religion, the driving force behind her every action.

By the time she was captured, she had accomplished two points of her mission—Orleans and Rheims. But the operation envisaged by the movement supporting her was on a far greater and more universal scale. Charles VII's consent to it in its fundamental aims, given during the mysterious meeting at Chinon, enabled the finance provided by the Third Order to be released. The ungrateful monarch abandoned the scheme however, and its realization was deferred.

But the Maid of Orleans remained faithful to the ideal which had been instilled in her. It consisted first in a strengthening of Christian unity, already aided by the election of Martin V, who hailed from Anjou and was a friend of Queen Yolanda; secondly, in 'a bold plan of universal understanding and of the pacific progress of nations'* which, under the aegis of St Francis, was to be translated into a westward, transatlantic expansion. The perseverence of the friars minor was rewarded in centuries to come. The United States owe them the foundation of two important towns: San Francisco—'Saint Francis'—and Los Angeles—'The Angels'.

As soon as she was freed from the tribulations of her trial, Joan had only one purpose. Immediately after her relegation to exile—rather than to captivity, if one accepts the Inquisitor Graverend's words 'she did not serve one day of her sentence'[2]—she did her utmost to continue the work she had started.

In order to dispose of the paradox, let us suppose that some adventuress, aware of her resemblance to Isabeau's daughter, should have wanted to pass herself off as Joan. As any other name might jeopardize the success of her imposture, she would, logically, have presented herself declaring: 'I am Joan the Maid . . . You recognize me . . .'

But the Dean of Saint-Thibaud stated specifically in his Chronicle that it was the Maid Jehanne who had been in France . . ., adding further on that she was calling herself Claude.

She did this for a variety of reasons. All the problems were entangled, and for prudence's sake it was essential that she should re-appear under a pseudonym. The choice of 'Claude' was made because of its religious associations.

In the seventh century, St Claude had been bishop of Besançon (where Colette of Corbie established her headquarters) and was more or less its patron saint. Attracted by her sisters in spirituality, the Maid, on leaving Savoy, came for a time to live 'discreetly' amongst the Clares of Mother Nicolette's convent.

'It is for us to retell the outpourings of Joan to St Colette,' exclaimed the *Manifeste du Comité de l'Appel au Tiers Ordre de Saint François*, issued at Saint-Dié on 27th December 1894.

And, conforming to the rule of the professed nuns, the heroine immediately adopted the name of Claude, spiritual father of Besançon. It was ideal for confusing the trails without destroying them.

* Author's note: See Bessonet-Favre. This has been confirmed by present-day Franciscans. The medieval programme of the Order was idealistic. It has now become practical.

By the treaty of Arras, signed at the end of 1435, civil war was ended in France, and England lost all confidence in her former ally Burgundy, who in early 1436 facilitated the liberation of Paris. Obviously, any immediate revelation of the enigmas of the trial could have jeopardized the results achieved. Public opinion could well have reacted in such a way as to compromise the coming negotiations. Also, John of Bedford had died at the end of 1435. Philip the Good had therefore granted Joan her complete freedom, thereby relieving her of her promise not to engage in further military action.

But it was the religious substratum which constituted the real pattern of her behaviour. Her first act was, understandably, to rejoin her former friends, the Franciscans. Consequently, starting from Metz in 1436 and using the religious ideal as a guide, one is inescapably brought back to the castle of Rouen on 13th May 1431. This was shortly before the abjuration, the inconsistencies of which are resolved.

On this 13th May, a luxurious reception was given by the Earl of Warwick, the castle governor. It was

> as important in the number of guests—over 100 of them—as in their status [wrote Régine Pernoud]. At the Earl's table sat several personages who were involved in the trial . . . including John of Luxemburg and the Bishop of Beauvais. Also present were the Grand Chancellor of France, Louis of Luxemburg, the Bishop of Noyon (the man whose memory was so poor in 1456), and two Knights of Burgundy, whose names are not given. Nevertheless one of them can, in all probability, be identified as Haimond de Macy.[3]

Amongst the guests, too, were Queen Catherine, her son the young Henry VI, and, significantly, Pierre de Menthon-Montrottier, emissary of Duke Amadeus of Savoy.

It is commonly acknowledged nowadays that formal receptions frequently serve as a blind for diplomatic negotiations of which the public remains ignorant, and can be more important than official conferences.

As Régine Pernoud suggests, it is logical to assume it was at the time of this feast that John of Luxemburg made his proposal to buy back the Maid in exchange for her promise to cease fighting the allies.

Nevertheless it would be a mistake to assume the scene took place immediately after the carousal. Our medieval ancestors certainly had rough manners and were hot-headed, but it is inconceivable that those who had so coldly planned a political trial would, rather childishly, have confronted the accused in her room.

Joan's reply to this offer, recorded for us by Haimond de Macy, has already been given: she vehemently protested against the principle of a transaction which annulled all her efforts. This did not prevent her from abjuring in public a few days later . . . thus permitting Philippe Erlanger to write that by 'putting her cross at the foot of the fatal document not only did the witch avoid the stake, but also the English failed to extract a single word against Charles VII'.[4]

Macy had been in love with the heroine ever since Beaurevoir, and although he had been brushed off several times his feelings towards her so persisted that 25 years later he was still expressing his devotion to her.

What is inexplicable about his statement is that it stops abruptly after the scene of the abjuration. There is no word of the condemnation, nor of the stake. Just as Monstrelet could remember nothing of Joan's meeting with Philip the Good, so the knight too seemingly lost his memory. This is strange coming from a lover who proved to be so faithful and who was necessarily well informed by virtue of his functions. His laconic conclusion was that he believed she was in paradise. He was, of course, in no danger of lying by saying this. In 1456, as it will be seen, the Maid of Orleans had been dead and buried for six years.

As can be deduced from these facts, the reaction of a man genuinely in love is to await an end to the painful events and, acting on instructions, keep silent about them.

After the substitution had been carried out according to plan on the morning of 30th May, the two 'Knights of Burgundy', Macy and his companion, waited for Joan in the underground passage of Gaalor. Having ridden some distance from Rouen, the three of them were joined by a new escort led by Pierre de Menthon, and they all then took the road to Savoy.

'Was it no more than a coincidence that the Council of Basle, electing a new Pope against the uncompromising Eugenius IV, should precisely choose Amadeus VIII of Savoy,* who was the old *compère* of the Queen of Sicily?'[4]

If not, what were the reasons then?

Eight kilometres from Annecy towered the formidable castle of Montrottier, which belonged to the Duke, but which he had given in 1427 to Pierre de Menthon. A year later, Colette of Corbie founded a convent of Clares at Evian, near the castle of Ripaille where Amadeus retired as a hermit in 1434. It comes as no surprise that a Franciscan author should have written on the subject of the saint and the antipope: 'Despite her links with him, Colette urged her daughters of Vevey to refuse him obedience.'[5]

A new chain of coincidences links Yolanda of Anjou, Amadeus

* Translator's note: Amadeus became Felix V in 1439. The last of the antipopes, he received little support and renounced his claims in 1449 to put an end to the schism. His daughter Marguerite had married Yolanda's eldest son Louis III of Anjou.

VIII, Colette of Corbie all in Savoy—in fact only Joan the Maid was missing.

The castle of Montrottier, described in a fine book by Joseph Sérand, had its legends.

> Thus the room of the keep . . . known as 'the chamber of the Alchemist', is reputed to have been the laboratory of one such man.
>
> It is also maintained that in the room situated above the preceding one, and called '*the Prison of the Maid*', a young girl was incarcerated for not acceding to the demands of her lord, and that she marked her days of captivity by engraving lines on the window-recess of her small room.[6]

Research has revealed that there were four or five lines. This would correspond to the years 1431–36.

In the preface to his book, Joseph Sérand emphasizes that he is not 'writing out of any predilection for the picturesque . . . but that *he knows* what each century has left in this courtyard, *and in this Chamber*'.

Why, in view of this, did he take care to spell Maid with a capital? Could not the advances of this unidentified 'lord' be those of the suitor rejected at Beaurevoir?

Legends are convenient to mask the true facts, and it seems credible that Macy, after being entrusted with the supervision of the exiled and turbulent girl, became a jealous lover.

But the Chamber of the Maid is not the only substantiation of Joan's exile in Savoy, and its likelihood is confirmed by other data. First of all the castle of Montrottier had a statue of the Black Virgin. Exceedingly old, it was in the oratory which adjoined the enclosing wall. Secondly, in Annecy itself, there still exists a presbytery which was consecrated at the end of the fourteenth century to Notre-Dame de Liesse. Thirdly, Pierre de Menthon, a councillor of Duke Amadeus VIII and a man of some importance, was deputed during this period to negotiate an agreement between Charles VII, Philip the Good and Charles of Orleans.

In 1432, he went to Rome to attempt a reconciliation between Eugenius IV and the Fathers assembled in Basle. But the Pope's difficulties were such that in May 1434 an insurrection forced him to flee from Rome and seek temporary refuge in Florence. The revolt of the Roman people was quelled bloodily by Francis Sforza.[7]

The Italian travels of the Maid Joan are mentioned without any date being given in the *Journal d'un Bourgeois de Paris*, and it seems logical to assume that she accompanied the lord of Menthon-Montrottier on this occasion.

'And for this reason,' wrote the chronicler, 'it was necessary for her to go to Rome. So she went there dressed as a man, and fought as a soldier in the Holy Father's war, twice committing homicide.'

Twice! It is a recognized fact that Joan loved war. As there were consecutive revolts against papal authority for several years in a country bordering on Savoy, there is full justification for thinking that the 'Third Order's envoy' indeed went to Italy to defend her ideal of Christian unity. It was an attitude not only strictly in character but also corroborated by the fact that St Colette supported Eugenius IV.

Meanwhile in Paris, the position of the occupiers steadily deteriorated although the young Henry VI had been crowned King of France and England on 16th December 1431. By the death of Anne of Bedford, Philip the Good had been relieved of family ties, and he gradually broke away from his brother-in-law the Regent.

By 1435, with the death of John of Bedford, which occurred at the same time as that of Isabeau of Bavaria, there was nothing to hold Philip back, and he signed the Treaty of Arras, which effectively reversed the alliances.

On the following 16th April, Paris was liberated by a Franco-Burgundian thrust. Charles VII did not enter it yet however, despite the prompt change in allegiances of the Parisians. 'They chased the English and collaborators with shouts of: *à la queue, à la queue*,' commented Monstrelet.

These happy events freed Joan from the oath she had pronounced before leaving Rouen, yet her liberty was still to be determined by the policy of the kingdom. The secret of Chinon had to be hushed up at all costs, for her condemnation had put the King's legitimacy in question once again.

And with popular opinion already unsettled by the coronation of Henry VI, it was out of the question for the Maid of Orleans as such to appear. Whence the imperative necessity of later promoting a second operation with a religious base: transforming the girl the English had condemned as a witch into an idol by a judgment of Rome. It was paving the way to the Rehabilitation.

Always sacrificed to the Reason of State, Joan submitted to the conditions, though not readily. For the sake of discretion, it was necessary for her to choose another name—that of Claude.

My hypothesis is supported by a text written in the eighteenth century by Abbé Baverel in Besançon. It is a genealogical table of the Girardots of Nozeroy, who were a collateral branch of my own line by a fourth son.[8] The document, which bears the reference 'Girardot' in the left-hand corner, mentions amongst others:

Robert des Armoises married
Jehanne du Lys the Maid of France,
died in 1450.

In view of the profusion of 'Armoises' branches, there is at first sight no logical reason for this document to include a special mention of the Maid of France. For Father Baverel to have noted it with such precision, he must undoubtedly have seen texts in Bresançon, probably in the archives of the Clare convent.

In defence of the integrity of ecclesiastics, I find it impossible to accept that Abbé Baverel was a forger, as has been claimed of Father Vignier or even Abbé Villaret. In any case, by the nineteenth century, the Girardots of Nozeroy had little contact with the Armoises—Ermoises—Sermoises, who were never particularly proud of this alliance.

And so, a few weeks after the liberation of Paris, the Maid Joan-Claude was at last able to leave Besançon, having arranged a meeting in Lorraine with Pierre and Jean d'Arc, and having exchanged her patronymic of Orleans for that of France. Orleans would have been far too revealing.

32

ELIZABETH OF GOERLITZ, DUCHESS OF LUXEMBURG

> And was recognized by several signs as the Maid Jehanne of France who took Charles the King to Rheims . . .
>
> (*Chronicle of Saint-Thibaud*)

When he later completed the Dean's narrative, Philippe de Vigneulles provided a detail which is highly significant: 'And on the 20th day of May, a young girl called Claude, being in woman's dress, appeared as Jehanne the Maid, and was seen in a place situated near Metz, named la Grange-aux-Hormes . . . and the two brothers of the said Maid were there and certified that it was she . . .'

The fact that she arrived 'in woman's dress' is readily explained by an analysis of the texts. Just as the name Claude was adopted because of her stay at Besançon, so it was logical for Joan to conform to the customs or recommendations of the Clares around her. And male attire had already caused her enough trouble for her now to adopt a prudent course. An 'impostor' on the other hand would undoubtedly have appeared in a page's costume so as to conform strictly to the character she wished to imitate.

> The Maid Jehanne went to la Grange-aux-Hormes, near Saint-Privat, *and was led there* to speak to some of the lords of Metz . . . [continued the Dean of Saint-Thibaud]. And on the same day there came to see her her two brothers, one of whom was a knight and was called Messire Pierre, and the other Petit Jehan, esquire. And they thought that she had been burnt. And when they saw her, they recognized her, and she too recognized them . . .

So Joan had not come alone to this strange meeting but had been given an escort until she was in the care of the d'Arc brothers. The Dean does not say who escorted her, but the fact is worthy of note.

Calumny is the weapon of the weak, and the opponents of the 'reappearance' theory find only one explanation for the behaviour of the d'Arc brothers: self-interest. It is to be wondered what purpose it could serve them. It is inconceivable that the loyal Pierre d'Arc, an honourable knight who had followed the Maid of Orleans throughout the whole of the saga, and in its most difficult times, should suddenly be a party to a crude imposture. And it is suggested that Petit Jehan did likewise!

The fact that their careers were divergent is of course glossed over. If Jehan d'Arc had been the individual stigmatized, how is one to explain the authority and the honours that Charles VII later conferred on him? He became bailiff of Vermandois, Captain of Chartres and Captain of Vaucouleurs after Robert de Baudricourt.

> And on the Monday, one-and-twentieth day of this month, they took their sister to Bacquillon,* and there, *Sir Nicolas Louve*, knight, gave her a horse costing thirty francs, and a pair of spatterdashes . . . And the lord Aubert Boulay, a hood, and Sir Nicolas Grongnait, a sword . . .

In other words, some of the highest notables and officers of Metz were taken in and made a spontaneous and motiveless contribution towards the basic needs of a supposedly unknown horsewoman . . .

In fact, they knew very well with whom they were dealing. In 1888, town councillors wrote that 'in January 1429, on the square of the castle of Nancy, Joan of Arc, astride a horse, ran a-tilt in front of the nobility and the people of Lorraine'.[10]

Nancy is only about 30 miles from Metz.

Who were these distinguished lords? It will be remembered that Nicolas Louve had been dubbed knight by Charles VII on the day of the Coronation, at the Maid's request. By 1436, Louve, whose known origins went back to the thirteenth century, had obtained important posts, such as councillor-chamberlain of the Duke of Burgundy. It is hard to believe that a man who was soliciting the post of chamberlain to the King of France—and was indeed successful—would risk ruining a brilliant career by lending his support to a deception.

The fact that he recognized Joan is indisputable, for he said so.

The other witnesses were equally reliable. Aubert Boulay, a lord, was the chief municipal magistrate of Metz in 1433. Nicolas Grongnait, nicknamed 'the good jouster', was governor of the city.

Before this assembly of notables, who were eminently capable of appreciating the qualities of a good knight,

> the said Maid mounted the said horse very skilfully . . . And she said several things to Sir Nicolas Louve by which he understood well that it was she who had been in France, and was recognized by several signs as the Maid of Jehanne of France who took Charles the King to be crowned at Rheims.

Therefore, proof of Joan's identity was provided not only by the

* Author's note: Bacquillon was the name of a family from Lorraine, which doubtless gave this place its name. Ancelin Bacquillon was a friend of Nicolas Louve and of the d'Arc family. . . . See G. Pesme, op. cit.

physical resemblance—the same voice, the same bearing—but also by these 'signs' witnessed by high-ranking officials.

Several sayings of Joan's, some of which are reproduced in the official trial record 're-written' by Cauchon, adopted symbols still in use by certain 'secret' societies.

After her answer to Jean Beaupère: 'I recognized two of my saints by the *sign* that they made me,' the Maid added: 'It is *seven years* since they started to govern my conduct.' These significant words reveal a knowledge of signs belonging to the ritual which, according to Béroalde de Verville, she had used on her arrival at Chinon: 'My age adds up to three times seven.'

This use of the two numbers together points once again to Joan's intensive initiation, already established by her utterance at Poitiers: 'I know neither A nor B, but I know how to work and pray.'

Is this not reminiscent of the modern attitude: 'I don't know how to read or write, but I know how to spell?'

As for the power of signs, who could enter a masonic lodge without knowledge of them?

Louve, future chamberlain of Charles VII, was not the man to perpetrate such a hoax, especially as this return to Lorraine was not made only in front of a selected audience. On the previous day, Sunday, a meeting with the d'Arc brothers had taken place quite openly.

'And some people said that she had been burnt at Rouen, and she spoke most often in parables, and said practically nothing of her intentions . . .' This is hardly surprising. She had just fought for the defence of the Holy See. The most important point of the mission conceived by the Franciscan movement was yet to be accomplished, but Joan for the time being had not the means to do so.

The Dean of Saint-Thibaud goes on to mention two significant points which show Joan's adherence to her religious ideal.

> And she said that she would have no power before St John the Baptist's Day.*
>
> But when her brothers had taken her away [they therefore did not leave her] she soon returned for the feast of Pentecost (27th May) in the town of Marville, and stayed there about three weeks at Jehan Quenast's house. And then left to go to Notre-Dame de Liesse . . .

In the course of the trial proceedings, when she was speaking of the certain victory of her party, and possibly referring to the liberation of Paris, the Maid had said: 'But I would like it to happen before St John the Baptist's Day.'

A comparison of the Rouen and Metz sentences begs the question how could an obscure adventuress possibly have known what was in

* Translator's note: Midsummer, 24th June.

the trial proceedings, not yet released by His Lordship Cauchon and still lying in the files of the archbishopric of Rouen?

Furthermore, why did she go on the Liesse pilgrimage? As we have seen, a confraternity had been founded by Charles VI to practise the cult of the Black Virgin, and united the princes and princesses of the blood.

'And when she wanted to leave, several people from Metz went to see her at the said Marville, gave her various jewels, and there, they *recognized that she was indeed the Maid of France*, and then, Geoffroy Dex gave her a horse . . .' So she was given a second horse, and valuable jewels . . .

The lord Geoffroy Dex was the scion of an important Metz family. A kinsman of his was the town treasurer in 1435.

Having returned from Liesse, Joan 'went away to Arelont,* a town which is in the duchy of Luxemburg'.

> While she was in Arelont, she was constantly with Madame de Luxembourg, and she was there some time, until the son of the Count of Warnenbourg took her to his father the Count.† And the said Count loved her greatly, so much so that when she wanted to return [to Arlon], he had made for her a fine cuirass to arm her . . .

This generous present completed the equipment.

'And then she came to the said Arelont.' She stayed here several months at her aunt's, the Duchess of Luxemburg. This exceptional welcome was attributable to yet another of those family connections which featured so much in Joan's life.

Despite the Emperor of Germany's high hopes that his niece, Elizabeth of Goerlitz-Luxemburg, would marry Charles of Orleans, the marriage did not come about, and Elizabeth became the wife of Anthony of Burgundy. She was therefore the aunt of Philip the Good and of the Bedford couple who could expect to inherit from her. She was also the sister-in-law of Duke Amadeus VIII of Savoy, who had married Mary of Burgundy, sister of John the Fearless. Amadeus VIII was therefore both Philip the Good's uncle and Joan's cousin. Furthermore, by her second marriage to John of Bavaria—one of Isabeau's brothers—in 1419, Elizabeth of Goerlitz had become Joan's aunt.

It is hardly surprising then that Joan should have stayed in Savoy. As soon as she was set free, and when the political considerations which had already been eased by John of Bedford's death permitted,

* Author's notes: The name Arlon was sometimes spelt Arelont, or even Erlon.

† The county of Warnenbourg, or Virnebourg, was situated between Trier and Cologne, a little to the west of Koblenz. Count Robert of Warnenbourg had in 1415 rendered services to Anthony of Burgundy, Duke of Luxemburg, and had remained on the best of terms with the Duchess. This explains his attitude to Joan. See Berthollet's *Histoire du Duché de Luxembourg*.

the Maid of France made her way to Arlon, passing by Besançon and Metz.

And these details prove that a deception would have been impossible to sustain in view of the close relationship between the protagonists. Philip the Good who kept well in with Elizabeth because of his expectations, would immediately have warned her, if only to spare her ridicule.

Quietly settled in with her aunt, the good Duchess, Joan then indulged in a spate of letter-writing. Had she been unsure of herself, this would have been incomprehensible. And, in view of the official outcome of Rouen, to write before having herself 'recognized' ought to have aroused mistrust. But this was in no way the case, as can be checked in irrefutable and readily available documents, namely the 1434–36 *comptes de Forteresse de la ville d'Orléans* of Jacques Largentier, receiver of public revenues, who was probably none other than Jacques Boucher, called *l'argentier*—'the treasurer'.[11]

The news was first sent to her former friends of Orleans, then to the King.

> To the said Jacquet Leprestre, the 5th day of the said month of August, on the morning, for ten *pintes* and *choppines** of wine . . . and presented to Jehan, brother of the Maid . . .

Jehan d'Arc was therefore the first messenger. He took wine with Jacquet Leprestre, who had been present at the official reception given for Joan in 1429.

A similar entry concerned a supper:

> To the said Jacquet Leprestre, on the Sunday evening, for twelve *pintes* and *choppines* of wine . . . given and presented to the said Jehan brother of Jehanne the Maid, and supped with him Pierre Baratin, Jacquet Lesbahy and the said Jacquet Largentier . . .
>
> —To Berthaut Fournier, merchant, for twelve chickens, twelve pigeons, two goslings and two hares, given and presented to the said brother of the Maid . . .

It is essential to quote here the relevant parts of these bookkeeping entries for the year 1436 if one is to understand the sequence of the journeys between Arlon and the King's residence, and the reasons for them. However, these rather tedious extracts have been abridged, and certain archaisms translated, without lessening their impact or their medieval charm.

> *9th August*: To Pierre Baratin and Jean Bombachelier, for a gift given to *Fleur de lilz*, *herald of arms* of two reals of gold, for having brought letters to the town from Jehanne the Maid . . .

* Translator's note: A French *pinte* was approximately equivalent to a litre, therefore to two English pints. A *choppine* was a half litre, just under an English pint.

There follows a list of items, of which three are highly significant.

A. Tuesday 21st August. An account of a visit to Charles VII by Jehan d'Arc, who for the first time in a contemporary text, is called 'Dulils' (or du Lys):

> ... for gift made to Jehan Dulils, brother of Jehanne the Maid ... of the sum of twelve *Livres Tournois*, for which the said brother of the said Maid came into the Chamber of the Town to ask the *procureurs* of the said town to help with a little money for him to return to his said sister; ... saying that he came from the King, and that the King had granted him a hundred francs, and commanded that it should be given him, but that this had not been done and only twenty francs were given him ... of which but eight francs remained to him, which was little to return ...

The same day, Jehan d'Arc again took wine with Jacquet Leprestre who received seven sous and nine deniers 'for ten *pintes* and *choppines* of wine bought from Jean Hatte, given and presented to the said Dulils ...'

B. 25th August:

> To Regnault Brunne, the 25th day of the said month, on the evening, for drink given to a messenger who brought letters from Jehanne the Maid and was on his way to Guillaume Bellier, bailiff of Troyes ...*

C. 28th October:

> To Coeur de Lilz (herald of arms), the 28th day of October 1436, for a journey which he made on behalf of the said town [Orleans] to the Maid who was at Arlon in the Duchy of Luxemburg, and for carrying to Loches, to the King who was there, the letters which he brought from the said Jehanne the Maid ... on which journey he spent forty-one days, to wit, thirty-four days on the journey to the Maid and seven days to go to the King ... The said Coeur de Lilz set out to go to the said Maid, on Tuesday, last day of July, and returned the second day of September, that is thirty-four days spent and occupied with the said journey ...

11th September:

> to Jacquet Leprestre ... for wine, chickens and nuts, dispensed in the chamber of the said town at the coming of the said Coeur de Lilz who brought the said letters from Jehanne the Maid, and for drink for the said Coeur de Lilz, who said he had a great thirst ...

There were therefore four messengers travelling between Arlon, Orleans, Blois and Loches, during the summer of 1436. And it is by no means certain, nor even likely, that Jehan d'Arc was the first to bring news of the Maid. The King's messenger Fleur de

* Author's note: But who resided at Blois. Bellier was one of Charles of Orleans' counsellors. His wife the lady of Bellier had been in charge of the Maid's household at Chinon in 1429. It is hardly surprising that Joan should have written to him after her exile was over.

Lilz, who had known Joan since the liberation of Orleans, had necessarily left some time previously, since he returned on 9th August with letters from Joan, four days after Jehan d'Arc's arrival on the 5th.

Meanwhile, Coeur de Lys had, in turn, left for Luxemburg, on 31st July.

It is inconceivable that Charles VII could have been deceived. He was necessarily well informed, if only through Philip the Good, with whom he was on better terms as a result of the Treaty of Arras. Furthermore, Joan's letters must have exhibited the usual distinguishing marks and seals.

Nevertheless, the King wanted an official confirmation, and sent Coeur de Lys to do so. Coeur de Lys, the second 'herald of arms', was by definition a public officer whose function was to intimate declarations of war, to bear messages, 'to verify armorial bearings, and whose person was sacred'.

To whom had Charles VII despatched these two heralds? The aim of the costly journeys was Joan the Maid of France, who was living at Arlon, with the Duchess of Luxemburg, their aunt.* I shall pass no comment; the facts speak for themselves.

Meanwhile, Jehan d'Arc had seen the sovereign, and received confidential instructions concerning the surname du Lys, which Joan and her foster-brothers were to bear. For this name would conceal the truth about her origins the revelation of which would have been dangerous for the security of the throne. It would conform to the rules of heredity, and moreover give her the complete freedom of a new identity.

'Joan the Maid of Orleans' became 'Joan du Lys, the Maid of France'. She was indeed never called d'Arc in her lifetime, but was first designated thus in the rescript of Calixtus III in 1455.

Finally, Jehan d'Arc, short of money, went through Orleans again before returning to Luxemburg, and was there called 'Dulils', as the King had instructed.

For all these reasons, Elizabeth of Goerlitz was able at last, in October 1436, to give her agreement and blessing to a ceremony which took place at Arlon.

> And there [wrote the dean of Saint-Thibaud] was celebrated the wedding of the Lord Robert des Harmoises, knight, and of the said Jehanne the Maid. And then came the said Lord of Harmoises with his wife, the Maid, to live at Metz, in the house of the said Sir Robert, which he had before Sainte-Segoleine . . .

For what reasons had Louis of Orleans' daughter been moved to

* Author's note: It will be remembered that Elizabeth of Luxemburg had married Isabeau of Bavaria's brother.

consent to this unconsummated marriage with a knight 'of obscure lineage'?

For half a century cousins of Sir Robert had been serving in the immediate entourage of the Dukes of Burgundy.

33
THE HOUSE OF ARMOISES

Gyronny of twelve Or and azure an escutcheon gules.
Armorial bearings of the senior line (ancient arms of the House of Flanders)*

To quote the Introduction to the Archives of the Castle of Nettancourt-Vaubécourt,[12] the Armoises 'can be considered to be the first family in Barrois, and one of the first in Lorraine, not only because of the military services they rendered and the public offices they filled throughout six centuries, but because of their possessions and alliances'.

A river and two villages in the Ardennes still bear witness to the long history of the Armoises, while their origins are revealed both by their armorial bearings and their motto *Flandria me genuit*—'Flanders engendered me'. This filiation is confirmed by the *Mesmoire pour la Maison des Armoises*, written around 1600 by an anonymous author and now in the library at Nancy, which also provides the key to a heraldic problem. It is all the more reliable a document in that it was primarily based on a treatise 'by Guillaume, Bishop of Tournai, Abbot of Saint-Bertin, and Chancellor of the Order of the Golden Fleece at the time of Duke Charles the Bold of Burgundy'. This treatise, which describes the institution of the order, is itself unimpeachable by virtue of the high functions of the author.[13]

> Which House [says the text] was descended from the *Anciens Forestiers* of Flanders, who were called thus until one of them married Judix, daughter of King Charles the Bold of France, [in 862] . . . and then were called counts, as can be ascertained in the Annals of Flanders which start with Ludwig [or Lidéric], the first *forestier* who . . . had been found in a wood by Dagobert, King of France . . .†
>
> . . . They bore the said arms [the gyronny] until the valiant Count Philip, husband of the Queen of Portugal, whilst in the Holy Land, vanquished Nobilion [brother of the king of Jerusalem under Saladin] who had treacherously attacked him, and stripped him of his arms, which were gold charged with a lion sable . . .

* Author's note: In the junior lines of the Armoises, the escutcheon is 'per pale argent and gules'. (See Husson l'Ecossais and Jules Chifflet.)

† Translator's note: Dagobert, King of the Franks in 628, the last of the Merovingian kings.

The *Mesmoire* goes on to say that the valiant Philip of Flanders decided to adopt the arms of Nobilion, and later abandoned his other arms to the junior line. These arms 'are those of the Armoises'. This is unequivocal, and is furthermore confirmed by the unquestionable fact that the lion as a heraldic figure appeared later than the gyronny.*

It was therefore to be expected that shortly before Philip assumed Nobilion's arms, a junior *forestier* should be designated for the first time by the name of his lands, his descendants thereafter inheriting the ancient armorial bearings of Flanders.

In 1137, Anselme-Nicolas of Armoises and Stonne is mentioned together with his brother Guillaume and their cousin Guy d'Autry, in the founding charter of the monastery of Mont-Dieu.[14] Ten years later, St Bernard retired to the new abbey to write a treatise 'on solitary life'. It is tempting to think that Anselme-Nicolas, who lived only ten minutes' ride away, knew the saint who drew up the rule of the Knights Templar.

In the thirteenth century, several generations of powerful knights bearing the famous gyronny won renown and, despite their mixed fortunes, invariably made illustrious alliances with such as the Charbogne, Coucy-Vervins, Grandpré, Hans, Ham, Flandre and Rethel families.

In 1282, Nicolas, called 'le Gueulars des Armoises'—'the bawler'—who was an astute diplomat, was nominated guarantor of the county of Rethel. Because of his military experience in the Mediterranean, he then accompanied Henry Count of Bar, who became Edward I's son-in-law, to Naples and Sicily. On his return, 'The Bawler' was entrusted with several missions to the great English king. He died in 1303, and a stele three and a half metres high which was erected to his memory shows that he belonged to the Order of Hospitallers, if not to that of the Temple.

At about the same time, a much remarked-on marriage took place between another Nicolas 'des Armoises de Charbogne' and Isabeau de Grandpré, Countess of Rethel. By this match, Nicolas became step-father to Countess Jeanne de Rethel, born of her mother's previous marriage with Hugues IV de Rethel.[15] As Jeanne de Rethel's son Louis II of Flanders married Margaret of France, daughter of King Philip V the Tall, Nicolas was by marriage the ancestor of the Dukes of Burgundy, John the Fearless and his descendants, and of course of Anthony of Burgundy, the first husband of Elizabeth of Goerlitz-Luxemburg.

* Author's note: This famous 'Lion of Flanders' taken from Nobilion of Albany by Philip of Flanders on the field of battle in the twelfth century gradually replaced the old 'gyronny Or and azure', which remained however in the Armoises branch.

In the early fourteenth century, at the time of the Templars' affair, the Armoises suddenly left most of their possessions in Champagne, and settled in Lorraine. Whether this was a coincidence or not, Colart I married Marie de Chambley and founded there a new line from which numerous well-known branches would spring.

Marie's brother, Ferri III de Chambley, also had well-known descendants, such as—through the Beauvau and the Bourbon-Vendôme lines—King Henry IV of France.

Robert de Baudricourt, Captain of Vaucouleurs, married Ferri's daughter Alarde de Chambley, and thereby became the cousin of Robert des Harmoises and also of Joan the Maid to whom he was already related by his first marriage.

Colart I, knight and lord of Fléville, who was a mercenary and something of a brigand, was beheaded in a war against Metz in 1368. Two of his children are of particular interest.

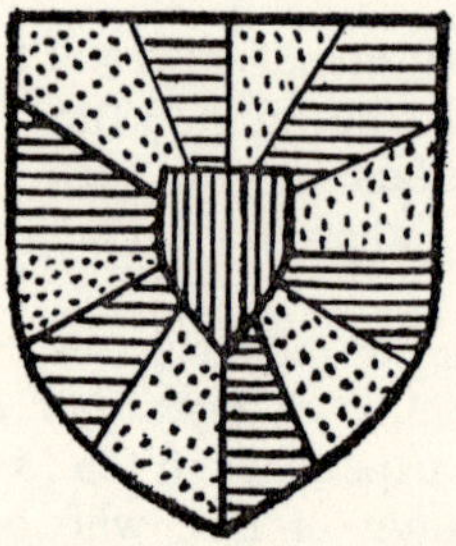

Fig. 5

Ancient armorial bearings of the Counts of Flanders and of the Armoises of the elder branch.

Armorial bearings taken from Nobilion by the magnanimous Count Philip of Flanders.

These two standards can be seen flying together on the Castle of the Counts, at Ghent. (See reproduction in *Histoire Universelle, tome 4, Collection Marabout: Mu 36*).

Robin, his second son, was the progenitor of a line in which many illustrious names feature: through the Haraucourt, Nettancourt, Lezay-Marnésia families and Stéphanie-Louise of Beauharnais (Napoleon's adoptive daughter who married the Grand Duke of Baden, Prince of Hohenzollern-Sigmaringen) the Neuville branch of the Armoises reaches down to ex-King Michael of Rumania and King Baudouin of Belgium; the branch of Charles des Armoises de Barisey-Savigny, which included the Ligniville, Simiane-Moncha, Sourdis, La Tour-d'Auvergne, Bouillon, and Rohan-Soubise families, ended upon the death of Louis de Bourbon-Condé, Duke of Enghien, who was executed in 1804 on Napoleon's orders; finally the Jaulny branch of the Armoises were forbears of the Marquis d'Aulnoy.

Richart I, Colart's fourth son, founded a separate branch by both marriages, the first in Burgundy, the second in Lorraine. They are the subject of the next chapter.

34

1436

Sweeping through cities in which flags are flying for her,
Here, in armour, comes the Lady of Armoises,
Wife of Robert, Lord of Tichémont.
He is 'the jouster', the lover of elegance,
She is Joan of Arc, the Maid of France,
Who, living, is reborn in the blue of his shield.
(Gaston-Nicolas de Sermoise, 1928)

Richart I's successive marriages brought about the close relationship between his grandson Robert and the 'Sermoise' branch, and so it is vital to give details of them.[16]

The first marriage with Marie de Gérardot, in Burgundy

Being the fourth son, Richart was a penniless knight and left for Dijon some time before 1345. There he married Marie, only daughter of Etienne de Gérardot, who was to become procurator of the town at the time of its negotiations with the English. Marie, a rich heiress, who was older than Richart, took particular pride in her origins,* and for this reason their three sons—Pierre, Jehan and Guillaume—did not bear only their father's name. Before her death, Marie insisted that her sons should add her name and arms to those of the Armoises.

The eldest, Pierre de Sermoise, went off at an early age to fight at the side of Du Guesclin. His courage was rewarded shortly afterwards when he married Marguerite de Cuignières, and Charles V granted him the office of captain of the 'fort and bridge' of Meulan as a wedding gift.

His younger brother, Jehan, 'squire of the Duke of Burgundy', respected his mother's wish, and by the time of his death in the Nicopolis massacre in 1396, he had already adopted the name 'des Ermoises et de Gérardot', and had marshalled the two coats of arms on his shield.† According to the great seventeenth-century heraldic

* Author's note: Etienne de Gérardot's (or Girardot) armorial bearings prove that he was a descendant of Girardus, or Girars de Manchecort who was mentioned in Villehardoin's chronicle of the Fourth Crusade.

† Quarterly, first and fourth, gules a chevron argent, second and third, argent a lion rampant sable (armorial bearings of the Gérardot). Over all, an escutcheon gyronny of twelve Or and azure, with an inescutcheon per pale of the second and first (the Armoises arms).

authority Pierre Palliot, 'these combinations . . . of names and arms were at one time frequent'.

This line remained loyal to the House of Burgundy and its descendants until the time of King Philip II of Spain. Several generations of 'Jean', 'Guillaume' and 'Pierre', are mentioned together with Burgundian marshals or great captains, such as Vergy (1405), Neufchastel (1412), Thoulongeon (1429), Dinteville (1431), Jacourt (1435).

Upon the death of Charles the Bold, Joseph-Denis Gérardot de Sermoise, having married Marie de Rochebaron who was the granddaughter of John the Fearless by his bastard daughter Philippine, decided to serve Maria of Burgundy and Maximilian of Austria. His loyalty made him their confidant. At first named Gentleman of the Chamber to the Duchess, he then received the hereditary title of Count Palatine of Gueldres. (Letters given in Ghent on 26th August 1477.) It was therefore to be expected that his son Jehan should become a councillor of Charles V, ducal governor of Bar, and a knight of the Golden Fleece. His titles, armorial bearings and prerogatives were confirmed by 'His Most Sacred Imperial Majesty', by letters patent given at Madrid on 15th May 1522.[17]

The following text is a good example of the variation in spelling because of regional pronunciation. All on the same page are:

Joseph-Denis *Girardot des Armoises* married
Marie de Rochebaron, from whom he had:
M. Jean Gérardot Count de *Sermoise* who had
M. Lois Gérardot Count *des Ermoises* who was *officier du Gobelet** of the king.

(This was at the time of Charles IX and Henry III.)[18] The name of this branch could thus be indexed under A, D, E, S or G.

The Sermoises made alliances with no less illustrious families than their cousins did: Le Bouteiller de Senlis, Rabutin, Rochebaron, Nozeroy, Hennequin d'Assy—whence Marillac and Montmorency—Romécourt, etc.

Finally, in the eighteenth century, Jean-Nicolas de Sermoise, chamberlain and lieutenant of the *Garde-Noble* of the Duke of Lorraine, allied himself to the Jaulny branch, descended from Colart I by his elder son Robin. On 4th July 1757, he married Anne-Catherine des Armoises, daughter of the Marquis of Aulnoy and Anne de Beauvau.

As for Pierre de Sermoise (the captain of Meulan already mentioned), his great-granddaughter, Marie Le Bouteiller de Senlis, married Henri-Auguste of Orleans, Marquis of Rothelin, who was a descendant of Dunois.

* Translator's note: The *gobelet du roi* was where bread, wine and fruit were provided for the king's table.

The second marriage of Richart I, with Anne de Sorbey

Soon after the death of Marie de Gérardot-Ermoises, Richart returned to Lorraine, married Anne de Sorbey, and became marshal of Barrois. Of the eight children of this second marriage, two are of interest here: Jean, the ancestor of the Autrey branch (which would later marry into the Bassompierre family), and Richart II des Armoises, lord of Tichémont, who also became a marshal, then governor of the duchy of Bar. His wife, Alix de Breux, gave birth to the Robert who was to become Joan the Maid of France's husband.

This marriage is certainly no cause for surprise. The Armoises were perfectly respectable, whatever calumnious aspersions have been cast by historians more anxious to preserve the legend than to accept the evidence.

Dubbed knight in about 1418, Robert, an enthusiastic jouster, was younger than has usually been suggested. He at first obtained the trust of his suzerain thanks to his father's good name. But in 1423 Robert's instability and independence caused him to lose his fief of Norroy, and ten years later, the lordship of Tichémont which he had inherited from his father was confiscated by René of Anjou, Duke of Bar.

Despite the strife between him and the Bishop of Metz, he nevertheless entertained good relations with the town's seven-strong 'war council'. His friendship with Nicolas Louve is clearly revealed in letters exchanged between them after 1426: 'Dear and great friend ... we recommend ourselves to you ...', and Robert replied in equally warm and genial terms.

It is naive to suggest that Louve and his entourage, all powerful people, knowingly let their friend fall into the net of an adventuress when they had known the Maid of Orleans since 1429. A letter written at the time of the coronation by Jean Dex states that 'many lords from Metz went to join Charles VII and Jehanne at Rheims'.[19]

It is even likely that Robert was present at the meeting at Bacquillon; a family record in my possession seems to confirm it.

It is incidentally worthy of note that all the wives mentioned in the family genealogies had distinguished origins. Had Robert's wife not been Joan the Maid, she would have been the exception—an anomaly impossible to explain. Who then might she have been?

When he met the Maid, the 'dear and great friend' of the Metz Council was in straitened circumstances. He was possibly hoping that, through his wife's influence, he would be able to regain his confiscated fiefs: after all, René of Bar was closely related to Joan through his brother-in-law Charles VII, and the thought of this must have been most attractive. But Joan did not succeed on his behalf.

As far as she was concerned, marriage to a nobleman from such a line was politically ideal: her residence outside the kingdom of

France would ensure the peace of mind of Charles VII, who was nervous by nature.

Shortly before this, during her residence in Cologne in the summer of 1436, the Franciscan heroine had ostentatiously shown her preference for one of the candidates to the archiepiscopal see of Trier. After fighting in Italy for the cause of the real pope, faithful to her ideal of Christian unity, she had arrived in the middle of the religious turmoil in which the partisans of Eugenius IV opposed the schismatics.

Surrounded by Dominicans and theologians, the General Inquisitor of Mayence did not hesitate to summon her, for no good reason, to appear before a tribunal. It was only through the friendship of the young Ulrich of Virnebourg that she was able to return safe and sound to Arlon, just before her wedding.

The religious motivation is blatant and provides a weighty confirmation of the facts. The Dominican Jean Nider, whose intolerance of heretics was notorious, knew with whom he was dealing and while he disapproved of Joan's attitude, he did not dwell on the identity of this girl who was claiming once again to have been 'sent by God'.[20]

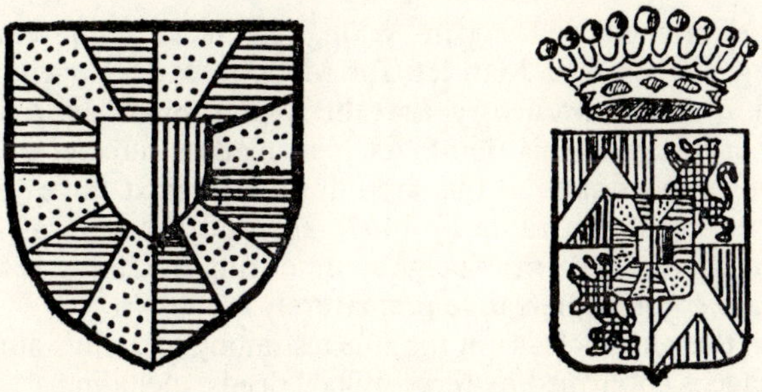

Fig. 6

Coat of arms of the Armoises of the junior lines.

Coat of arms of the branch of Armoises and Gérardot, Counts of Sermoise.

Their common motto: *Flandria me genuit.*

35
THE MARRIAGE CONTRACT

> And then came the said Lord of Harmoises with his wife, the Maid, to live at Metz. . . . And they stayed there for as long as it pleased them.
>
> (Conclusion of the *Chronicle of the Dean of Saint-Thibault*)

According to Abbé Jacques Choux, custodian of the *Musée Lorrain*, little is known about the author of this chronicle. 'One thing however is certain: in 1443, he was *curé* of Saint-Eucaire of Metz, and finished his chronicle in 1445. He was therefore in a good position to be well informed about the events which took place in the region of Metz in 1436.'[21]

Shortly after their wedding in Arlon, celebrated at the court of Luxemburg, Robert and Joan left for Metz, in early November. It seems odd, if not contradictory, that the Dean should have abruptly ended his narrative at this point. As Joan made a number of fairly ostentatious appearances in this area during the next three years—before returning to Lorraine in 1440—she and the curé of Saint-Eucaire must have been near neighbours during this time. Why did the Dean interrupt his narrative prematurely?

Happily, this chronicle is not the sole testimony to Joan's survival. Her marriage is confirmed by three official deeds, including a *vidimus* in my possession. And the continuation of the saga is supported by other documents in so categorical a fashion that Abbé Cochard and Abbé Vergniaud-Romagnési were moved to write: 'If these facts were not supported by authentic documents, it would be impossible to believe them!'

In any event, Robert's income did not stretch to raising troops and going off on a new campaign, and so, in need of money, the couple stopped halfway between Arlon and Metz, at Marville. There Robert went to a notary and mortgaged the profits that would later arise from a quarter of one of his properties for the considerable sum of just over 350 francs in Lorraine money.*

Although the deed was entitled 'purchase of the 1/4 of Haraucourt

* Author's note: By way of comparison, Joan's luxurious suit of armour had cost 100 francs.

by Colart de Grand-Failly and Poinsette d'Ancelrue, his wife . . .', it represented no more than four years' purchase of the income and was not an outright sale of the fief.

> We, Robert des Armoises, knight, lord of Tichémont, and Jehanne du Lys, the Maid of France, lady of the said Tichémont, the wife, licenced and authorized, of the above named Robert . . .

Dated 7th November 1436, the document clearly reveals the motive of the transaction: Robert consented to rent land for the benefit of Joan. And it is a fact that in 1445 the Lady of Armoises repaid the loan at the time agreed.[22] The name *Jehanne du Lys, la Pucelle de France* is repeated many times throughout the five-page document, the authority of which is established beyond doubt in its last paragraph.

> As witness to the truth of the above-mentioned and our acceptance thereof, we Robert des Armoises and Jehanne du Lys, the Maid of France, our aforementioned wife, have appended our seals on these present letters; and have begged and asked our very great friend Jehan de Thoneletil, and Saubelet de Dun, provost of Marville, to affix their seals on these present letters. And we, Jehan de Thoneletil and Saubelet de Dun, aforementioned, at the prayer of our very dear and great friends, the aforesaid Robert and Lady Jehanne, have appended our seals with theirs for purposes of witnessing, on these present letters which were done and given the year of grace of our Lord one thousand four hundred and thirty six . . .

Two important witnesses thus acted as guarantors not only for their friend Robert but also for the lender, Colart de Grand-Failly, who was another friend of theirs: Jehan de Thoneletil was a powerful lord in the region, while Saubelet de Dun was the provost—by definition a royal or lordly magistrate and a spokesman of justice.

It is a common saying that questions of interest or money ruin friendship, but this transaction proved an exception. Yet it was a hazardous one. The sum amounted to several thousand pounds sterling, or more than a thirtieth of the 'prince's ransom' paid by Bedford. And as the first interest would only accrue after five years, the loan would only be repaid at the end of a decade.

Despite the risks, both parties accepted, signed, and appended their seals, as did the officer of justice. They would certainly have known that the King's heralds, Fleur de Lilz and Coeur de Lilz, had checked at Arlon the seals of the Lady they knew so well.

It is inconceivable that Robert, already in bad odour with his suzerain, the Duke of Bar, would deliberately have taken the risk of eventual conflict with the law. And did he mortgage his lands, his friendships and his honour, for the sole reason of pleasing a woman who had no name and no origin?

Until recently, 'the 1/4 of Haraucourt' was only known by the transcription made by Dom Calmet, probably from the original document, in the eighteenth century. However, I have in my personal possession a *vidimus* which is of paramount importance because of the place where it was drawn up. Indeed, the village of Fresne-en-Woëvre which is mentioned in the appendix brings new dimensions to the affair:

> Copied by us notaries sworn to the *tabellionage* of the Episcopal See and County of Verdun, from the original drawn up on sound and whole parchment, with four pendent seals in green wax . . ., and collated by us, it being consistent word for word, executed at Fresne-en-Woëvre, the fifteenth day of July [1598] . . .
>
> signed Purmiers and Marty.*

The original of the marriage contract, a document which bears no relation to the '1/4 of Haraucourt', was still at Fresne-en-Woëvre in 1907, with Maître Marty's successor. Already in the seventeenth century, Father Vignier of the Oratoire claimed he had found it in the archives of Jean des Armoises, lord of Jaulny. It was a surprising discovery and there was a report about it in the *Mercure Galant* in 1683. A letter followed, from Father Vignier's brother to M. de Grammont, informing him of all the facts. This discovery should however be disregarded for the time being, for Father Vignier's integrity has too often been impugned. And some contemporary authors go so far as to contest the existence of the document, suggesting that the priest confused the marriage contract and the '1/4 of Haraucourt'.

Are the integrity and intellectual honesty of Albert Bayet, President Edouard Herriot and Count Robert de Labessières, who all claimed to have seen the contract, also to be challenged?

Albert Bayet, a teacher at the Ecole des Hautes Etudes, and the author of orthodox works on the period, was so impressed by a discovery he had made that in 1920 he thought fit to call a press conference. In 1907 he had seen the marriage contract bearing a signature identical to the one on Joan's letter to the inhabitants of Rheims. On his death-bed, Albert Bayet confirmed these facts to M. Yves Lavoquer, a journalist who had been one of those summoned 25 years earlier.

President Edouard Herriot, a former pupil of the Ecole Normale Supérieure, was a personal friend of my maternal grandfather.

Finally, Count Robert de Labessières who lived at Ancemont, a village near Fresne-en-Woëvre, had also been brought up to believe in the legend, but on seeing the document, his agitation was such that thereafter, he repeatedly informed his family of its tenor. His

* Author's note: This *vidimus* was annotated by Denu in 1775.

cousin M. Jacques Guérillon, an expert on medieval arms and armour, heard the disclosures on many occasions and has certified the fact to me in two letters.[23]

To look at it objectively, even conceding that Father Vignier was mistaken, as many others have done, it is inconceivable that these eminent people should all have mistaken a commercial agreement for a marriage contract.

The truth must surely be that the archives of the Fresne-en-Woëvre notary contained two different documents which for a long time lay together.

In possession of a large sum of money, Joan and her husband left Marville. On arriving at Metz, the Maid's one thought was to join Gilles de Rais, her 'very dear friend of heart'. The marshal alone of her former companions would still support her hope of taking up the fight again for her ideal.

36

THE PSEUDO-SIEGE OF LA ROCHELLE

> The Maid of France, being near La Rochelle, sent to ask for help from the king [of Spain], and this the Constable of Castile did for her.
>
> (*Chronicle of Don Alvaro de Luna*)*

Although Quicherat said that Spain's good faith could not be questioned, historians are unanimous that after July 1436, there was no siege at La Rochelle for many years to come. What then are the true facts behind this Spanish chronicle? They are complex and have frequently been refuted by authors who have failed to discriminate between them and patent errors in the texts. How, in particular, did the king of Castile know that Joan, as is mentioned in another chronicle,† had been in Savoy? Who had told him?

A cross-checking of the available data provides a corroborative reconstruction of events near La Rochelle between 1436 and 1437. Though it seems unlikely at first sight, it is supported by documents, establishing once more that every historical event is linked to motivation.

FIRST DATA: THE SPANISH CHRONICLE;

> The Maid of France being near La Rochelle, there took place an event of great importance.
>
> She wrote to the king [of Spain] and sent him her ambassador, together with those whom the king [of France] was sending, begging him

* Author's notes: Don Alvaro de Luna was Constable of Castile. The chronicle was written some time between 1460 and 1562 when, according to Quicherat, it was printed in Burgos. Jean de Saint-Jean mentions an edition published in Madrid in 1784.

As Don Alvaro was a highly placed personage, his words are worthy of credence, especially as he knew Jehan d'Aulon.

† See *Ciudad de Dios*, by Father Miguelez, mentioned in an article by Marcellin Desfourneaux entitled 'Joan of Arc in Spain' published in the *Revista Espanola de Historia*, Madrid 1943. '. . . And then, when she was safe and liberated, because the brother of the Duke of Savoy who had guarded the camp . . . After the Maid was liberated, she took back what the King of England had won whilst she was a prisoner . . .'

> to send her a few ships from the Armada, which it was incumbent on His Majesty to do by virtue of the confederation existing between His Majesty and the king of France . . .

Influenced by his favourite, Alvaro de Luna, John II of Castile had always respected his treaty of friendship with France. However, Charles VII never received any help from Spain at critical moments. With this in mind, the sudden decision to send a large fleet at a time when Charles VII was not in trouble is hard to understand. But it is highly significant that Don Alvaro de Luna, who was all-powerful at the court, belonged to the Franciscan movement; in the Chapel of Santiago at Toledo Cathedral there is a portrait of him kneeling at prayer with St Francis.

> And these ambassadors having been sent to Valladolid, where the king was in residence in his said year 1436, they were grandly received, and numerous feasts were given in their honour . . . [continued the chronicle]

It is strange that Jehan d'Aulon, confidant of Yolanda—Queen of the Four Kingdoms, one of which was Aragon—should have spent several lengthy stays in Spain, after his liberation. This is according to his descendant, M. Bernard-Jean Daulon: in 1436, Jehan d'Aulon was apparently given several missions, and between 1452 and 1454 he was entrusted by Charles VII with official embassies to the Courts of Castile, Savoy and Navarre.[24]

> And having handed to the king the letter that the Maid had written, the Constable [de Luna] showed it to the grandees of the Court, as though it were a most venerable relic. For, being courageous and valiant in great manner, he loved those who were likewise. For this reason he showed much respect for the deeds of the Maid.

As Joan's letter would undoubtedly have caused a sensation at the Court of Castile, it could hardly not have been seen by the French emissaries subsequently delegated and in particular by her former squire to whom it would have been shown with pride—assuming, of course, that he had not brought it in the first place.

Why did Jehan d'Aulon, the 'most honest and most capable knight', who knew Joan's signature and codes better than anyone, not deflate the enthusiasm of the Spaniards? The affair was still talked about over a hundred years later.*

In the event,

> the Constable who governed with the king his lord, and on his order decided immediately to send to the Maid a fleet such as to give good

* Author's note: The *Direction Générale des Archives et Bibliothèques* in Madrid said in 1958: 'This letter doubtless passed into the archives of the royal crown of Castile, which disappeared without trace at the beginning of the sixteenth century, at the time of the popular uprising against the Emperor Charles V.'

> succour to the king of France, and satisfy his needs. He had twenty-five ships (some say thirty-five big ships) and fifteen carvels prepared, the best that could be found, and armed with the best equipment . . . and, as the fleet was ready, the ambassadors left the Court of the king pleased and joyous.

However, this fleet did not take part in any engagement throughout this period.

SECOND DATA: THE TEMPLAR PORT OF LA ROCHELLE

The order had founded a Provincial House here, and planned the construction of its famous fortifications. Intrigued by this powerfully defended and isolated port, Louis Charpentier had the ingenious idea of linking up on a map all the preceptories and commanderies of France. The drawing showed that six great Templar routes fanned out from La Rochelle from north to south, covering the whole country.

The reason for constructing this port nevertheless proved elusive, and we are indebted to Jean de la Varende disclosing it: 'The Templars regularly went to America whence, from the mines they were exploiting there, they brought back silver, rather than gold. Because of this the people said that they had money.'[25]

This assertion is corroborated by the fact that this rare metal, until then more or less unexploited in Europe, suddenly made a full-scale appearance in the Middle Ages. Although a novelist, Jean de la Varende is obviously imparting hard facts in this instance. He is in any case well enough known as a man of integrity not to be challenged. His sources were not only family and local traditions but also the archives of old Normandy families to which he had access.

However none of all this is in fact surprising in the light of modern archaeological discoveries. Celts, Scandinavians, and Normans were already landing on the coasts of America at the dawn of the second millennium of our era. 'Greenland had been discovered in the tenth century by the Scandinavian Eric the Red, coming from Iceland, and a settlement and a bishopric had been organized there,' writes Marianne Mahn-Lot. Then, 'Leif Ericsson explored Newfoundland, Labrador and the mysterious Vinland—later identified as Cape Cod in the United States.'[26]

When the Order of the Temple was suppressed, numerous knights regrouped in Spain and Portugal. Their knowledge, handed down, contributed to the departure of Christopher Columbus' carvels, bearing on their sails the cross of the Order of Christ—which was also Joan's cross.

THIRD DATA: THE NAUTICAL MAPS OF THE AMERICAN CONTINENT, of Greenland, and the Antarctic (without its ice).

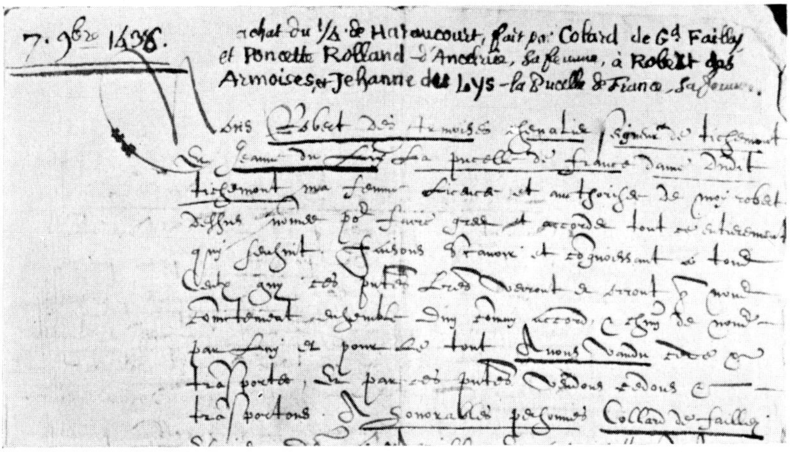

Vidimus of the 'purchase of the ¼ of Haraucourt'. (*above*) The first page: 'We, Robert des Armoises, knight, Lord of Tichémont, and Jehanne du Lys, the Maid of France, my wife. . . .' (*below*) The final page: 'Copied by us notaries sworn . . . to the episcopal see and County of Verdun . . . executed at Fresne-en-Woëvre . . . signed Purmiers and Marty'.
(Author's collection. Photos by Michel de Sermoise)

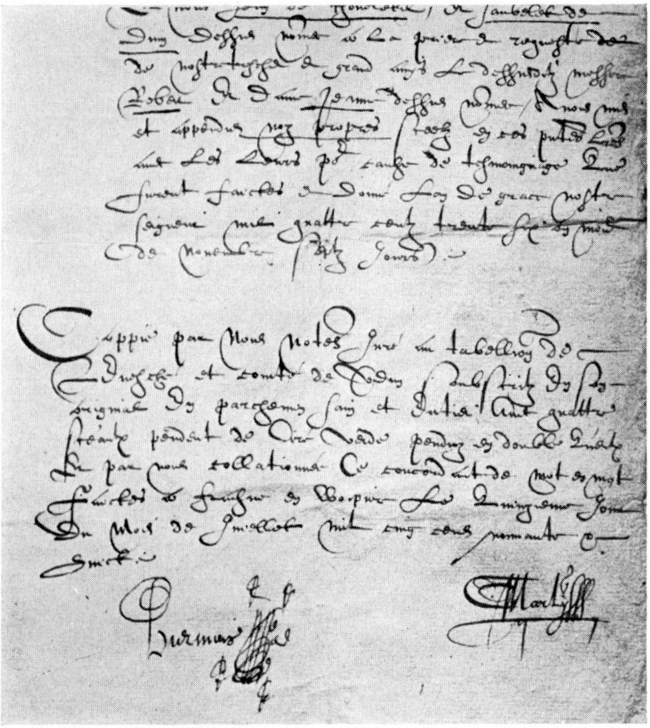

(*above*) Medallion of Joan the Maid of France, Lady of Armoises, on the left-hand side of the coffered chimney in the medieval castle of Jaulny (near Thiaucourt, Meurthe-et-Moselle). The face is identical to that depicted on the sculpted panel in 'Le Grenier' at the Metz Museum. (Photo by J. J. Ceccarini)

(*left*) Louis de Maele, Count of Flanders, the grandson of Countess Jeanne de Rethel (daughter-in-law of Nicolas des Armoises de Charbogne) and the grandfather of John the Fearless and Antony of Burgundy.
(*Recueil d'Arras.* Photo by Giraudon)

(*above*) Medallion of Robert des Armoises at Jaulny.
(Photo by J. J. Ceccarini)

(*right*) Joan the Maid and her standard—a sketch made in the margin of a Paris Parliament register for the years 1428–36 by the clerk Fauquembergue.
(Photo by Giraudon)

(above) Part of Joan's tomb hidden under a step of the chancel of the church at Pulligny-sur-Madon, near Joan of Arc's statue. To the right of the inscription is the cross inscribed in a circle, symbolizing the mission's completion.

An angel in the 'lotus' position—a medieval sculpture on a keystone in the church at Pulligny.
(Photos by J. J. Ceccarini)

Mentioned in the nineteenth century by Bessonet-Favre, the Tertiary of St Francis, these documents would be no less shattering for a positivist. 'The Franciscans had found these nautical maps in their archives, and they were handed a few years later to Christopher Columbus (one of the most valiant and famous members of the Third Order), to aid his search for the lost route from Europe to the West Indies.

'America was already known to the Ancients. Pliny mentions it clearly in his works and, in the twelfth century, an English navigator had landed in Northern America, after stopping in Iceland.'*

In the nineteenth century one could easily have been considered a crank for making such statements. But now all the old assumptions have been shattered by the discovery in 1929 of the sea maps of Piri Reis in the Topkapi Palace in Istanbul. Their origin is revealed by Piri Reis himself, an admiral of the Ottoman Fleet in the sixteenth century:

> In the course of a naval battle in 1501 with the Spaniards, a Turkish officer . . . made prisoner a man who had taken part in the three historical journeys of Christopher Columbus. The prisoner was in possession of a number of most interesting maps. With these maps, Christopher Columbus had been able to define the object of his voyage.

How had he come into possession of them? In a biography of his father, Ferdinand Columbus wrote that the explorer 'took careful note of all the directions that sailors or other persons were able to give him'.[27]

These surveys written in code would admittedly not constitute sufficient proof had not the geological branch of the American Army become interested in them in 1957. With the aid of specialists such as seismologists and glacierists, they studied, deciphered, checked and dated these maps, in the interests of American National Defence.

Task Force 43, Walters, Paul-Emile Victor, and Father Daniel Lineham, established that these maps had been drawn from ancient documents, and confirmed categorically that they gave meticulously accurate coast-lines from Greenland to the Antarctic, the interior and mountain ranges only 'discovered' in 1952.

Finally, the scientists gave the date of the basic details as going back to between 5 000 and 10 000 BC.[28]

Bessonet-Favre was right: at the end of the Middle Ages, the Franciscans received information not only from the Templars and the Orient, but also, in all probability, from the West through the

* Author's note: Bessonet-Favre (*op. cit.*) adds that the Cordeliers led by Jean de Baëza had by 1417 already reached the Canary Islands (expedition of Jean de Béthencourt). The principal church was elevated to a diocese in 1424 by Pope Martin V.

Celtic movement, which had certainly instructed Breton and Norman sailors on the subject.

A synthesis of these elements points to the purpose already mentioned. 'One must consider the politics of the time (the fourteenth and fifteenth centuries) as a whole,' says Bessonet-Favre. 'After the links between French, Burgundian and English, then Spanish, friars minor had been tightened, the next step was to bring into effect the bold plan of universal understanding, and the pacific progress of nations, and to turn towards foreign missions.'

It was the last but most important point of a mission evolved years previously and agreed on at Chinon. It was the purpose of the Franco-Spanish Confederation, but Charles VII let it drop despite the efforts of Joan, who had been prepared for this last task.

Meanwhile, to bring about this pacific development of Western Europe, it was no longer possible to look towards the East because of the strength of the Turks. And so, whilst the royal power was slowly taking over from the English occupiers, the prime concern had become to lead westwards the mercenaries and soldiers who were still ransacking the countryside. The plan failed, either through the inertia, avarice or complacent pride of an ungrateful king.

In any event, the Spaniards took up the scheme again fifty years later when they entrusted it to Christopher Columbus. With the same mission, in 1555, a Burgundian captain of the Spanish armies named Girardot des Armoises was killed by the arrows of the Indians of Columbia, outside a town to which he gave his name.*[29]

No surprise should now be felt at a Hispano-Peruvian painting of the sixteenth century, which is in the Pedro de Osma Collection. Presenting a complete synthesis, the painting depicts *Jhoana d'Arco* holding a standard which bears the cross of the order of the missionaries, with a motif of artemisias† (see illustrations).

* Translator's note: The town Girardot is about sixty miles from Bogota.

† Author's note: In Christian Symbolism, the red artemisia is dedicated to John the Baptist. According to F. de Saucy in his book *Les Templiers de Metz*, a beam in the oratory of the Templars in Metz depicted knights in combat on a background of red artemisias (see illustrations). At the castle of Jaulny (Meurthe et Moselle), the walls of the room which contains the frescos of Joan and Robert are covered with fleurs-de-lis and artemisias. The frieze is decorated with artemisias and with Crosses of the Eight Beatitudes—the cross of the Franciscan monogram.

37

GILLES DE RAIS

> Later, he financed the extraordinary adventure of the Lady Desarmois . . .[30]

When the Maid of France left Metz in December 1436, she did not go directly to La Rochelle.[31] The organization of a campaign, this time beyond the seas, demanded considerable funds, a subject that the correspondence recently exchanged with Charles VII, through Jehan d'Arc and the herald Coeur de Lys, could not have failed to mention.

The contract completed at Chinon had been recalled. Orleans and the coronation were part of a five-point programme of which the last point had caused astonishment tempered with scepticism to appear on the Dauphin's face. In the fifteenth century, to go on a voyage of discovery to a land unknown seemed crazy. However, moved by expediency, Charles agreed to start the programme: 'We shall see about the rest later . . .' he must have said to himself. He reckoned without Joan.

Honour bound to make a token gesture, the King had consented to ambassadors being sent to solicit help from the Castilian Armada.[32] After having given vague assurances, he had evaded the issue of how the operation was to be financed as indeed was his habit each time money was required.

Joan's first objective was therefore to get to Tiffauges, one of the residences of her friend Gilles de Laval, Lord of Rais, who she remembered to be immensely rich. The welcome she was given on her arrival did not belie her host's famous hospitality. In her honour, Gilles had prepared in the precinct of the castle a fantastic pageant which she had not seen before: the *Mystère d'Orléans*. It is known that in one year he spent over eighty thousand gold crowns (*écus d'or*), this figure including a series of performances.

What detractor of the Maid of France can give a satisfactory explanation for the fact that Gilles, who was chamberlain-councillor of the King, and usually so choosy about people, welcomed her unhesitatingly?

Until 1957, when it was established that men in ancient times had precise knowledge of the geography of America, the question of the arrival of a large Spanish fleet in front of La Rochelle was incomprehensible.

As Bessonet-Favre, who found references to it in the Franciscan Order's archives, wrote in the nineteenth century, this vision of the conquest of lands across the Atlantic provides all the answers. It not only permits the verification of the relevant passages in the Spanish texts, but also explains in particular Gilles de Rais' otherwise incomprehensible enthusiasm in spontaneously obeying the call of the 'Maid of Armoises'.

The motivation is elementary: the lure of gain.

The Marshal, whose prodigality had already brought him in 1436 to the verge of financial ruin, could see that by becoming a professional soldier his fortunes would be rapidly restored. No one was better qualified to provide the leadership of troops in the conquest of new lands which, rumour had it, were overflowing with silver and gold. Assured of the command by the Maid, to whom he was already indebted for his nomination as marshal of France, Gilles did not hesitate to contribute towards the expenses necessitated by the organization of the expedition. It was an entirely satisfactory solution from the point of view of the King and his entourage, who were only too relieved to be rid of a man who aroused both alarm and jealousy.

When the enterprise eventually failed, Gilles, in desperate financial straits, was obliged to resort to alchemy, in which he was passionately interested, to attempt the manufacture of gold. These facts are confirmed by dates: it was towards the end of 1438 that Francesco Prelati—the 'black magician'—came to join the alchemists taken on by Joan's former companion. Gilles was about to embark on a series of heinous, lunatic crimes.

It was thus from Tiffauges that Joan's ambassador left, bearing the famous letter addressed to the King of Castile. Whether the fleet agreed to by John II on the advice of his favourite actually went to La Rochelle is not established by any texts other than the Spanish chronicles, which indulge in a detailed description of the former Templar base. All that is known is that several ships of the Armada cruised in neighbouring waters in 1436.*

The last point of the mission conceived by the Friars minor failed in France through Charles VII's default, and it was not he who

* Author's note: According to L. de Richemond in his book *La Rochelle au temps de Charles VII*, and several anonymous texts, a few Spanish ships had in the spring of 1436 been ordered to protect from English ships the arrival of the Scottish princess Margaret Stewart, daughter of James I of Scotland, who was to marry the future Louis XI.

received 'the sceptre of the seas'[33] but, thanks to Christopher Columbus, the Emperor Charles V.

Thereafter forced to limit her ideal to France alone, the Maid's sole remaining objective was to rid the country of the *Grandes Compagnies* who had re-formed because of unemployment and were engaged in the worst kind of depredation south of the Loire. Joan pursued them and on the way attacked a few strongly held English forts in Guyenne. Gilles provided the money, and a few lines of the *Mystère d'Orléans* show that he had long since made up his mind on the matter:

> And, Lady, do not doubt,
> I wish but to do your will.
> My allies and underlings,
> Lady, know that all shall come,
> And your will we shall do,
> In everything, at your inclination.
> And if you wish we shall depart,
> Acting at your device.

In March 1436—the last month of the medieval calendar year—about 400 men from La Rochelle went down into the south-west. A few years after the final liberation of the city of Blaye by Dunois in 1451, Leon of Rozmital, Grand-judge of Bohemia, stayed there awhile and heard from the inhabitants of Joan's arrival in 1436. There is no doubt that she entered the town but was unable to stay there, for it changed hands several times before its deliverance.

After Blaye, Bordeaux and then Bayonne were besieged, as is described in abundant detail in the *Chronicle of Lorraine*.

> They rode so far that they arrived outside Bordeaux, made preparations for war, . . . and besieged it most fiercely with artillery, and made approaches . . . The English in the town were all astounded to see so great a number of people . . . and at the end of six weeks to them surrendered . . . leaving horses and equipment there, . . . and went off . . . The Maid entered the town, and left a garrison to defend it well. They then all went off to Bayonne, and besieged it with great shots of artillery, saying: 'English, surrender or you will all die!' The English concluded that if they held out a long time, woe would befall them. They started to parley, asking leave, and safety for their bodies and luggage. All this was granted them, and so they took them and all went off . . . The Maid by her power of war has chased them all out.

Quite apart from the threatening phrase 'surrender or you will all die', which is reminiscent in tone of her attack on Paris in 1429, the name 'the Maid', used in the chronicle, is significant.

Shortly afterwards, Xaintrailles the Gascon took part in the cleaning-up operations. He was one of the last companions of the heroine, whom he had followed (with Baretta) after the disintegration of the royal forces. Would he have tolerated the presence of a 'so-called adventuress' when he had known the Maid of Orleans so well?

The Spanish chronicle ended with the claim that 'the fleet of Castile won much honour, as can be seen in the *Coronica de la Poncella* . . .'* Exaggerations or errors in dates are obviously attributable to distance and oral transmission of information. In addition, the Spaniards were trying to justify the mobilization of part of their fleet, which had not served any purpose. This explains the inapposite conclusion.

However, excluding the bombast, the basic facts are there to corroborate events.

Towards the end of this long campaign, while the expedition was going round Poitou,[34] the rumour started that the Maid had died after having been wounded for the third time. There are two extant documents attesting to the measures that the news brought about.

The first, dated 29th June 1441, is a letter of remission granted by the King to Jehan of Siquenville. It provides the proof that two years earlier, Joan had handed over command to one of her companions-in-arms:

> We, Charles, by grace of God King of France, inform all present and to come, that we have received the humble supplication of Jehan de Siquenville, squire of the Gascogne country, containing that, two years ago or thereabouts [therefore in June 1439], the late Lord of Raitz, in his lifetime our Councillor, Chamberlain and Marshal of France, under whom the said supplicant served, said to this supplicant that he wanted to go to Le Mans, and that he wanted him to take charge and government of the men of war that a named Jehanne who called herself Maid then had, promising that, if he [Siquenville] took the said town, he would be its captain. Which supplicant, to obey the said late Lord of Raitz, his master . . . agreed to it and took charge a certain time in the countries of Poitou and Anjou . . .
>
> Given at Saint-Denis, in France . . .†

The King thereby revealed, though reticently, that Joan was still at the side of Gilles in 1439. This is confirmed by Vallet de Viriville who says that at this time the Lady of Armoises was accompanying the Marshal across Poitou. Secondly, the text indicates clearly that the order to seize Le Mans was given by Rais, and not by the Maid, contrary to what has been claimed.

* Author's note: This problem was treated in the last chapter. According to Quicherat (Volume V), it was the edition printed in Burgos in 1562.

† Author's note: *Trésors des Chartes, Archives Nationales* J176—document 84. Quoted by Quicherat, Jean Grimod, etc. Jean de Saint-Jean adds that Siquenville 'had been guilty of ransoming several villages of Anjou and Poitou', but that he did not take Le Mans. This town was only delivered in 1448.

The other document, an extract from the Orleans Accounts of Gilet Morschoasne, provides completely different data.

After the trial, the townspeople had organized a solemn procession on 8th May every year in memory of their liberator. The last one had been in 1436, the year of Joan's reappearance.

Suddenly, two days before Corpus Christi in 1439, eight masses were ordered, not to the memory, but 'for the obsequies' of the late Joan the Maid:

> To Gilet Morshoasne, for nine pounds and a half of wax . . . to make four candles and a flare for the obsequies of the late Jehanne the Maid, two days before Corpus-Christi . . .
>
> To the prior of Saint-Sanson . . . for eight low masses which were sung during the said obsequies . . . to Thévenon de Bourges . . . to Jacquet Leprestre . . . to the churchwarden of Saint-Sanson . . . who rang the vigils and the mass . . .[35]

Nevertheless, the town's grief was short-lived. Joan recovered so quickly and so well, that barely two months later, other book-keeping entries were made, dispelling the established ideas.

38

THE TOWN OF ORLEANS' GRATITUDE

Maid, *ma mie*, be you most welcome back . . .
(Charles VII, in Pierre Sala's account)[36]

Ten years after the first official reception given in Joan's honour during the liberation of Orleans, a second reception given on 18th July 1439 was proof of her return to the town. Jacquet Leprestre was once again responsible for organizing it:

1. To Jacquet Leprestre, the 18th day of July, for ten *pintes* and a *choppine* [nearly ten litres] of wine presented to Lady Jehanne des Armoises, for this 14 *sols parisis.**

For over two months, the townspeople were able to come up to her and converse with her as in the past, and it never occurred to anyone to contest the obvious truth that the Maid of France was indeed the Maid of Orleans.

As Philippe Erlanger has written, the Town Council felt 'neither scepticism nor uncertainty. The liberator was found again, acclaimed and revered.' [37] The town councillors, warned of her arrival in 1436 by the letters bearing her seal and signature, had no reservations. They fêted her nearly every day, and within a fortnight had made her the gift of a considerable sum.

Morschoasne's entries are so embarrassingly authentic that Abbé Cochard and his friend Vergniaud-Romagnési were unable to deny the facts and stated: 'They are inexplicable, but it is repugnant to us to admit it.' This seems a strange conception of objectivity.

There was a succession of receptions at which wine and meat were served.

2. To him [Jaquet], on 29th day of July . . . *to the said My Lady Jehanne.*

* Author's note: The eight entries quoted in this chapter, taken from Morchoasne's *register of the Accounts of the Fortress of Orleans* for the year 1439 (CC.655) are numbered 1 to 8 for convenience. They are quoted by most dissident authors including Jean Grimod.

The possessive used in this second entry, as in the following one, denotes the affectionate respect of the townspeople for her.

> 3. To the said Jacquet, the before-last day of July, for meat bought from Basin . . . to present *to the said My Lady Jehanne des Armoises* . . .
> 4. To the said Jaquet, the last day of July . . . to dinner and to supper . . .
> 5. To him, the first day of August, for ten *pintes* and *choppines* of wine, to her presented when she left this town . . .

For Joan went away for two or three weeks. The people of Orleans, possibly fearing she would not return, took the opportunity of showing her their belated but heartfelt gratitude:

> 6. *To Jehanne d'Armoises, for gift to her made* the 1st day of August, *after deliberation done with the Council of the Town, for the good which she did to the said town during the siege* . . .

Joan was presented with 210 *livres* in memory of the liberation, while the rent of a fine middle-class house cost at the time between 10 and 14 *livres* a year.[38] Luillier, Thévenon de Bourges, Leprestre, Lesbahy and others including several churchmen, felt neither hesitation nor compunction about dipping into the treasury of Luillier's brother-in-law, the Intendant Boucher, who made no protest. The Maid of Orleans received forthwith the equivalent of two and a half months of the pension granted to the Lord Bastard.

Dunois, in fact, arrived on the scene at this point. But he does not seem to have been scandalized when informed of the matter by Jacques Boucher. Their mutual discretion is readily explained: they could not make an official acknowledgement of Joan without betraying the King. But honour and loyalty prevented them from denouncing her.

There were further receptions on the Maid's return:

> 7. To the said Jaquet [Leprestre], for eight *pintes* of wine dispensed at a supper at which were Jehan Luillier and Thévenon de Bourges, for they thought to present it to the said Lady Jehanne, who left before the said wine had come . . .

Whatever the reason for Joan leaving the table, and there are numerous possibilities, conformist writers have expatiated on this trivial matter. After a superficial reading of documents, and doubtless preferring his own feelings to hard facts, Maurice Garçon has placed the following interpretation on the situation: 'It seems pretty obvious that the Lady of Armoises appreciated the necessity to disappear rapidly.'[39]

Happily, there is another entry by Morschoasne establishing that the Lady in question did not disappear:

> 8. To Jehan Pichon, the *4th day of September*, for six *pintes* and *choppines* . . . presented *to the Lady Jehanne des Armoises* . . .

An intelligent summary of the matter was expressed some fifty years ago in the *Bulletin Syndical des Instituteurs*: 'Is it not rather presumptuous of us to say . . . five hundred years after the event, that it was not the real Joan of Arc . . . and that the people of Orleans, who actually saw her, made a foolish mistake?'[40] If they did, they were by no means the only ones to do so. Charles VII arrived in these parts before 24th August for he presided a Great Royal Council on that day. With him were Dunois, Charles of Anjou, the Lord of Chaumont, the Archbishop of Vienne, and in particular Rabateau. It will be remembered that Jehan Rabateau was Joan's host at Poitiers, and that the famous *Book of Poitiers* had been written at his house. As the King's Advocate General, and shortly to assume his position as President of the Paris Parliament, he would surely have been the first to denounce a fraud.

The illustrious assembly only left Orleans on 5th September, and so for these two weeks Joan, Lady of Armoises, was in the town at the same time as Charles VII. The reception of 4th September took place under his very nose. How is one to explain this surprising tolerance on the part of a monarch who was the most distrustful of men?

The sequence of events shows the connivance between Joan and her brother, and makes it possible to determine where the meeting described by Pierre Sala took place. Although his account is intentionally confusing for the reasons already given, it is possible to state categorically that the meeting took place during the summer of 1439 in Jacques Boucher's garden.

Ten years after the first part of the saga, the King having expressed the wish to meet 'this Maid who much resembled the first', it happened that, at the time of the meeting, 'he was in a garden, under a great vine-arbour . . .'

Was it to impress those present that it was decided to repeat the stratagem used in Chinon in 1429? The scene is perfectly recounted by Philippe Erlanger.

> As at Chinon, the young girl went to fetch the King, deliberately lost in the crowd of his courtiers; as at Chinon, Charles saw kneeling at his feet a beautiful, robust girl with her hair cropped, and a mystical look on her face. He was moved, overwhelmed . . . He was in no doubt that he was looking at the miraculous shepherdess . . . and ensured that no harm was done her.[41]

Indeed, the Maid was never troubled and neither was her retinue, her so-called accomplices—on the contrary, they were rewarded.

According to information given to Sala by Charles's Chamberlain Guillaume de Boissy, Joan

> came straight to the King, which dumbfounded him so that he knew not what to say apart from greeting her kindly and saying: Maid, *ma mie*, be you most welcome back, in the name of God who knows the secret which is between you and me. Then, miraculously, after hearing these words this false maid knelt down . . .

God and the secret were the reasons for yet another 'abjuration', this time at Orleans. It is the crux of the matter. A martyr to political realism, Joan had to sacrifice herself once again in the interest of the security of the throne, and agreed to denounce herself in ultimate self-abnegation. She was moved to this last renunciation by the religious faith which had conditioned her and been the driving force of her life. From that day no more was heard of her.

An item from the accounts of the town of Tours[42] reveals however that Joan remained at Orleans some time after the date given by Morschoasne.

> To the Receiver, by an order given the 27th day of September, the year above said [1439], and here recorded, the sum of 4 *Livres Tournois* that by our command and ordinance has been paid and given, namely to Jehan Drouart . . . for a journey which he made in this present month to Orleans . . .
>
> To carry sealed letters that the Lord Bailiff was writing to the King our sire, on the subject of Lady Jehanne des Armoises . . . and a letter that the said Lady Jehanne wrote to the said Lord Bailiff . . .*

These sealed letters were accordingly accompanied by a demand for money that Joan had sent to the bailiff, after her meeting with Charles VII. The King had granted her a certain sum to enable her to return to Metz, and had told her to ask the Bailiff of Tours for it. The latter's sealed letters thus assume their full significance: he would not pay out any money without authorization. This did not prevent him from continuing to designate the author of the demand in terms of respect: 'Lady Jehanne . . .'

And a few days later, in the presence of the King who had returned to Orleans on 30th September for the Estates General, of Queen Marie, Yolanda of Anjou and the whole court, a performance of Gilles de Rais' spectacular pageant was given in the heart of the town. In it Gilles appeared in a particularly glorious role, while Joan was described as follows:

* Author's note: This bailiff was Harduin de Champagne who filled the post from 1425 to 1444 and therefore knew Joan well.

Lady Jehanne, Noble Princess,
Most Noble and Powerful Lady
Most Noble and excellent Princess . . .*

It is most likely that Joan was present, before her departure for Lorraine.

* Author's note: From the 1862 edition. The presumed author of it is Jacques Millet.

Gilles de Rais spent between 80,000 and 100,000 *livres* on this new series of fêtes in 1439. See Vallet de Viriville and Abbé Bossard.

39

THE 'SWINDLER' REWARDED

> The funeral service, reinstituted in 1439, just before Joan's return to Orleans, was again suppressed after 1440.
> (A note in Grillot de Givry's book *La Survivance et le mariage de Jeanne d'Arc*)

According to the *Journal d'un Bourgeois de Paris*, a 'false' Maid appeared in the capital in 1440. On her arrival, the Parliament, presided over by Rabateau, summoned her, preached to her and questioned her . . . 'She said that she was not a maid but had been married to a knight and had borne him two sons . . .'

The *Journal* however cannot be accepted unquestioningly. The Bourgeois, violently opposed to the Armagnacs and consistently hostile to Joan, indulges more than once in rancorous fictional narrative.

In any event, identification with the Lady of Armoises is patently impossible. She did not, as far as I know, go to Paris at this time, and there are certainly no documents in Paris archives showing her to have done so. Secondly, Joan des Armoises' incessant campaigning after 1436 would almost certainly have prevented her from keeping the birth of a child in 1439 secret from the inhabitants of Orleans.

This question of imaginary children can be settled by official genealogies of the House of Armoises which state that Robert had none from this marriage with Joan, whereas he had had some from his first marriage with Alix of Manonville. Thus, in a document in my possession, Chérin notes with precision:

> Robert des Armoises, died without descendants
> wife: Jeanne the Maid of France[43]

As Abbé Villaret had written, Joan had only the outward appearance of her sex. The doctors consulted for the checks on her virginity carried out at Poitiers and Rouen were categorical on this point, as may be seen from Doctor Delachambre's testimony in 1456. Summoned by Warwick and Winchester to look after the Maid at the castle of Bouvreuil, he had professedly appeared before them together with Master Guillaume Desjardin and other doctors:

> Then, we went to see Jehanne . . . myself, by virtue of my medical profession, I was able to ascertain that she was a virgin and intact, having seen her almost naked . . . I felt her loins; she was very narrow, so far as I could see . . .[44]

In short, this diagnosis was made after Joan had done much riding astride, and clearly describes what the modern gynaecologist would define as a malformation of the genital organs, complicated by a contracted pelvis in the form of a vase. The last point alone makes childbirth practically impossible, other than by a Caesarean section.

It is easy to imagine Robert's disappointment when he discovered on his wedding night that Joan's long-standing nickname was sadly only too accurate. To this insuperable sexual impasse were soon added other irritations. The Maid of France imperiously informed Robert of her intention of leaving forthwith, and demanded financial help to this effect, so that she could join Gilles de Rais and other companions-in-arms.

Disorientated, and bound by the secret of State, the poor knight, as a last resort 'retired into the Celestine monastery in Metz', according to Jean-Julien Barbé.[45] Although this author quotes erroneous evidence in support, it is a plausible hypothesis, particularly in view of the fact that Robert disappeared for several years. And although there is no further document referring directly to the couple, this hypothesis is verified chronologically by other significant and corroborative data.

In 1440, Isabelle Romée, who was ill in Orleans, was nursed and subsequently received a pension. A few authors have suggested that she had been living in the town for several years. This 1440 document is the first to establish the fact and, even so, would only have been of passing interest had not Isabelle's adoptive daughter been described as Jehanne the Maid, who was therefore not yet 'deceased'.[46]

At about the same time, despite his supposed participation in a hoax, Pierre du Lys was granted by Charles VII 'the privilege of collecting the tolls of Chaumont', so that he was able to settle in Orleans.[47] Pierre took charge of his mother, and was furthermore on the spot to welcome back another of his benefactors, Duke Charles, who was liberated in December of that year by the part payment of a ransom of 200,000 *escuz* of gold.

Pierre d'Arc—who at this point was not yet called 'du Lys'—had long benefited from signal favour, having been created a Knight of the Porcupine by the Duke's command. The significance of this distinction is considerable.

> The Order of the Porcupine was founded in 1394 by Louis of Orleans, on the occasion of the christening of his son Charles[48] . . . who later became its Grand Master.

A rival of the Golden Fleece and of the Garter, this Order above all observed strict rules: its knights, who were limited in number, had to be nobles of four quarters.

For example, Eustache de Rochebaron, a relation of the Sermoise branch, became a member of the Order in 1437, and Philip the Good became one on the occasion of the marriage of Charles of Orleans and Mary of Cleves in 1440.

One can only assume that this honour conferred before 1436 on Joan's foster brother, cancelled the patently faked act of ennoblement of the d'Arc family dated 29th December 1429. Otherwise, Pierre du Lys' lineage would not have satisfied the requirements.

In fact, his line was of noble extraction,* and the family's state of derogation had been secretly abrogated by the King. The d'Arcs therefore did not need to be ennobled, and their present-day descendants can but rejoice in the fact.

This is corroborated by the two following points. The *vidimus* of the act, drawn up in the sixteenth century, during the reign of Henry II, states that the original did not bear the usual great royal seal.

Secondly, the spelling of d'Arc as *Day* poses a definite problem. Of course in different circumstances it would be of trifling importance, but in this case it is surprising enough for Quicherat to insist: 'It is disconcerting that the Maid's surname should have been altered thus in so important a document.'

These flagrant anomalies change matters, particularly when so many precautions were taken in other directions. The issue was once again deliberately confused.

On 29th July 1443, by special grace, the Duke of Orleans granted to Messire Pierre du Lys, as well as to his son Jehan, the emblements, profits, usufructs, revenues and emoluments from an island situated on the River Loire.

'Which Isle-aux-Boeufs, the said My Lord Duke has given' in compensation (to the said Pierre) for the loss of his wife's possession duly sold to pay his ransom. After the privilege granted by the King, the Duke's generosity to Pierre du Lys ran to more than mere honorary distinctions, however prized these might be.

The deed of gift[49] informs all good folk:

> Having heard the supplication of the said messire Pierre du Lys, stating that to acquit himself loyally towards the King . . . he left his country to enter the service of the King our said Lord and of His Grace the Duke, in company with Jehanne the Maid his sister with whom until

* Author's note: In the course of my research, I discovered so many eminent members of the d'Arc family before this period that I have only been able to mention a small number of them in this book.

his absentment and thereafter until the present time, he has exposed his body in that said service . . .

The expression *son absentement* has given rise to much discussion and hasty judgments. Some authors claim that it refers to Joan; others, with grammar on their side, say quite rightly that it refers to the subject of the sentence, namely to Pierre du Lys. They have all missed the point. Thorough analysis shows that it is the expression 'with whom' which dominates the whole sentence. It can be broken up thus: 'with whom (until his absentment), and thereafter (this absentment) until the present time . . .' Or better still, *with whom . . . until the present time.*

An eighteenth-century scholar made the pertinent comment that if Joan the Maid had been dead in 1443, Pierre would not have failed to stress the fact in his supplication.[50] It would have been an additional claim on the Duke's favours. Therefore, happy to reward the faithful knight who had more or less escorted Joan up until his return from London, Charles of Orleans would have rewarded him for perpetrating a fraud. It is to be wondered why someone of such high order would have associated himself with a deceit organized in his own town. Furthermore, it is difficult to conceive that he would have allowed Pierre du Lys to remain a knight if he had indeed been guilty of such a breach of honour.

40

NICOLAS LOUVE THE FRANCISCAN

. . . By which he understood well that it was the Maid Jehanne . . .

(Dean of Saint-Thibaud)

Until the plans for Joan's canonization were afoot, it was openly rumoured that the people of Metz had given her a tremendous welcome. And despite the unkind insinuations of her detractors, the tale is still told in a few villages of Lorraine that the Lady of Armoises was kind and generous, and that she behaved very well for the rest of her life.

On Joan's return to Metz at the end of 1439, Robert, now sporting a beard and a moustache, left the Celestines. They then settled 'in the house that the said Lord of Harmoises had opposite Sainte-Segoleine, and they stayed there for as long as it pleased them'. This is according to the Dean of Saint-Thibault who lived in the presbytery of Saint-Eucaire, about five hundred metres away. Nearer still was the Celestine monastery and also, at the bottom of the rue des Récollets, the Franciscan convent.

Rising above a row of arcades exposed to the daylight, the knight's *Hostel* bordered the actual *place des Maréchaux*. From the first floor, the view took in the square in front of Sainte-Segoleine, which, curiously enough, is now *place Jeanne d'Arc*. The keystone of the great porch was decorated with two coats of arms in sculpted stone: on the left, the armorial bearings of the Maid, on the right, those of the Armoises.*

Joan's exemplary goodness during the last nine years of her life is witness once again to her unswerving fidelity to the instruction she had received. Respect for promises made, and the spiritual ideal, finally broke in her passionate character which had unceasingly devoted itself to the pursuit of the goal. Other than pious duties and domestic life, the couple merely spent their time riding to visit close relatives and friends amongst the nobility.

* Author's note: This was until the Revolution when, according to local lore, they were scraped away.

Military campaigns and political preoccupations were now things of the past for Joan. And Robert, marked by years of fasting and matins, docilely followed his wife's instructions: no more tournaments, no more feudal-type raids on his neighbours' lands.

Joan was not, in fact, acting thus in isolation for she was part of a close group of friends originally brought together by religion. Nicolas Louve, the leading figure of the republic of Metz, had belonged to the Third Order for at least thirty years. An influential member of the Friars of the Strict Observance, he too professed the ideology preached by St Colette and adopted by the Maid. Like them, he had fought wholeheartedly for Christian unity, in support of the true Pope Eugenius IV.

> There has died the Lord Nicole Lowe [Louve], Knight, Chamberlain of the Emperor, and of the King of France, and of the Duke of Burgundy, who was a man wise and prudent in all his deeds, and who was a founder of the Cordelier Fathers of the Observance of Metz . . .*

A necrology which follows the chronicle describes his obsequies on 10th February 1461: 'and was then buried dressed in religious habit, to wit, half celestine and half cordelier, but with a knight's hood'.[51]

It is known from other sources that he devoted his life to the Franciscans with their good-natured simplicity, to the Celestines in their austerity and to public duties. Like the 'brothers, angels, and saints' of the Third Order charged with contributing to the realization of their social programme, this important notable knew everybody. Able by virtue of his status to move around freely, he regularly met the eminent figures of the movement—Yolanda of Anjou, Mother Nicolette, and Isabelle Romée who had come specially from Lorraine to the pilgrimages at Puy.

Louve was, without doubt, one of Joan's 'voices'.

It seems extremely likely that he intervened with Robert de Baudricourt on Joan's behalf, particularly in view of the support of the *clerks minor* at the time of her second attempt, and of the fact that Baudricourt was then closely related to Robert des Armoises by his first wife.

Just before the start of the saga, Louve had gone to Nancy 'with the lords of Metz who displaced themselves to see the Maid'. And it was thanks to Joan that he had been dubbed knight in Rheims cathedral by Charles VII on the day of his coronation.

Fifteen years later, in 1444–5, at the time of the siege of Metz by French troops, he was charged with conducting negotiations on behalf of the people under his administration with the King and

* See *Monastica Metensia* by E. de Bouteiller. The author states that the Third Order of Metz was affiliated to the confraternity of the Strict Observance.

René of Anjou.* 'And the said Lord Louve answered so valiantly and honestly that he was praised and esteemed by the princes and other personages present . . . and they said that it was long since they had heard a knight reply as wisely and prudently on each article as had done the Lord Nicole Louve . . .'[52] This text, which brings to mind the praise lavished on Jehan d'Aulon, is all the more authoritative in that it had no cause to defend.

Louve, a tertiary of uncompromising honesty, and considerable political experience, did not stultify himself in 1436 and told the Dean the absolute truth: 'By which he understood well that it was the Maid who had been in France; and she was recognized by several signs as Jehanne of France who took Charles the King to be sacred at Rheims . . .'

The mention of Notre-Dame de Liesse, of John the Baptist, and Jehanne of France by the Dean is proof that Louve knew all the secrets: Joan's birth in 1407 as well as the King's intention to change the patronymic of *Orleans* into that of *France*.

In 1445 the Lady of Armoises was still alive; and faithful to her commitments she repaid Colart de Failly's widow Poincette the loan made for the 'quarter of Haraucourt'.[53]

The portraits of her, often mentioned, present no less conclusive evidence. Grillot de Givry first wrote that M. de Haldat du Lys owned one which resembled Joan of Arc, and had been painted 'at the time of her reappearance in Lorraine'. Vergniaud-Romagnési identified it by the armour, quite unlike the one depicted in the Orleans portraits. This is explained by the fact that she had been given another suit by the Count of Virnebourg.

Detractors then countered that 'the adventuress' had been so successful because she bore a close resemblance to Joan of Arc, and that she had merely benefited from a coincidence.

This argument is without foundation and can be dismissed instantly, for a physiognomical study of extant works shows that Jehanne des Armoises bore an astonishing resemblance not only to the Maid of Orleans, but also to her nephew Louis XII, to Charles V as seen in the profile of his statue, and to many other members of the house of Valois.

Whilst it may just be possible to accept the first point of similarity as coincidence this cannot be said of the second: two such points must be conclusive proof. In any event, there are at the present time, for all to see, two sets of effigies depicting her looking at her husband.

A sculpted panel, one of a collection of remarkable medieval

* Author's note: René, Duke of Anjou, Bar and Lorraine, sometimes called Good King René. As he was Queen Marie of Anjou's brother, he was Charles VII's, and Joan's, brother-in-law. His daughter Margaret of Anjou married Henry VI of England.

exhibits, is on show in the room called *Le Grenier* in the museum at Metz. At the castle of Jaulny in the department of Meurthe-et-Moselle, the ancient fortress of Simon des Armoises, two striking frescos decorate a splendid coffered chimney.

The sculpted medallions of the Metz museum are set in the lower part of a gate salvaged from the *Hostel* opposite Sainte-Segoleine before its demolition in 1852. The style of the Gothic motifs in the top part of the panel betray typically fifteenth-century treatment, with appropriate symbolism used for each figure.

The medallion of Joan is borne by two dolphins,* with their mouths closed, and between them is a sun with the face of a man. The Maid's features, delicately done, are identical to those of the Jaulny portrait. The only difference is in her headwear which is here constituted by a human-faced dolphin, beneath a sort of calotte.

Robert, who wears a moustache as well as a beard—whereas in the Jaulny portrait he only has a 'Tyburn collar'—is supported by two dolphins, with their heads downwards. A hood and two symbolical animals linked together by a ring, complete the portrait.

These differences, notably in the dolphins and in the absence of symbolism, seem to indicate that the Jaulny frescos were not done by the same artist as the sculptures at Metz.

It was in any case only in August 1447 that a Richard des Armoises, from another branch of the family, officially entered into possession of half the fief of Jaulny, after his marriage to Agnes, daughter of Simonin, lord of Jaulny.

Apart from hearsay, there are therefore no grounds for supposing that the castle was the second home of Robert and Joan, particularly two years before their death. It is known however that they visited here frequently, and it is logical to assume that the object of the chimney portrait was to commemorate their visits as much as this brilliant alliance.

Much more important for us is the branch of Autrey. Already a century previously, this fief had been raised in favour of Rodolphe des Armoises.

* Author's note: In his *Vocabulaire des symboles et attributs*, Abbé Corblet indicates that the dolphin is not only an allegory of salvation and diligence, but is an emblem of conjugal love, and also of Christ in Christendom.

41

THE TOMB AT PULLIGNY

> The Lady of Armoises—Joan of Arc—is buried here, with all her jewels . . .
>
> (M. Girot, Mayor of Pulligny-sur-Madon, Meurthe-et-Moselle)

At the time Joan was settling in Lorraine, Philip des Armoises—son of François who was Robert's first cousin—married Isabelle du Fay, and she brought him the lordship of Autrey as a dowry.[54]

The Maid of France, who had just renounced all public activity, at once conceived great affection for her second cousins. This phenomenon of compensation is psychologically straightforward. With the creation of a family nucleus, of which she had been completely deprived ever since becoming conscious of her mission, her affective energy was transferred and her behaviour was thereby modified. Thereafter she was able to give vent to her maternal instincts, which had been repressed for the reasons we know. These instincts manifested themselves intensely when she became the godmother of the first born of the branch of Autrey, and gave the child the Christian name 'Louis'—Louis I des Armoises of Autrey.[55]

'I believe it was the first time in the family's history that the name Louis appeared, but it seems to have been given thereafter to the eldest of each generation,' wrote Léon Germain de Maidy quite accurately, adding that he did not know the reason why it was adopted. It is certainly not generally known.

Joan naturally chose for her godson her father Louis of Orleans' Christian name. In the light of this, further details provided by Germain de Maidy assume their full significance.

> It is likely that the Autrey branch modified their coat of arms by adding a small charge . . . There are reasonable grounds for believing that it was a fleur-de-lis: possibly because of the name Louis, which was the one most frequently borne by the kings of France . . .[56]

For one who has always denied that the Lady of Armoises was Joan, this insistence is strange, if not revealing. Especially as the Armoises only supported the French kings periodically, the sum total of their service amounting to no more than 54 years throughout the centuries.

In 1449, for the first time in a decade, an official document bore the word 'deceased' in front of the Maid's name. 'To Isabeau bereaved of the late Jehanne the Maid, for a gift that the town is making her . . .'[57] Joan had therefore died between April and July, and the town of Orleans, having learnt the news, took the opportunity when making the gift to Isabelle Romée on Tuesday 20th August 1449 to acknowledge the fact. Her death was confirmed a year later by Charles of Orleans when granting a new favour of Pierre du Lys.

Traditions about her still prevail in a village close to Autrey.

> The Lady of Armoises was passionately devoted to her godson. Every day, she rode to Pulligny and was seen to pray in the small church she loved so much because of its chapels, one of which was dedicated to the Virgin, and another to John the Baptist.*

When Philippe des Armoises took possession of Autrey, the interior of the church had not yet been completed and it is often said that the Lady of Armoises paid out large sums towards its decoration. She later expressed the wish to be buried there, as did her husband.

Despite a few ugly changes tastelessly made in the last hundred years, the church still has an intimate atmosphere, conducive to mysticism, with its late Gothic nave and aisles facing east. A few surprising symbols remain.

Many years ago, my uncle Gaston-Nicolas de Sermoise, a diplomat and former *Chargé-de-Missions*, had been enlightened on the subject through members of our family. In 1929, he decided to investigate the traditional accounts and went to Pulligny with a friend. Abbé Pian who was *curé* at the time, handed him a pamphlet and provided further details himself, imparting all he knew.

> The Maid Joan, by then Lady of Armoises, was buried in this church, with her rings and jewels, at the far right-hand corner of the chancel and nave. Robert rests beside her, dressed in his knight's armour.

The fact that Robert died after Joan is confirmed in a genealogical table drawn up at Besançon for the Girardots of Nozeroy-Armoises: 'Robert des Armoises, Lord of Tichémont . . . died in 1450.'[58]

> At the end of the seventeenth century [Abbé Pian continued], members of the family had a memorial tablet placed on a wall near the tomb, which was becoming worn under the feet of the faithful.
>
> In 1890, when proceedings for the Beatification were started, the memorial was taken away. However, the iconoclasts forgot to remove

* Author's note: The church had been built by Perrin de Pulligny who, as is recorded on his memorial tablet, was buried there in 1436. It has been suggested with some justification that the Pulligny family was the same as the Poulengy. A Latin text quoted as a source gives *Ludovici de Pulengy* for Pulligny.

its moulding, and it can still be seen in the small deconsecrated chapel to the right of the chancel.

Shortly afterwards, the ancient flagstones of the church were replaced by kitchen tiles! Joan's and Robert's tombstone then disappeared from sight, partly under the flooring, partly under a step of the chancel which now extends to the end of the nave.

A year before his death, my uncle told me briefly the essential family data, and then bequeathed to me the results of all his research and the family documents. A few years passed, and then Abbé Pian died too.

In 1968, pressed by a group of friends, I decided to investigate, and one Saturday in November of that year, I went over to Pulligny with them.* We were received by M. Girot, the mayor, and M. Florentin, a former master-builder, who were both born in the village and had been familiar with the tomb's history since childhood. They had also known Abbé Pian intimately, and were thus all the more favourably inclined towards our project. Point by point, they enthusiastically confirmed my uncle's revelations: Joan, godmother of Louis; the jewels in the coffin; Robert and his armour; and finally, the location of the tomb. They added further details which we tape-recorded: 'The Maid's armorial bearings were sculpted on the keystone of a vault near the tomb. But these were scratched during the Revolution.'

Curious to know what remained of the original inscriptions on the ledger after all the depredations, we were given valuable assistance by the present incumbent, M. l'Abbé Chrétien who generously allowed us to remain the whole afternoon.

After two hours' hard work, a step was loosened, and an angle of the tomb, stripped of its cement, gradually appeared. There were Gothic inscriptions which from the letters we were able to identify as being fifteenth-century in style. This was therefore one of the oldest tombs in the church.

A few words half rubbed out followed by a sign, were sufficient for us to understand.

PRIEZ POUR LAME D LLE  **CI**

We know the lady in question. As for the sign, with its multiple symbols, it constitutes the keystone of our discovery.

* Author's note: The group consisted of: M. Jacques Lesinge, a journalist; M. Jean-Jacques Ceccarini, a photographer; M. Gérard Pesme, whose book on Joan I have had occasion to refer to many times; and M. Jacques Guérillon, a writer and an expert on medieval arms.

As already mentioned, the Cross of the Eight Beatitudes, with equal arms and eight equidistant points, is painted on all the monograms of the Franciscan movement and figured on the sails of Christopher Columbus' ships. It also figures in the Peruvian painting of Jhoana d'Arco, on her standard sprinkled with artemisias (see illustrations).

At Pulligny, this cross of knighthood is inscribed in a circle, and so becomes the 'quartered circle of Celtic tradition', the significance of which is completion of the mission, and thus the attainment of perfection which animates substance. It is a millennial symbol to be found throughout the Christian world, often placed behind the head of 'Christ in Majesty'. It can be seen clearly at Notre-Dame in Paris, set back a little from the two Christs on the great portal.*

Finally, the cross has been so placed in the circle that it resembles the cross of Burgundy, the *croix de Saint-André.*

All this is conclusive evidence that Joan the Maid represented union, and a quest for peace.

In his book on Pulligny published in 1893, Abbé Eugène Martin claimed to have described all the features of interest. It is therefore surprising to find an omission on his part. The Lady of Armoises was after all the first benefactress of the church, but not one of the words engraved on her tombstone corresponds to those of the Abbé. Why did he omit this important ledger? And why was it horribly mutilated with a chisel, in 1920, at the time of the Canonization?

The answer was already outlined in the course of the preliminary investigation of the Trial of Rehabilitation by the Inquisitor Jean Bréhal: 'It is up to you to guess if you are able!'

Like kings, the Church never completely effaces the traces of its secrets. And so the symbol of which Joan had said to her judges: 'The sign of my mission will last a thousand years,' was engraved after her death.

The endless succession of strange facts marking the Maid's life proves that these coincidences cannot be attributed to chance, by very reason of their number.

Next to the Maid of France's tombstone in the church of Pulligny is an altar bearing a statue of Joan of Arc dressed in brown Franciscan frieze decorated with fleurs-de-lis.

Is it surprising to find another statue of Joan in the principal church in Charmes, in the chapel to the right of the porch, until the end of the nineteenth century called the 'chapel of the Armoises'?[59] The

* Author's note: A 'Christ in Majesty' with the sign may be seen in the entrance hall of the convent of the 'Franciscan Missions', 7 rue Marie-Rose, Paris, 14e.
The significance of the Latin cross is of course quite different.
See the bibliography.

statue is next to a 'piscina decorated with the conjoined armorial bearings of the Armoises and the Dukes of Lorraine'.

It becomes abundantly clear that from the day the national heroine consented to live far from the profane world—to *migrare a saeculo*—it would only be possible to identify her through the use of symbols. That is why the ledger of Pulligny still bears a special cross—the sign of the completion of the mission—and that other complementary revelations subsist, such as those of the panel at the Metz Museum—the sun accompanied by three dolphins which are a symbol both of her origin and of 'the Christian who has taken refuge in God's bosom through the mediation of Christ'.*

* Author's note: On the subject of the human-faced sun, the heraldic authority Pierre Palliot wrote in 1660: 'Also the Holy Scriptures have held it to be the figure of Jesus-Christ, saviour of our souls.'

NOTES TO PART IV

1 See *Metz Ancien* by Baron Gérard d'Hannoncelles, first president of the royal court of Metz between 1820 and 1830. The original manuscript of the Dean of St Thibaud was in the hands of the Reverend Fathers of Nancy
2 *Journal d'un Bourgeois de Paris, op. cit.*
3 See Régine Pernoud's article 'Jeanne d'Arc prisonnière' in *La Revue de Paris*, June 1960
4 In *Charles VII et son mystère*, Philippe Erlanger
5 *Les Clarisses*, J. Ancelet-Hustache
6 *Le Château de Montrottier*, Joseph Sérand
7 See *Dictionnaire d'Histoire et de Géographie ecclésiastique*, tome II. *Imprimatur* of Cardinal Dubois, *Ed. Letouzey*, Paris 1924
8 *Collection Baverel* (Files 112, 113, 117) in the Besançon Library
9 See *Metz Ancien—Chroniques*, Baron Gérard d'Hannoncelles, *op. cit.*
10 See *Bulletin de la Société d'Archéologie et Musée Historique Lorrain*, Nancy 1929
11 Number CC 654 folio 34, verso. Quoted by Grillot de Givry and Jean Grimod, *op. cit.*
12 Archives of Bar-le-Duc
The general sources for §33 are: ancient and modern armorials, Pierre Palliot (*op. cit.*), *Cabinet des Manuscrits* (d'Hozier), Bibliothèque Nationale; collections in archives and libraries in Paris (Bibliothèque Nationale), Nancy, Metz, Rheims, Bar-le-Duc, Besançon, Dijon
13 Other sources quoted in this *Mesmoire* (Manscript 22, in the library at Nancy) are: *Annals of Flanders; Chronicles* of du Haillan, Münster's *Cosmography*, and titles by M. d'Annoncel (sixteenth century)
14 Quoted by Henri Vincent. The records of Mont-Dieu are in the Archives des Ardennes, reference number H277
15 *La Maison des Armoises*, Henri Vincent
16 General sources for §34 are: Armorials by Father Anselme, Dom Calmet, Pierre Palliot (1660); Moreri's *Grand Dictionnaire Historique*, and the *Histoire Générale et particulière de Bourgogne* by the Religieux de St-Bénigne; Bibliothèque Nationale (Cabinet des Manuscrits); Libraries and archives in Besançon (Mss Baverel 111–112–117) Dijon, Bar-le-Duc, Metz, Nancy; Archives of the King of Arms of His most Catholic Majesty, Madrid, and of the civilian Tribunal of Briey; and the personal archives of the author
17 His arms, first registered in Madrid in 1522, were confirmed in 1669, 1726, 1770 and 1928. Also, document of the creation of the county of Sermoise, in March 1669, Library of Bar-le-Duc, *Coll. Bellot-Herment*, MSS 131, File 111
18 *Coll. Baverel*, MSS 111 (499) Besançon

19 See Quicherat, *Procès*, tome V, and Jean de Saint-Jean, *op. cit.*
20 See the extract from Jean Nider's *Formicarium*, which he wrote in 1437, in Quicherat's *Procès. Histoire ecclésiastique de Cologne*, C. A. Ley, 1883. *Dates sur la vie et les fonctions des Archevêques de Trèves*, Kurt Löhnert, 1908
21 In *Annales de l'Est* No. 2, Nancy 1963
22 See *Histoire d'une famille de Lorraine*, Comte Geoffrey de Failly
23 Albert Bayet is quoted by Gérard Pesme; both he and Edouard Herriot are quoted by M. David-Darnac. Personal archives
24 See *Jehan d'Aulon, écuyer de Jehanne d'Arc*
25 See *Les Mystères Templiers*, Louis Charpentier. Most of what is related here about the Templars at La Rochelle has been taken from this interesting book
26 In her book *Christophe Colomb*
27 *The Life of the Admiral Christopher Columbus* by Ferdinand Columbus, Rutgers University, New Brunswick, NJ, USA, 1959. *The Oldest Map of America* by Dr Afetinan, Ankara 1954
28 See *Les secrets de L'Atlantide* by Andrew Tomas; English edition *Atlantis—From Legend to Discovery*, London, 1972. Also, *Histoire Inconnue des Hommes depuis cent mille ans* by Robert Charroux
29 Family Archives. An article appeared on the subject in the *Figaro* (28th December 1968) entitled 'Les communautés de base en Amérique latin' by Abbé René Laurentin
30 Letter of the Marquis de la Torre, *Annales de la Société Scientifique et littéraire de Cannes* (Volume XIV) and conference on Gilles de Rais
31 Other sources for §37 are to be found in the general bibliography
32 The Spanish Chronicle aready quoted, and the article 'Jeanne d'Arc en Espagne' by Marcellin Desfourneaux, *op. cit.*
33 Bessonet-Favre, *op. cit.*
34 *Histoire de Charles VII* by Vallet de Viriville, quoted by Jean de Saint Jean
35 Extracts from the accounts of Gilles Morchoasne, June 1439. Orleans, register CC655, folios 53, 56, 74. Quoted by Quicherat, Jean Grimod etc., *op. cit.*
36 *Les Prouesses de plusieurs Roys*, dedicated to Francis I by Pierre Sala. *Manuscrits français, Bibliothèque Nationale*, No 10420. Quoted by Jean Grimod, *op. cit.*
37 Philippe Erlanger: *Charles VII et son Mystère*
38 In *Courrier des Chercheurs et des Curieux*, *Miroir de l'Histoire*, issue number 172 (April 1964)
39 See *Les Deux Jeanne d'Arc*, by Claude Pasteur
40 André Bourrier: *L'Idée Libre*, 1925, and *Bulletin Syndical des Instituteurs*, October 1924
41 Philippe Erlanger, *op. cit.*
42 Years 1438–39, Municipal Archives. Quoted by Jean Grimod, *op. cit.*
43 Author's archives, File No 12 892
44 *Trial of Rehabilitation*, *op. cit.*
45 In *A travers le Vieux Metz*
46 See the *Archives du Loiret*, *Registre de l'année 1440*, CC 655, folio 76

47 See *Le Dossier de Jehanne*, Maurice David-Darnac

48 See the Larousse Dictionary in two volumes, and *Le Camail ou le Porc-Espic* by H. de Brémond-d'Ars

49 Extract from the *Trésor du Domaine d'Orléans*. Deed executed in the Chamber of Accounts by Mâitre Robin Gaffard on 29th July 1443, quoted by Pasquier and Jean Grimod, *op. cit.*

50 D. Polluche, *Société Littéraire d'Orléans*, published by Vandebergue 1749

51 *Monastica Metensia*, E. de Bouteiller

52 *Chroniques de Metz de l'an 900 à 1552*, by Huguenin de Metz, published in 1838

53 *Histoire d'une famille de Lorraine*, by Comte G. de Failly

54 Various genealogies, including Dom Calmet, Chérin and personal archives

55 *Recherches sur la famille des Armoises de la branche d'Autrey*, by Léon Germain de Maidy: M.S.A.L., Volume LXV (1920–22)

56 *Ibid*

57 Archives du Loiret, Accounts of the Town of Orleans. Reg. CC 661, folio 19, verso

58 MSS Baverel Nos 111–112–117, in the library at Besançon. It should be noted that the ecclesiastical administrative division headed by the Archbishopric of Besançon comprised Saint-Dié, Nancy and Pulligny etc. This is why numerous documents from Lorraine are still to be found in this important archive centre

59 See *La Famille des Armoises* (*Branche de Neuville*) by M. Lemercier de Morière

V

THE MAKING OF A LEGEND

42

THE REHABILITATION

> Finally on Jean de Montigny's advice the promoters of the Rehabilitation persuaded the king of France to keep in the background . . . and let the d'Arc family speak . . .
>
> (*Comment Jeanne d'Arc est montée sur les autels*, Chanoine Chollet)[1]

The King's motives had to be exceptionally strong to make him adopt such a subtle course of action. In the event it proved to have been indispensable, for the Holy See's decision on a new case remained in abeyance from 1450 to 1455 because of the Turkish menace overshadowing Christendom. Although France remained 'the eldest daughter of the Church', Pope Nicholas V wanted to conciliate England, hoping for her support in the event of a new crusade.

For five years Rome therefore turned a deaf ear to France's demands for a revision of the Trial of Condemnation. This obliged Charles VII to 'transfer the cause from the political arena to the domain of private honour', concluded Chanoine Chollet, a professor of theology, at the beginning of this century.

Despite the transfer, the trial which opened to declare His Lordship Cauchon's conclusions invalid was again a political one. But it took the King's men six patient years to succeed in quashing the 1431 sentence. The security of the dynasty was thereafter assured, and the succession to the throne was conclusively restored *according to divine right*, for this was indeed the whole purpose of the operation.

A few months after the Maid's actual death, her brother Charles VII made a much remarked on entry into Rouen on 10th November 1449. Morbidly tormented by a 30-year-old fear, he lost no time after his arrival in giving strict instructions for the archives of the archbishopric to be searched.

A long time had passed since the coronation and the nickname of 'so-called dauphin' had been forgotten, but only through the agency of 'this creature in the form of a woman', subsequently condemned as a heretic, witch and relapse, by an important faction of the Church: the Rouen Tribunal, with the approval of the University.

And so every means had to be adopted to correct as soon as possible the disastrous psychology of the situation. Now that the turbulent Maid had finally left the scene, a judgment which would have the Pope's blessing could be envisaged. The enterprise, the profound political nature of which has never been sufficiently stressed, was facilitated by circumstances.

First of all, by the fact that England was undermined by internal strife. Despite important victories, John of Bedford had already encountered difficulties after the death of Henry V in 1422. Palace quarrels and divergent interests had set Gloucester, Warwick, etc. one against the other within the ruling family. The end product by 1450 was civil war, a prelude to the Wars of the Roses.

France had little to fear therefore from England at the time of the reconquest of Rouen. Furthermore, Burgundy had changed sides, and just as he had prudently absented himself from his cousin Charles' coronation at Rheims, so Philip the Good did not attend the coronation of Henry VI in Paris in December 1431.

Secondly, following the liberation of Paris, the University had changed allegiance, and the King had been wise enough to overlook the past.

On 15th February 1450 he wrote to the Rector, Guillaume Bouillé, a letter fraught with meaning and authority. Joan the Maid was designated thus, without any allusion to the d'Arc family, or to the name. The Rector and his subordinates were expressly enjoined

> to inform yourselves well and diligently on the said trial [of 1431] ... And ... all those whom you know to have any writings, trials or other things touching on the matter, constrain them by all due means and that you see to be necessary, to hand them over to you, so that they may be brought or sent to us ... (Oursel)

After this threatening letter, what men were chosen to help unravel the truth but seven turncoats from the Bishop of Beauvais who miraculously became the first witnesses in favour of the dynastic cause. After Manchon, the notary, had been examined on 8th March, the Brothers Toutmouillé, Isembard de la Pierre and Ladvenu, Massieu, and even Jean Beaupère were questioned.

For 'they had to know the truth of the trial,' writes Régine Pernoud. 'Until then, they knew nothing of it, except what their enemies had allowed to become known.'[2]

After the condemnation, the University itself had only been informed by two sources: the letter of Henry VI, inspired by Bedford who not being religious had full scope for falsifying the facts; and the woolly sermon bristling with contradictions preached by the Grand Inquisitor in Paris on 4th July 1431, in which he had supported the theory of the stake.[3] In the circumstances, it seems difficult to trust a man who refused to preside over the Rouen tribunal and was present at none of the sittings.

On the basis of all this, the learned theologians concluded that Joan *migravit a saeculo*. This is acceptable inasmuch as Latin dictionaries do not all agree on the normal meaning. A literal translation gives, in this order: Joan left the century, the profane world, worldly life, and, finally, the world.[4] Death was therefore not necessarily meant by this phrase, which was why it was used to notify the Pope. Latin offers the advantage of exceptional richness and variety of expression, with countless nuances. It enables one to cheat without lying and hide conveniently.

In fact, the Rouen archives revealed no more than the English and His Lordship Cauchon had decided to let be known. Having rigged a trial for political reasons, they would not have been imprudent enough to permit the existence of documents liable to cancel the results achieved. There only remained the voluminous account re-written over the course of five years under the direction of the Bishop who, it should be remembered, was chaplain-confessor to John of Bedford.

There is no doubt that these minutes, a product of Cauchon's Machiavellian genius, are authentic, at any rate in form. But it is unlikely that they are so in spirit. Our most eminent specialists, worried by this point, confirm that the notaries charged with drawing them up refused to sign the last pages of a copy in existence today.

It seems imprudent to assert there were no other pages. It is to be wondered what became of the original documents in the first place, such as the act of abjuration bearing Joan's signature, and the cross inscribed in 'a sort of circle'. None of them has ever seen the light of day, suggesting that they had only been rough drafts never to be revealed.

As the first trial served as a basis to the second, the validity of these two juridical edifices is therefore highly contestable, if not wholly suspect.

In 1452, the papal legate Guillaume d'Estouteville, was still pressing the reluctant Nicholas V in the King's name. D'Estouteville secured the co-operation of Jehan Bréhal, Inquisitor of France, and on 31st December, the latter sent a letter to a Dominican brother of the convent in Vienne, in which he did not hesitate to reveal very clearly the King's real motives.

> The honour of His Royal Majesty once suffered from his English enemies an enormous hurt, from the fact that after they had captured the simple and pure Maid who, by the grace of God—it is evidence itself—had fought for his cause, they drew up a trial in matter of faith, at the termination of which, to the censure of the King and the kingdom, they made her ignominiously die by fire . . . (Oursel)

The Inquisitor was not of course actually lying either. As he had not been present at the events of May 1431, he was merely reporting what he had been told. And, in any case, the attorney Prévosteau was to elevate dissimulation to the height of an institution.

One viewpoint on the subject had already been expressed by the Bishop of Verden, Dietrich von Nieheim, when he wrote in 1411: 'When her existence is threatened, the Church is relieved of the commandments of morality. Unity as a purpose sanctifies all means—craft, treachery, violence . . .'[5]

At the time of these first steps towards the Rehabilitation, the Roman Empire in the East was disintegrating, whilst the unity of faith was threatened by disturbing rifts appearing in both England and Germany. And so Bréhal seized the opportunity and did his utmost to convince the Pope to set a permanent seal on the union of Rome with her 'eldest daughter' France. Charles VII had sanded the floor for the Inquisitor's abandonment of his last scruples by making an advance payment on account of his expenses. In December 1452, the King had generously granted him 'the sum of 37 *livres*, ten *solz*, in *escuz* of gold, to him given to help him to live whilst busying himself with the examination of the trial of Jehanne the Maid . . .',[6] who was still not called d'Arc.

That Bréhal, who had never been one to retreat from the exigencies of the Church's temporal policy, was still troubled in his conscience is shown by the *Summarium* he wrote on the case. 'We are not to guess the secrets ignored by everybody, and which are known only by Jehanne and the King. It is not up to us to probe these mysteries too deeply.'

These texts make the reasons for the new proceedings stand out clearly. The first text in particular shows an instance of that potent psychological measure which has been used at various times throughout history, the transformation of national heroes into martyrs. Transcended into a Superior Being, the hero who by his sacrifice accomplished far more than most for the public weal, galvanizes citizens into obedience in defence of common interests.

Like a scapegoat, the hero-martyr furthermore absolves the nation from past sins, and his sacrifice attracts all extroverted sado-masochistic death impulses accumulated in the collective unconscious.

That is why, in the pattern of all religions, Charles VII (as, later, the Republic would do) immediately took upon his own account the theme of death at the stake in which symbols mingled: fire, the water of the Seine which engulfed the martyr's remains, the white dove—a Franciscan emblem—which 'escaped towards the country of France'. These symbols are so deeply rooted that they can only be explained by psychoanalysis.

In 1455, Alfonso Borgia succeeded Nicholas V, after years of waiting, and under the more discreet name of Calixtus III, immediately subscribed to France's wishes. He nominated several commissioners to conduct the inquiry, the best known of them being the Archbishop of Rheims, Juvénal des Ursins, who was Jehan d'Aulon's brother-in-law.

Meanwhile, the King was tending his reputation by maintaining or granting prebends and honours. The most surprising case was undoubtedly that of Thomas de Courcelles, the former Rouen judge who had declared himself in favour of Joan being tortured: he 'received thus the simple title of dean of the chapter of Notre Dame of Paris; and was honoured, not only by the favour but by the friendship of Charles VII whose funeral oration he had to pronounce'.[7]

These anomalies can be summarized by a sentence taken from an analysis of Rheims cathedral archives: 'The men of this period acted in concert, at Poitiers, Orleans, Rheims, Paris . . . but only showed up at the end of events.'[8]

In the light of this, it is hardly surprising that the Trial of Rehabilitation concluded that Pierre Cauchon 'was actuated by immoderate ardour'. And this was substantiated by the fact that despite the unspeakable liberties he had taken with procedure, the Bishop was never excommunicated by the Holy See.

Calixtus, a Borgia and a realist, did not allow the case to drag on, and two months after his accession, in June 1455, he sent off his pontifical rescript. In it, the Church adopted a standpoint by officially substituting the name Joan of Arc for Joan the Maid.

It was then that Prévosteau, the attorney, was able to speak in the name of her adoptive family. It was a piece of subtlety in that the d'Arcs, inasmuch as they were plaintiffs, would not have to testify under oath.

The rescript concluded quite simply that Joan 'having been condemned by an iniquitous sentence, at the end of an illegal trial, had been doomed to execution by the secular arm'. (Oursel)

This, as we know, is untrue. To be 'doomed to execution' has, in any case, never meant to die, and this ambiguous statement would make it possible to avoid questions on the consequences of this promise of death.

For five months from 12th December 1455, summonses, enquiries and ceremonies guaranteed to move the most hardened hearts, took place in the cathedrals of Paris and Rouen, in front of the lords of the kingdom. The Rouen judges were carefully and speedily questioned. An interrogatory was taken in Lorraine and it seems most surprising that Nicolas Louve was never consulted although he was very much alive in 1456. The town of Orleans answered with edifying generalities. After 112 witnesses had been heard, the Investigation which had been scamped in the King's interests, closed in Paris and Rouen.

The unanimous findings were that Joan was a good Catholic—therefore no heretic—and that her trial had been entirely rigged. 'It appears that the English proceeded more by hatred and by passion than by love of the truth. They sought to have her deemed a heretic and thereby to reach the King of France, our Lord . . .' Such were the words of Brother Pierre Miget, professor of theology, who had been questioned twice. (Oursel)

What official history fails to say is that there was at the time a sharp disagreement. Speaking for the convents of Preaching Friars of Beauvais and Evreux, who had nevertheless long since rallied to the King, Master Renaud Bredouille declared in substance that the 'twelve articles'* did not seem to him to conform to the truth; that things had not been processed by the Lord Bishop Pierre Cauchon in the way that was related; he added that it was his intention to appear no more at the trial, leaving it to the conscience of the witnesses . . . that their oath should in no case be affected by this decision! (Oursel)

It was obviously rather embarrassing. And the trial was concluded with the utmost speed and judged; and on 7th July 1456 Joan, rehabilitated, mounted the pedestal of eternal heroes.

* Author's note: See Part III, Chapter 6: 'Cauchon's Forgeries'.

43

CANONIZATION

Mgr Verde attacked the actual value of the Trials of Condemnation and Rehabilitation, stressed the contradiction of certain statements, and denied the supernatural side of the mission . . .

(Rome, solemn session, on 6th January 1904)[9]

The Vatican therefore still had reservations at the beginning of the century. 'Joan appeared in history more like a heroine than a saint; either because she was more worthy of admiration than imitation, or because there were no miracles . . .' Such were its conclusions reported by Chanoine Chollet.

The reasons for both trials have indeed been apparent to scholars ever since 1456. Thus, D. Polluche wrote in Orleans in 1749: 'If the commissioners delegated by Calixtus III did not divulge the happy outcome of 1431, it was because their purpose was not to show that Joan had escaped death at Rouen, but to examine whether there had been any grounds for condemning her to it . . .'

The Maid was forgotten. Then in 1803, Napoleon became her passionate admirer and wrote, 'The illustrious Joan of Arc has proved that there is no miracle that the French spirit cannot operate when national independence is in jeopardy.'[10]

Auguste Comte,* who hated the Emperor as well as the monarchy, retorted to this by appropriating the Maid of Orleans and making her into an idol of atheistic positivism. In a letter to John Stuart Mill which is a monument of fatuity, he wrote: 'I hope that a celebration in honour of Joan of Arc will soon compensate for the shameful apotheosis of Bonaparte . . . On the subject of the positivist's natural aptitude for systematizing all glories, I have been led to recommend to my audience the due glorification of our heroine Joan of Arc, whom theology has been unable to arrogate.'[11]

Insulted to the quick by this misappropriation, Mgr Dupanloup, Bishop of Orleans, was honour bound to take up the challenge, and Joan's cause was seized upon for the third time in history. The

* Translator's note: Auguste Comte (1798–1853), the mathematician and philosopher who founded positivism.

prelate's counter to atheism was that she could only have acted on God's orders.

It was a brilliant idea. In the face of the combined assaults of growing rationalism and free-thinking, the inspired virgin would act as a unique stimulant for the tottering faith of the times.

In 1870, the war against Germany ended in catastrophic defeat followed by the fall of the Second Empire. France had to pay a tribute of five thousand million *francs-or*, and worse still had to hand over two provinces to Germany. Wilhelm I, influenced by Bismarck, claimed that Alsace and Lorraine were German not only in heart but in reality. The reasons for the demand were in fact economic rather than territorial. Wilhelm had precise plans for the iron mines of Lorraine, which seemed indispensable to the expansion of German industry.

The issue was furthermore complicated by a psychological factor in that Lorraine had only been French for a hundred years, and, quite possibly, there was a residue of the autonomist feelings prevalent at the time of union with France. A report addressed to Cardinal Fleury in 1736 had revealed how precarious was the French position. 'When public opinion had been sounded to find out how many members of the Ancient Knighthood would react favourably to a possible reunion with France,' the findings were inconclusive.[12]

There was an urgent need then to make people forget that the Lorrainers had not been unanimous, and the leaders of the Third Republic considered no sacrifice too great. The hymns of praise sung by the Bishop of Orleans and the Church over the previous twenty years were now augmented by the chorus of the anticlerics; and Léon Gambetta,* momentarily overcome with religious feeling, peremptorily exclaimed: 'Joan of Arc must not be touched.' And with good cause: by the miracle of a spontaneous political transmutation, Joan, who had been brought up in Barrois, became 'the good Lorrainer'.

What could be a better answer to Bismarck's empty claims than this heroic virgin from Lorraine who four centuries previously had sprung to the defence of the King of France. The crudely idealized conception of Joan that Charles VII had invented was then developed to the full. With Quicherat's works used as a basis, the Maid was refashioned according to the historical exigencies of the century; and it was of course forbidden to disagree.

Led by the *Ligue des Patriotes*, all parties joined in singing the *Chants du soldat* in support of Paul Déroulède's spirit,† and to

* Translator's note: A poet and politician (1846–1914). He was President of the *Ligue des patriotes*, and was the author of the *Chants du soldat*—patriotic, high-flown poems.

† Translator's note: A politician whose inflamed patriotism and eloquence earned him a prominent place in the government of the Third Republic (1838–82).

exacerbate nationalist feelings. Under the pontificate of Leo XIII, in 1895, a 'call to the 800,000 tertiaries of St Francis of Assisi' was proclaimed at Saint-Dié. The 'Pope of the workers' propagated the typical symbol of proletarian heroism: Joan of Arc, a humble peasant-girl, and shepherdess to boot. The shepherd and his flock: such would be the archetype, the purveyor of miracles, dear to both temporal and religious powers.

Disputes were bound to arise in all this fervour. The question of the 'false maids' who imitated Joan is of no interest here. These two or three impostors whose real identity is not known can be eliminated instantly by a close look at the dates. There is no point of resemblance between their case and that of Joan du Lys the Maid of France.*

And revealing evidence was made to disappear. For example, a file concerning the marriage of Robert des Armoises in 1436 literally vanished from the archives of the castle of Nettancourt. On 23rd September 1889 the box which contained it and some other deeds was found to be half-empty.[13]

A few of my great-uncle's notes put me onto the track. Mgr Mathieu, who had written magnificent encomiums about Joan of Arc, and who was a friend of Leo XIII, did not hesitate however to express his doubts and his disappointment as a professor of history. 'What a sad thing it is, at my age, to see proved wrong all one has believed and to see crumbled a foundation which seemed so solid. One no longer knows what to think,' he confided to his biographer, Edmond Renard.

My uncle's agitation was confirmed by the newspaper *La Croix*† when it said that 'the cardinalcy allowed him full scope to search the Vatican archives . . .' A euphemism which speaks for itself.

Despite the evident advancement of Joan's 'modern cause', Rome took no action. Then, in 1905, there was a rupture between the Church and State. Illogically, this political hiatus was in fact to serve the Beatification far better than unity in the Catholic ranks, for an exchange of good services took place.

The heroine was beatified on 18th April 1909, despite the heated discussion which had preceded this action. All had not gone smoothly. In the words of Chanoine Chollet, speaking of the strong objections made on the occasion:

* Author's note: It has been advanced that the Lady of Armoises was the daughter of Jean d'Arc. As according to chronology Robert was already advanced in years in 1436, he would therefore have married a young child. This little girl could not possibly have displayed her horsemanship in front of Nicolas Louve and put on the armour given her by the Count of Virnebourg—unless she was even more precocious than the Maid!

† Translator's note: A daily Catholic paper founded in 1883. It is now an evening paper.

> Mgr Verde, the Devil's Advocate, attacked the authenticity of the trials [of Condemnation and Rehabilitation] which all [modern] witnesses quoted as evidence, and stressed the contradictions of certain statements [of the fifteenth century]. He denied the supernatural side of [Joan's] mission saying that there was more in her that was strange and morbid than supernatural. He claimed that she had not been heroic . . . but had on the contrary seriously failed by her attempt to escape, by her attitude towards the Church, and by her abjuration.

Mgr Verde finally added that there were no miracles.

And so some were found—vague healings of leg, chest and stomach ulcers, noted in convents. After special inquests in Orleans, Evreux and Arras, three out of five suggested miracles were accepted, although there were serious doubts about the genuineness of the instantaneous cure of an irremediable illness.

We will see why, and in particular by what *circumlocutione verborum* the difficulty was bypassed.

At the same time that anglophobia was dying out in France, thanks to Edward VII, to the Entente Cordiale and to the British rôle in the First World War, hatred of the Germans reached its peak.

Following Péguy's hymns to Joan, Léon Bloy's* *Jeanne et l'Allemagne* synthesized, in 1915, the state of mind conditioned towards revenge. 'The vilest nation in the world has dared lay hands on the very homeland of Joan of Arc, on Lorraine . . . Since 1870, the Lorraine of Joan of Arc'—which we know to be false as she only lived in the occupied part after her marriage—'has been trampled on by the brutes, a profanation which is intolerable to God and to man . . . Today would she hear voices to rid our godless Republic of the Germans?'

The war was won, and when the Armistice was signed on 11th November 1918, the crucial operation of canonization was already in hand. On the cessation of hostilities, discussion about three new miracles was immediately resumed. One of those retained is worthy of note—the others being exemplified by the case of Marie-Antoinette Mirandelle, who had suffered from a perforating ulcer of the foot. The case of Marie-Thérèse Belin, however, for whom doctors had given up hope, is incredibly ambiguous. Suffering from pulmonary tuberculosis and tuberculous peritonitis, she also had a diseased mitral valve.[14]

* Translator's note: Charles Péguy (1873–1914), a poet and prose writer who combined Christian mystical lyricism with militant nationalism and polemic socialism in his writings. Born in Orleans he was haunted by the idea of Joan the simple peasant-girl and in 1910 wrote *Le Mystère de la Charité de Jeanne d'Arc*. He was killed in the First World War.

Léon Bloy (1846–1917), another Catholic writer, author of the autobiographical novel *Le Désespéré* and of a long *Journal*, who was both a revolutionary and a prophet of apocalyptic doom.

If ever there was a specious case in the history of miracles, it was that of Thérèse Belin. It was found so 'embarrassing' by the Sacred College that Pope Benedict XV, his conscience committed, was forced to restate the question. And in an address on 6th April 1919, a year before the French saint was added to the list, he clarified how miracles by substitution of the intercessor worked.

> The memory of Mary must never be excluded, not even when a miracle seems to be attributable to the intercession or mediation of one of the Blessed or a saint. Such is the teaching that We believe should be drawn from the fact that Thérèse Belin obtained her instantaneous and complete cure at the sanctuary of Lourdes.

In these conditions, was it Joan or Mary? I shall leave the reader to decide.

While discussion was coming to an end in Rome, the radical-socialist party found itself in a minority in Paris. In order to satisfy the demands of both the new government and the French episcopate the 'Joan of Arc Pope'* pronounced the sentence, and Joan was canonized on 16th May 1920.

It was a total victory, on a number of counts. Externally, the 1918 victory was consecrated, and Lorraine irrevocably united with France by Joan's transcended figure.† Secondly, by virtue of the reciprocal services rendered, the Vatican was able to renew diplomatic relations with France, 'her eldest daughter'.

The internal results were no less advantageous. For the second time in history, Joan had brought about the unity of the country. Following the canonization now at one were: the right (the extremist party faithful to the fleurs-de-lis), the centre (an indeterminate mass, but favourable to order), finally, the left, reassured and taken with the symbol of a humble peasant-girl which could not fail to win the hearts of the people.

It was for all these reasons, for these borderline miracles, that the Maid of Orleans was canonized as a 'politicized' virgin, and not as a martyr.

* Author's note: Benedict XV was so described by a Cardinal wishing to express his overwhelming gratitude. Highly embarrassed from every point of view, and certainly shocked by this servile and inopportune demonstration, the Pope redressed matters in his speech of 6th April 1919.

† Translator's note: Lorraine had been returned to France by the Treaty of Versailles in June 1919.

44

CONCLUSION JOAN AND KNIGHTHOOD

> The sword has only been given you to defend the poor and the weak.
>
> (*St Bernard to Thibaud de Champagne*)[6]

By what device was the Maid of Orleans inscribed in the martyrology of Rome when she was not canonized as such?

The answer is to be found in the words of a well-known preacher whose euphemisms, inspired by Guillaume Prévosteau's technique, border on the sublime in this case. Just as in 1456 Brother Ladvenu had subscribed to Joan's death at the stake by laying responsibility for his statement on the executioner,* so the Reverend Father Kraemer takes refuge behind the authority of St Jerome.

> Joan's martyrdom [he writes] testified to her fidelity to her voices. It is a martyrdom by analogy. In one of his sermons, St Jerome declares of the Virgin Mary: 'I say without fear of being in error that the mother of God was both virgin and martyr, although she did not end her life by violent death.'[17]

Thus, copying Benedict XV with regard to Marie-Thérèse Belin, the Reverend Father shelters behind the Virgin by means of a substitution. This parallel drawn between Joan's martyrdom and that of the Virgin Mary who did not die a violent death is of obvious significance.

The case of Joan's virginity is no less remarkable. Texts authenticated by the signatures of three cardinals of the Holy Congregation of Rites in 1919 quote in italics, and without a break, the virgin 'very well known under the name of Maid of Orleans'.† Surprisingly it is the name Joanna de Arc which mainly figures in the titles and elsewhere, although in a distorted form. Joan was therefore canonized as

* Author's note: This Rouen executioner, Geoffroy Thérage, was a paradoxical man. His conscience was supposedly troubled by the execution of a witch who was an enemy of those who employed him, while a year later he beheaded, unmoved, 140 French prisoners in defiance of the laws of war.

† Author's note: *Aurelianensis Puellae pernotam nomine*. Cardinal di Belmonte, *op. cit.*

a virgin. In addition to the medical description of the time, which could be disputed, an example drawn from religious practice happily brings a categorical confirmation . . . by analogy.

Acting upon the advice of a Franciscan friar minor towards the end of the thirteenth century Elzear of Sabran had married, after his wife Delphine had made a vow in front of this friar, their mutual confessor, to preserve her virginity after the wedding. Both of them then entered the Third Order, and these 'Virgin-Spouses' remained so faithful to the vow that Elzear was canonized and Delphine beatified.[18]

In view of this it would be unjust and illogical to deny Joan the Maid the same recognition, all the more so in that Joan had promised to remain a virgin 'as long as it pleased God' and that, immediately after his wedding, Robert spent three years with the Celestines who demanded perpetual abstinence.

'Divine or human intervention—which, I would not like to say.' Such was, in his Memoirs, the judgment of Pius II, a former colleague of Thomas de Courcelles and of Jean Beaupère at the Council of Basle. At that time the Maid was fighting by the side of Sforza for the cause of Eugenius IV. It is clear that the incumbents of the Holy See were always well informed of the deeds of the heroine—not only Eugenius IV, but Martin V, Nicholas V (a friend of the Franciscans) and, more recently, Leo XIII between whom and the king of Italy the friars minor had brought about a rapprochement.

That is why any reservations were hidden by the use of ambiguous Latin expressions which would always make it possible to gloss adroitly over the business of the stake which does not diminish Joan's evident saintliness. For the Church is ever infallible in her domain. The Curia, which had long ago come into possession of the major part of the contemporary documents dealing with Joan would not have made a mistake in an affair which was no more advanced than the nationalistic policy of a Christian State. It was impossible for Rome to sanction unreservedly an operation which could one day be questioned at the whim of some government and make the Holy See lose face.

The question of money has also been brought up: indeed, France paid thirty million *francs-or* in 1920. The sum is justified by Father Roguet: 'Who need be scandalized? One must bear in mind the very heavy expenses of the trial and canonization ceremony of our national heroine.'[19]

I have no intention of participating in the periodical debates about the existence of the *Book of Poitiers* in the Vatican Archives. This work is only concerned with the psychological analysis of facts, events and behaviours. However, I have seen sufficient documents, evidence and information to be able to say that there are many other details on the Maid in Rome. Cardinal Mathieu's sad remark has been corroborated by a great Catholic writer. 'There, a few years ago, I had the unexpected luck to come across the document that you know, thanks to a very high personage who has since died. His successors have not been similarly disposed . . .'

This extract from a letter, of which I have a photo-copy, from Edouard Schneider to M. Gérard Pesme provides double proof of the existence of hidden documents. At the time when the author went through the file, and read, in particular, the report of the two monks delegated by the Poitiers commission, Pius XI was Pope. It is an accepted fact that he had pro-German sympathies, and so he could only look favourably upon the eventual divulgence of these documents supporting the German claims to Lorraine. Should it ever be revealed that Joan did not really come from this province but was in fact of French royal blood, all the resistance to Bismarck would have been in vain and the whole question would be raised again. The attitude of the next two Popes, Pius XII and John XXIII, was different and this verifies Edouard Schneider's words.

The universalist mission conceived in the fifteenth century has survived, in these conditions narrowly limited to French politics. The prisoner both of dynastic problems and of the financial interests of his entourage, Charles VII whom Joan and her friends had saved from ruin, soon deviated from the prescribed path and transformed an ideal that had been conceived for the whole Western world into nationalism. All was not lost however. The Benedictine R.F. Dom Gasquet emphasized the important rôle played by the Franciscans in the social revolution in Western Europe after the Black Death of 1348. He also stressed the hostility of the Lancastrians to the disciples of St Francis in general, and to the Observants in particular.[20]

France's resentment against England was fed by her burning nationalism. No occasion was and still is lost to throw the business of the stake in the face of the English, whose subconscious defence mechanism has made them sympathize with the heroine.

As for Germany, if the urgency of the situation in the nineteenth century understandably kindled the fire of patriotism, all these national reactions were superseded when it was a question of creating a United Europe.

Joan is an idol who was conceived chiefly to accomplish a programme of pacification in Europe. This was indeed the goal after the fourteenth century: a regeneration of the nations of the West under the banner of Jesus-Maria. 'To destroy the English is the least of the deeds reserved for the Maid. She has a loftier purpose: that faith should not perish,' wrote Christine de Pisan.*

* Translator's notes: A woman of letters and a prolific poet, born in 1363. She died between 1431 and 1440.

This Franciscan faith founded on social justice took its inspiration from the dogma of the Virgin Mother, the Immaculate Conception, which the Dominicans then opposed. Chartres, Puy-en-Velay, Notre-Dame de Bermont, Notre-Dame de Liesse were centres of a cult of the Black Virgin (Isis, Mother-goddess of humanity), which had astrological origins in times immemorial.

None of all this was fortuitous. In 1137, St Bernard had reinstated this cult as well as a particular veneration for John the Baptist. These beliefs emanated from the important and powerful alliegance of the presentiment of the Ancient Druids and of the feeling of Christian thinkers.'[21] Its originator is known to be St Colombanus.* This Irish saint was the monk of genius who brought about the harmonious synthesis of Druidic idealism and disciplined Christian thought, and who left his esoteric knowledge to the Benedictines. Colombanus set out from Ireland and founded a monastery at Luxeuil, near Lorraine. This explains the persistent Celtic manifestations in the region. These however unfortunately degenerated.

These Celts and Druids are excellently defined by Louis Charpentier: 'The Druids attached particular value to the profession of arms and are to be considered the creators of the Knighthood of Arms, such as the Red Branch Knights of Ulster . . . a knighthood of defenders and liberators.'[22]

The influence of Celtic groups was still considerable in the Middle Ages, and customs survive to this day. In Britanny, bards, druids and their followers—all Christians nevertheless—gather every year at ceremonies called *Gorzelts.*

As Sessevalle informs us that the Franciscans 'were equally the heirs of St Benedict',[23] it was easy for them, faced with the moral disintegration of Europe, to combine these elements in a common programme. The heritage of St Bernard adopted by the Knights of the Temple thus merged with the social and esoteric organization of the Celtic movement of the West. It was under the control of the Druids and the 'Ladies', and was refounded by the *Franciscan International.*

The fraternities of St Francis therefore took up the idea of a 'pact of Christian States with the Christ-regnant, a pact that the Church merely embraced through its sovereign sanction.'[24] The friars minor, from then on the monastic incarnation of the people, could, in an essentially social programme, work for peace and justice founded on Christly love and fight against privilege.

The five points of Joan the Maid's mission having been formulated accordingly, it was only necessary to turn to the sources and choose two prophets who would then be seen to prophesy the saga.

If one remembers that 'the coming of Christianity to the Celts is

* A contemporary of St Columba. He was the most influential of the Irish missionaries (543–615).

allegorically told in the legend of the Holy Grail,'[25] the Prophet Merlin then represents the whole tradition of Celtic knighthood. As for the Venerable Bede, he swept along all those Christians already instructed by the Benedictines.

For these reasons, Joan's spirit of knighthood transcends all the other religious orders to which some have mistakenly tried to affiliate her. Being a tertiary, all that counted for her was the realization of the ideal of the party of the poor and the weak: the defence of the people. As well as the participants—Ladies and knights—no means to success was neglected: psychological means, deeds said to be supernatural! Thus, shortly before leaving for Chinon, Joan is supposed to have had a revelation of the defeat of Rouvray on the day of the battle. But this overlooks the fact that all castles had dovecotes abundantly provided with carrier pigeons. The news could therefore have been transmitted in three hours.

A look at the ancient right which had preceded feudal practice, and at the pacts made under Clovis shows, finally, that Joan the Maid's real mission was to re-establish a regime of a truly democratic nature. The truth about her identity, her real feelings and her motives, can therefore today work towards the unification of Europe. I believe more in 'truth' than in the 'virtues' of dissimulation.

It is not enough to protect, hypocritically, those who are indifferent and devoid of an ideal; or else to limit the dangers of aggression to 'some neck of the woods'. The West will only achieve happiness by respecting others and their way of thinking.

Then, when hatred amongst nations has been abandoned, peace can be achieved by a way of life modelled on that of Joan the Maid of France who signed only with her Christian name, like kings.

Paris, December 1969

NOTES TO PART V

1 In his *Etude Générale sur les Procès de Béatification et de Canonisation de Jeanne d'Arc*
2 In *Jeanne d'Arc par elle-même et ses Témoins*, *op. cit.*
3 *Journal d'un Bourgeois de Paris*, *op. cit.* See also part III, §28
4 Quicherat, and Goelzer's Latin Dictionary
5 See *De schismate libri III.* Quoted by Arthur Koestler in *The Nought and the Infinite*
6 Quicherat, *op. cit.*
7 See *Mélanges et Notes sur les juges et assesseurs de Pierre Cauchon* by Charles de Beaurepaire
8 *Tableau du Chapitre de Reims* . . . by M. Jadart, *op. cit.*
9 Chanoine Chollet, *op. cit.*
10 Quoted in *Jeanne d'Arc* by Régine Pernoud
11 *Eglise et apostolat positiviste du Brésil* in the Bibliothèque Nationale, Paris
12 *Archives de famille et Histoire d'un Château de Lorraine*, by Baronne de la Chaise, Metz 1912
13 Archives of Bar-le-Duc, number 76.J.60
14 Cardinal Pignatelli di Belmonte, Rome 1919: *Documents sur la canonisation de Jeanne d'Arc*
15 *Actes de Benôit XV*, p.22 Ed. La Bonne Presse, Paris 1926
16 Quoted by Louis Charpentier in *Les Géants et le Mystère des origines*
17 Quoted by Claude Pasteur in *Les Deux Jeanne d'Arc*
18 *Vie des Saints*, Bibliothèque Nationale
19 *Message de Sainte Jeanne d'Arc*, Bulletin No. 74, Paris 1967
20 R. F. Dom Gasquet: *Henry VIII et les Monastères anglais*
21 Bessonet-Favre, *op. cit.*
22 Charpentier, *op. cit.*
23 In his book *Histoire Générale de l'Ordre de Saint-François*
24 Bessonet-Favre, *op. cit.*
25 *Etudes sur le Celtisme*, Patrice Genty

ADDENDUM

Discovery of important evidence in 1973

In the course of recent research on the period, I found three entries in the *Accounts of The Fortress of Orleans* which have hitherto been ignored. They concern the presence in Orleans of Regnault de Chartres, Chancellor of France, in 1439 when the Lady of Armoises was being fêted as Joan of Arc, thus corroborating the evidence put forward in § 38, and providing conclusive proof of her identity.

> To the said Jehan Luillier for the purchase of a luce and two jacks for presenting to the Lord Chancellor of France, the said day [26th May 1439], because he was once more bishop of this town, and was lodged in the outskirts because he had not yet made his entry . . . for this . . . 12 *sols parisis*. [folios 39 verso, 40 recto]
>
> To him for ten *pintes* and *choppines* of light wine and ten *pintes* of red wine presented at dinner and at supper to the said Lord Chancellor . . . for this . . . 24 *sols parisis*.
>
> To Jehan Baudoin for having been with Guiot Long to buy three barrels of wine to give (this 27th May 1439) to the said my lady Catherine [daughter of Charles VII] and to the Lord Chancellor . . . for this . . . 6 *sols parisis*. [folios 40 verso, 41 recto]

Regnault de Chartres had entered Orleans on 27th May 1439 in order to take up his duties as bishop of the diocese, after being archbishop of Rheims for over twenty years. He was therefore a member of the Orleans Town Council, and indeed would be until 1444. It must be remembered that Regnault de Chartres, one of the authors of the saga, had been one of the first to receive the Maid at Chinon, and had played an active part in the famous scene at which the 'crown brought by the angel' had been handed over to Charles VII (see above pages 126 and 129). He had then been in her entourage for about a year, so that no one could have known her better. His tolerance of the gift of 210 *livres parisis* made by the Orleans Council to the Lady of Armoises, and of the eight official receptions given in her honour, is inexplicable unless he knew her to be Joan of Arc; particularly as such receptions were ordinarily reserved for princes and princesses of the royal house, as is shown by other entries in the *Accounts*. The highest spiritual authority of the country would hardly associate himself with a gross deceit.

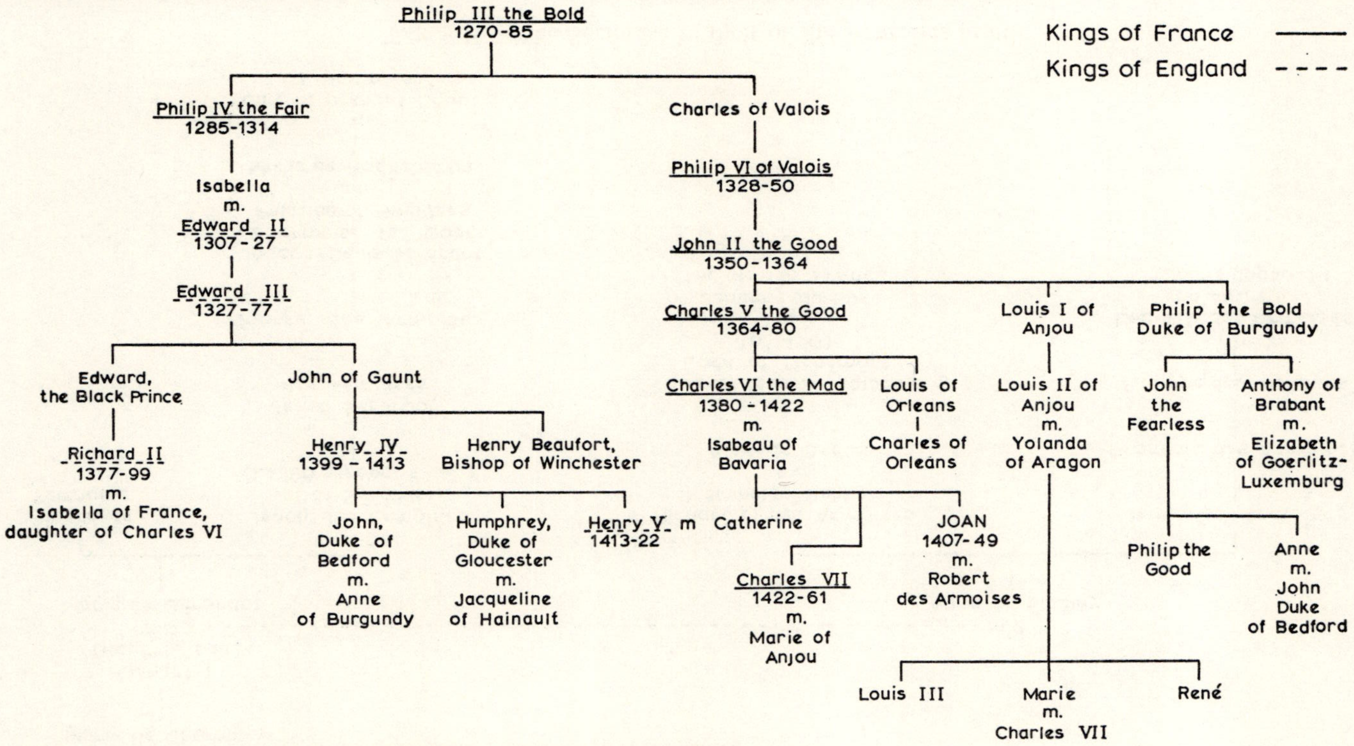

TABLE I. The relationship of the Plantagenet and the Valois lines.

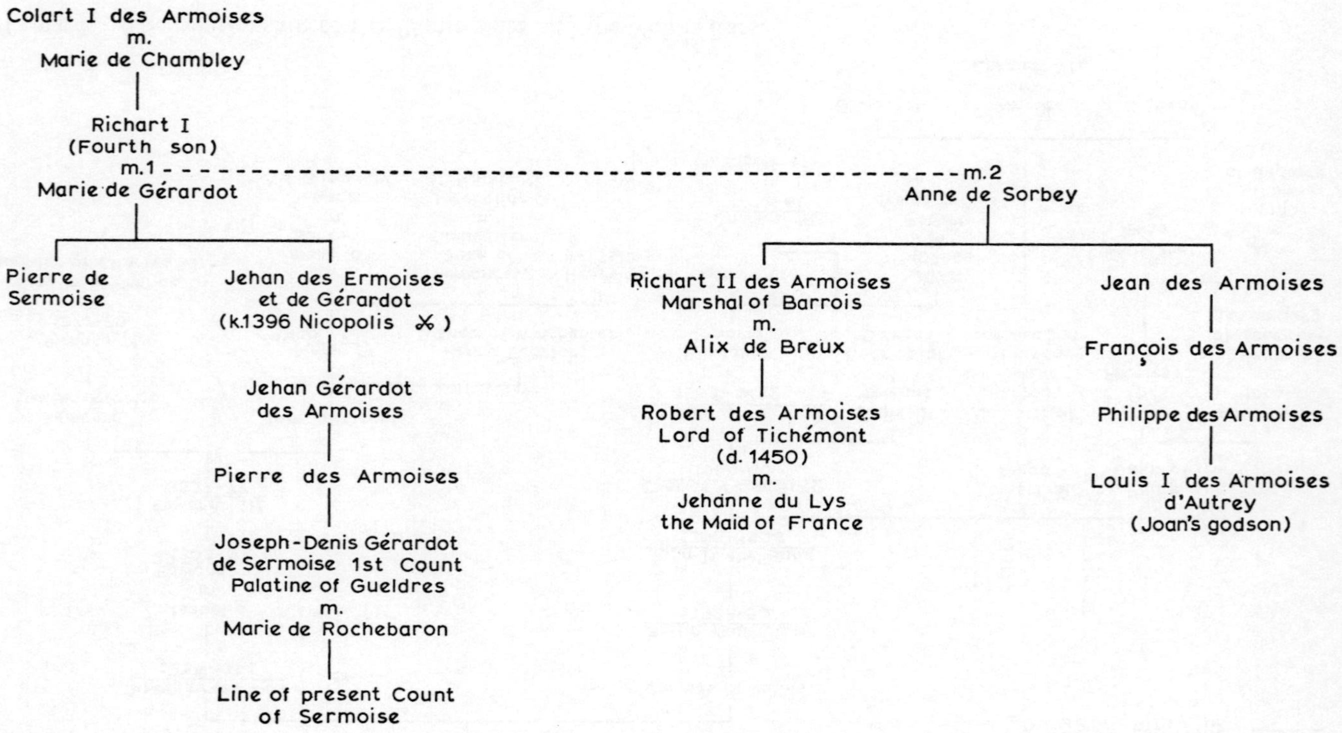

TABLE II. The Sermoise branch of the Armoises family.

BIBLIOGRAPHY

GENERAL

Abrégé Chronologique de l'Histoire de France. Prault, Paris, 1749.

Huguenin de Metz, *Chronique de Metz de l'an 900 a 1552.* Collection Du Puy, Metz, 1838.

Etat de la France, Vol. 1–4, 6. Wood & Palmer, London, 1752.

Auguste Bailly, *La Guerre de Cent Ans.* Arthème Fayard, Paris, 1941.

G. de Barante, *Histoire des Ducs de Bourgogne.* Paris.

Joseph Calmette, *Les Grands Ducs de Bourgogne.* Albin Michel, Paris, 1949.

Dom Calmet, *Histoire de Lorraine*, 7 vols. Nancy, 1745–57.

Dom Gasquet, *Henri VIII et les Monastères Anglais.* Librairie Lecoffre, Paris.

Gabriel Hanotaux, *Histoire de la Nation Française.* Paris.

Ernest Lavisse, *Histoire* (*XIVe et XVe siècles*). Hachette, Paris, 1902.

Ferdinand Lot, *La France, des origines à la fin de la Guerre de Cent Ans.* Gallimard, Paris, 1948.

Mac Farlane and Thompson, *The Comprehensive History of England.* London, 1861.

André Maurois, *Histoire d'Angleterre.* Arthème Fayard, Paris, 1937.

Halphen and Sagnac, *La Fin du Moyen Age.* Collection Peuples et Civilisations, Alcan, Paris, 1931.

Jules Michelet, *Histoire de Françe*, Paris.

Enguerrand, de Monstrelet, *Chroniques* (*XVe siècle*). Paris, 1854. Trans. as *Chronicles of Monstrelet*, by T. Johnes, London, 1840.

Louis Moreri, *Grand Dictionnaire Historique.* Paris, 1759.

Religieux de l'Abbaye de Saint-Bénigne de Dijon, *Histoire Générale et particulière de Bourgogne.* 1749.

Religieux de Saint-Denis, *Chroniques. Documents inédits sur l'Histoire de France*, Paris, 1839.

Vallet de Viriville, *Histoire de Charles VII.* Paris, 1858.

Velly, Villaret and Garnier, *Histoire de France en 30 vols.* Paris, 1765–86.

DISSIDENT BOOKS (in order of publication)

1667—Heine and Bignon, *Problème Historique sur la Pucelle d'Orléans, et Notes curieuses.*

1749—D. Polluche, *Problème Historique sur la Pucelle d'Orléans.* Vaudebergue, Orleans.

1819—Pierre Caze, *La vérité sur Jeanne d'Arc ou Eclaircissements sur son Origine.*

1889—Ernest Lesigne, *La Fin d'une Légende, Vie de Jeanne d'Arc.* Bayel, Paris.

1893—Gaston Save, *Jeanne des Armoises, Pucelle d'Orléans.* Nancy.

1898—Francis Andrée, *La Vérité sur Jeanne d'Arc.* Paris.

1914—Grillot de Givry, *La Survivance et le Mariage de Jeanne d'Arc.* Albin Michel, Paris.

1930–31—Abbé Ambroise Ledru, *Quelques erreurs des historiens de Jeanne d'Arc.* Revue des Provinces du Maine.

1931—Jean Jacoby, *Le Secret de Jeanne d'Arc.* Mercure de France, Paris.

1952—Jean Grimod, *Jeanne d'Arc a-t-elle été brûlée?* Amiot-Dumont, Paris.

1952—Edouard Schneider, *Jeanne d'Arc et ses Lys.* Grasset, Paris.

1957—Jean de Saint-Jean, *Jehanne.* Privately printed, La Baule-les-Pins (Loire-Atlantique).

1960—Gérard Pesme, *Jehanne d'Arc n'a pas été brûlée.* Ed. Balzac et La Ruche Ouvrière, Paris.

1961—André Guérin and Jack Palmer White, *Operation Shepherdess.* Heinemann.

1962—Prof. Jean Bosler, *Jeanne d'Arc était-elle la soeur de Charles VII?* Ed. Scorpion, Paris.

1962—Claude Pasteur, *Les Deux Jeanne d'Arc.* La Palatine, Paris.

1965—Maurice David-Darnac, *Histoire Véridique et Merveilleuse de la Pucelle d'Orléans.* Editions de la Table Ronde.
Translated as *The True Story of the Maid of Orleans*, by Peter de Polnay. W. H. Allen, 1969.

1968—Maurice David-Darnac, *Le Dossier de Jehanne.* J. J. Pauvert.

TRANSLATIONS AND COMMENTARIES OF THE TWO TRIAL PROCEEDINGS

In French

Colonel A. Billard, *Jeanne d'Arc et ses Juges.* Picard, Paris, 1933.

Pierre Champion, *Procès de Condamnation* (Latin text and translation), 2 vols. Paris, 1920–1.

Raymond Oursel, *Les Procès de Condemnation et de Réhabilitation de Jeanne d'Arc.* Editions Denoel, Paris, 1959.

Jules Quicherat, *Procès de Condamnation et de réhabilitation de Jeanne d'Arc, dite la Pucelle*, 5 vols. Société d'Histoire de France, Paris, 1841–9.

Régine Pernoud, *Jeanne d'Arc, par elle-même et ses Témoins.* Editions du Seuil, Paris, 1962.

In English

A translation of this last work is available, by Edward Hyams, published by Macdonald & Co., 1964, and Pelican Books, 1969.

W. P. Barrett, *The Trial of Jeanne d'Arc*, a complete translation of the Trial of Condemnation proceedings. George Routledge & Sons Ltd, 1931.

W. S. Scott, *The Trial of Joan of Arc*, a translation of the Orleans Manuscript (the original French minutes). Folio Society, 1956.

Régine Pernoud, *The Retrial of Joan of Arc—The Evidence at The Trial for her Rehabilitation 1450–56*. Translated by J. M. Cohen, Methuen, 1955, from the French *Vie et Mort de Jeanne d'Arc—témoignages du Procès de Réhabilitation*, published by Hachette, 1952.

ADDITIONAL BIBLIOGRAPHY

Le Mystère du Siège d'Orléans. Bibliothèque Nationale, Paris.

Jeanne d'Arc a-t-elle existé? a-t-elle été brûlée a Rouen? E.G.F., Orleans, 1866.

Jeanne n'a pas été brûlée a Rouen. Trois Ecrits, 1872.

Mgr Charles Aimond, *Histoire de Marville*. Presybtère de Marville, 1958.

G. Ambroise, *Les Moines du Moyen Age*. Picard, Paris, 1946.

Jeanne Ancelet-Hustache, *Les Clarisses*. Grasset, Paris, 1928.

Margaret Aston, *Panorama du XVe Siècle*. Flammarion, Paris, 1969.

Rev. F. P. Ayroles, *L'Université de Paris au temps de Jeanne et la cause de sa haine contre la libératrice*. Editors Rondelet, Paris, 1902. With an introduction by Pope Leo XIII.

Jean-Julien Barbé, *A travers le Vieux Metz*, Metz, 1913.

Charles de Beaurepaire, *Mélanges et Notes sur les Juges et Assesseurs de Procès de Condamnation*. Rouen, 1890.

E. Begin, *Guide de l'Etranger* (*de Metz*). Paris and Metz, 1834.

Pope Benedict XV, *Actes*. La Bonne Presse, Paris, 1926.

Bessonet-Favre, *Jeanne d'Arc Tertiaire de Saint-Francois*. Bloud & Barral, Paris, 1896.

Abbé Bizouard, *Histoire de sainte Colette et des Clarisses*. Besançon, 1888.

Léon Bloy, *Jeanne d'Arc et l'Allemagne*. Mercure de France, Paris, 1915.

Abbé Eugène Bossard, *Gilles de Rais*. H. Champion, Paris, 1886.

J. A. Bost, *Pèlerinage à Notre-Dame de Liesse*. Genève, 1890.

Boucher de Molandon, *Pierre du Lis, troisième frère de la Pucelle*. Paris, 1890.

Paul Bourrieu, *Au Pays des Sept Vallées*. Marrimpouey-Jeune, Pau, 1969.

E. de Bouteiller, *Monastica Metensia, Les Récollets de Metz.* Rousseau-Pallez, Metz, 1869. In the municipal archives of the town.

C. Buet, *Les Ducs de Savoie au XVe et au XVIe siècle.* Tours, 1878.

Caron, *Jeanne d'Arc au Crotoy.* Amiens.

Yves Cazaux, *Marie de Bourgogne.* Albin Michel, Paris, 1967.

Louis Charpentier, *La Cathédrale de Chartres.* Robert Laffont, Paris, 1966.

Louis Charpentier, *Les Mystères Templiers.* Robert Laffont, Paris, 1967.

Robert Charroux, *Histoire Inconnue des Hommes depuis Cent Mille Ans.* Robert Laffont, Paris, 1963.

Jacques Choffel, *Le Duc Charles d'Orléans.* New edition, Bresse, 1968.

Chanoine Chollet, *Etude Générale sur les Procès de Béatification et de Canonisation de Jeanne d'Arc.* Lille, 1910.

Auguste Comte, *Apostolat du Brésil. Jeanne d'Arc—Lettres à la Comtesse de la Vaux et à Stuart Mill.* Rio, 1910.

Jacques Cordier, *Jeanne d'Arc, sa personnalité, son rôle.* Table Ronde, Paris, 1948.

Guillaume Cousinot, *Chronique Normande et Chronique de la Pucelle.* Paris, 1859.

Bernard-Jean Daulon, *Jehan d'Aulon, écuyer de Jeanne d'Arc.* Privat, 1958.

Dr Deguerre, *Notice sur l'Abbaye d'Autrey.* Epinal, 1884.

Abbé Gorges Dottin, *La Religion des Celtes.* 1904.

Philippe Erlanger, *Charles VII et son Mystère.* Gallimard, Paris, 1945.

Comte G. de. Failly, *Histoire d'une Famille de Lorraine.* Virton, Belgium, 1967.

Philippe de Forceville, *Sainte Colette de Corbie.* Picard, 1958.

Léon Germain de Maidy, *La Famille des Armoises de la Branche d'Autrey.* Humblot, Nancy and MSAL, 1922.

Léon Germain de Maidy, *Epitaphe de Mahaut des Armoises, abbesse des Clarisses de Neufchâteau.* Nancy, 1925.

Abbé Grancher, *Ceffonds, lieu d'origine de Jacques d'Arc.* Saint-Dizier, 1895.

R. F. Henri de Grèzes, *Jeanne d'Arc franciscaine.* Pousielgue, 1895.

Baron Gérard d'Hannoncelles, *Metz Ancien.* Rousseau, Metz, 1856.

Adrian Harmand, *Jeanne d'Arc, ses costumes, son armure.* Editions Ernest Leroux, Paris, 1929.

Raban de Helmstadt, *Jacques von Sierck, hérétique.* Trier.

Richard Hennig, *Les Grandes Enigmes de l'Univers.* Robert Laffont, Paris, 1966.

Jean Jacoby, *Scènes de la Vie de Jeanne d'Arc.* Mercure de France, 1942.

Labourasse, *Vouthon et ses Seigneurs*. Bar-le-Duc, 1890.

Lefèvre-Pontalis, *La Fausse Jeanne d'Arc*. Paris, Orleans, 1895.

Lemercier de Morière, *La Famille des Armoises* (Neuville Branch). Crépin-Leblond, Nancy, 1881.

C. A. Ley, *Histoire ecclésiastique de Cologne*. Köln, 1883.

Jean Linel, *Pèlerinage de N.-D. de Liesse au Diocèse D'Annecy*. Revue des Alpes, Grenoble, 1939.

Kurt Löhnert, *Dates sur la vie et les fonctions des Archevêques de Trèves du Xe au XVe siècle*. Trier, 1908.

Chanoine de Longueville, *La Famille de Jeanne d'Arc était-elle originaire d'Arc-en-Barrois?* 1958.

Siméon Luce, *Jeanne d'Arc à Domrémy*. Paris, 1887.

J. Macquart, *Histoire de N.-D. de Liesse*. Abbeville, 1904.

Marianne Mahn-Lot, *Christophe Colomb*. Let Temps qui court, Editions du Seuil, Paris, 1960.

Jean Markale, *Les Celtes et la Civilisation Celtique*. Payot, 1969.

Abbé Eugène Martin, *Pulligny*. Nancy, 1893.

Cardinal F. D. Mathieu, *Les derniers jours de Léon XIII et le Conclave*. Paris, 1904.

A. Morosini, *Chroniques*. Fifteenth century.

Vicomte du Motey, *Jeanne d'Arc à Chinon*. H. Champion, 1927.

Vicomte du Motey, *Jeanne d'Arc à Vaucouleurs*. Alençon, 1929.

Jeanne d'Orliac, *Yolande d'Anjou, reine des Quatre Royaumes*. Plon, Paris, 1933.

Régine Pernoud, *Jeanne d'Arc*. Le temps qui court, Editions du Seuil, Paris, 1959.
Translated as *Joan of Arc*, by Jeanne Unger Duell. Evergreen Books, 1961.

Régine Pernoud, *Les Gaulois*. Le Temps qui court, Editions du Seuil, Paris, 1965.

A. Perrin, *Histoire de Savoie*. Chambéry, 1900.

Pius X, *Actes*. Bibliothèque Nationale.

Cardinal Pignatelli de Belmonte, *Documents sur la Canonisation de sainte Jeanne d'Arc*. Rome, 1919.

Marcle Poete, *La Confrérie de N.-D. de Liesse*. Nogent-le-Rotrou.

Edmond Renard, *Le Cardinal Mathieu*. Editions de Gigord, Paris, 1925.

L. de Richemond, *La Rochelle au temps de Charles VII*. 1878.

Raymond de Rigné, *La Vraye Histoire de Jehanne-la-Pucelle*, 2 vols. Privately printed, 1929.

F. de Saucy, *Les Templiers de Metz*. In the Bibliothèque Nationale, no publication date.

Joseph Sérand, *Le Château de Montrottier*. Gardet & Garin, Annecy, 1942.

F. de Sessevalle, *Histoire Générale de l'Ordre de Saint-François*. 1935.

Andrew Tomas, *Les Secrets de l'Atlantide.* Robert Laffont, 1969. A translation of *Atlantis—from Legend to Discovery.* Robert Hale, 1972.

Roland Villeneuve, *Gilles de Rais.* Denoël, Paris, 1955.

Henri Vincent, *La Maison des Armoises*, Henri Menu, Paris, 1877.

Henri Wallon, *Jeanne d'Arc.* Firmin-Didot, Paris, 1876.

Colette Yver, *Sainte Colette de Corbie.* Editions Franciscaines, 1945.

ARTICLES ETC.

Pour une Politique de Jeanne d'Arc. La Nouvelle voix de l'Alsace-Lorraine, Strasbourg, 1945.

Aux Tertiaires de St Francois d'Assise. Diocèse de St-Dié, 1895.

Jeanne d'Arc à Nancy. 1894. Bibliothèque Nationale.

Pierre Cauchon, Son origine, ses armoiries. Paris, 1890.

Pierre Cauchon de Sommièvre, Origine, armoiries, mort, sépulcre. Reims, 1898.

André Bourrier, *L'Idée Libre.* Paris, 1925, Bibliothèque Nationale.

Bourdeault, 'Chantocé et Gilles de Rais', *Mémoires de la Société d'Archéologie de Bretagne*, 1924.

Dr A. Cerné, *L'Enceinte et les tours du vieux château de Rouen.* Bulletin de la Société des Amis des Monuments Rouennais, 1928–31.

Abbé Jacques Choux, *Robert des Armoises, sire de Tichémont.* Annales de l'Est, No. 2, Nancy, 1963.

Marcellin Desfourneaux, 'Jeanne d'Arc en Espagne', *Revista Espanola de Historia.* Madrid, 1943.

Siméon Luce, 'Jeanne d'Arc et les Ordres Mendiants', *Revue des Deux Mondes.* 1881.

Jean-Marcel Paul, *Conférence sur Gilles de Rais. Annales de la Société Littéraire de Cannes* (A.M.) tome XIV.

Régine Pernoud, 'Jeanne d'Arc prisonnière', *La Revue de Paris*, No. 6, 1960.

M. Jadart, 'Tableau du chapitre de Reims et présence de Mgr Pierre Cauchon', *Bulletin du Comité de Travaux historiques*, 1892. Archives of the cathedral of Rheims, in the Bibliothèque Nationale, 8.LC18.347A.

GENEALOGIES AND ARMORIALS

Original documents, from the archives of the Sermoise family and in the author's personal collection.

Archives of the King-of-Arms of His Most Catholic Majesty, Madrid (Don Luis Rubio y Ganga y Brù).

Archives and documents consulted in libraries and archive centres of towns mentioned in this bibliography.

Armorials and genealogical documents: Father Anselme, Chérin, d'Hozier, Jean Cayon, Pelletier, Husson l'Ecossais, Dom Calmet, La Tour Varan, etc.

Pierre Palliot, *La Vraye et Parfaicte Science des Armoiries*. 1660.

Manuscripts, *Collections Baverel*, *Chifflet*, *Dunod de Charnage*, at Besançon, and other collections at Metz, Nancy, Bar-le-Duc, etc.

Modern works on heraldry etc.

SYMBOLISM AND MISCELLANEOUS

H. de Brémond d'Ars-Migré, *Les Chevaliers du Camail ou Porc-Epic*. Macon, 1938.

Jules Boucher, *La Symbolique Maçonnique*. Dervy, Paris, 1948.

Louis Charpentier, *Les Géants et le Mystère des Origines*. Robert Laffont, 1969.

Abbé Bertrand, *Etude de Symbolisme dans le Culte de la Vierge*. Limoges, 1947.

Eugène Droulers, *Dictionnaire de Allégories*. Turhout, no publication date.

Abbé J. Corblet, *Vocabulaire des Symboles et attributs*. Paris, 1877.

Jacques Duchaussoy, *Le Bestiaire du Divin*. La Colombe, 1958.

Histoire Secrète des Templiers ou Chevaliers de Malthe. Amsterdam, 1730.

Fulcanelli, *Le Mystère des Cathédrales*. Paris, 1957.

G. Gautier-Walter, *La Chevalerie et les Aspects de l'Histoire*. Editions de la Table Ronde, 1967.

Patrice Genty, *Etudes sur le Celtisme*. Editions Traditionnelles Villain & Belhomme, 1967.

Paul Naudon, *Rabelais Franc-Maçon*. La Balance, Paris, 1954.

Jean Palou, *La Franc-Maçonnerie*. Petite Bibliothèque Payot, 1964.

Oswald Wirth, *Le Tarot des Imagiers du Moyen Age*, Paris, 1927.

R. F. Baudot and R. F. Chaussin, *Vie des Saints*, 13 vols. Letouzey, 1935.

Dr Ernest Dichter, *La Stratégie du Désir*. Arthème Fayard, 1961.

Vance Packard, *The Hidden Persuaders*.

Henri Poincaré, *La Science et l'Hypothèse*. Flammarion, 1906.

Paul Ricoeur, *Histoire et Vérité*. Editions du Seuil, 1955.

Dictionnaire des Symboles. Robert Laffont, 1969.

Dictionaries and various works on psycho-analysis: Freud, Jung, Mullahy, etc.

Dictionnaire de l'Ancienne Langue Française, by La Curne de Sainte-Palaye.

Dictionnaire de l'Ancienne Langue Française et de Tous les Dialectes du IXe au XVe Siècle, by F. Godefroy, Paris, 1884.

INDEX

Agincourt, battle of, 40, 73
Albret, lord of, Count of Dreux, 91, 96
Alençon, Jean, Duke of, 59–61, 62, 63, 83, 89, 90, 91, 95, 98, 118, 126, 140
Alice-la-Rousse, 144
America, 156; discovery of, 184–185, 188
Anjou, Louis II, Duke of, 21n.
——, Louis III, Duke of, 43
——, Margaret of, 203
——, Marie of, 21n., 55, 96, 195, 203
——, René of, 48n., 176, 179, 203
——, Yolanda of, 21, 28, 32, 34, 35, 38, 42, 43, 47, 48, 54–5, 62, 65, 66, 67, 70 72, 97, 98, 115, 118, 156, 158, 183, 195, 202
Arlon, 82, 165, 166, 167, 168, 177, 178, 179
Armagnac party, 40, 42, 43, 104, 108, 109
Armoises, Robert des, 15, 54, 92, 160, 168, 169, 172, 174, 176, 178–9, 197, 201, 202, 204, 206, 207, 223, 227
Armoises family, genealogy of, 33, 160–1, 170–6, 177, 180, 186, 201, 204, 205, 206, 208, 209
Arras, 110, 111, 224
——, Treaty of, 157, 160, 168
Artemisia, symbolism of, 186, 208
Autrey, branch of: *see* Armoises family

Bacquillon, 163, 176
Bal des Ardents, 20
Baratin, Pierre, 166
Barbette, Hôtel, 23, 24–5, 27, 28, 37
Barrois, 13, 22, 32, 35, 38, 47, 48, 94, 170, 176, 222
Basle, Council of, 54, 64, 137, 158, 159, 227
Baudricourt, Robert de, 34, 48, 54, 58, 71, 76, 163, 172, 202
Bavaria, Jacqueline of, Countess of Hainaut, 117
——, John of, 165, 168
——, Louis the Bearded, Duke of, 27, 28
Beaufort, Henry, Cardinal of Winchester, 108, 132, 135, 136, 197
Beaugency, French victory at, 73, 89
Beaulieu-en-Vermandois, fortress of, Joan imprisoned at, 110
Beaupère, Jean, assessor at Trial, 136, 137, 138, 164, 216, 227
Beaurevoir, castle of, Joan imprisoned in, 104, 110, 111, 158, 159

Beauvais, Bishop of: *see* Cauchon, Pierre
Bede, the Venerable, 39, 230
Bedford, Anne of, 43, 80, 104, 109, 114, 115, 155, 160, 165
——, John, Duke of, 42, 47, 48, 71, 80, 89, 97, 104, 109, 112, 114, 115, 117, 118, 135, 136, 143, 157, 160, 165, 179, 216, 217
Belin, Marie-Thérèse, miracle of, 224–5, 226
Bellier, Anne de, 59, 167
——, Guillaume de, 59, 167
Benedict, Saint, 229
Benedict XV, Pope, 225, 226
Benedictines, 229, 230
Bermont, Notre-Dame de, 13, 108, 229
Bernard of Clairvaux, Saint, 16, 30, 109, 171, 226, 229
Besançon, 47, 156, 160, 161, 162, 166
Bismarck, 222, 228
Bizet, Jean, 33
Black Death, 18, 228
Black Virgin, The, 16, 94, 108, 159, 165, 229
Blois, 67, 69, 70, 74, 75, 76, 87, 97, 167
Bloy, Léon, 224
Boisguillaume, clerk at Trial, 139
Boissy, Guillaume de, 195
Bombachelier, Jean, 166
Boucher, Charlotte, 77
——, Jacques, 36, 76, 77, 78, 88, 89, 97, 166, 193, 194
Bouhier, Pierre, 135
Bouillé, Guillaume, Rector of University of Paris, 216
Boulainvillers, Perceval of, 29, 30, 37, 44
Boulay, Aubert, 163
Bouligny, Régnier of, 96
Bourges, Thévenon de, 77, 78, 191, 193
Bourges, 42, 96
Bournel, Guiscard de, 98
Boussac, Marshal, 70, 91
Bouvreuil, castle of, Joan imprisoned in, 14, 111, 112, 113, 114–15, 135, 136, 138, 141, 147, 157, 197
Bréban, Clignet de, 69
Bredouille, Renaud, 220
Bréhal, Jean, inquisitor of France, 16, 22, 53, 208, 217, 218
Brimeu, David de, 93
Brunne, Regnault, 167
Burgundy, Anthony of, 165, 171
——, Charles the Bold, Duke of, 19, 149, 170, 175
——, House of, and Burgundians, 19, 20, 23, 33, 40, 41, 42, 61, 70, 95, 97, 98, 99, 103, 104, 105, 107, 110, 149, 173, 174, 175
——, John the Fearless, Duke of, 19, 27, 28, 41, 42, 104, 165, 171, 175
——, Philip the Bold, Duke of, 19, 20
——, Philip the Good, Duke of, 19, 24n., 42, 43, 48, 62, 71, 72, 76, 83, 89, 92, 93, 97, 99, 109, 112, 117, 118, 144, 149, 157, 158, 159, 160, 163, 165, 166, 168, 199, 202, 216

Caboche, Jacques, 41, 103
Cagny, Perceval de, 140
Calatrava, Order of, 17
Calixtus III, Pope, 14, 120, 124, 168, 219, 221
Calot, Laurent, 134
Capet, Hugh, 19n.
Capetian dynasty, 17, 18
Caroline-la-Ferté, 144
Castile, 182, 183, 186, 190
Cauchon, Pierre, Bishop of

Beauvais, 14 37, 42, 90–1, 103–6, 108, 109, 112, 113, 116, 117, 118, 119–20, 121, 122, 123, 128, 129, 130, 131, 132, 133, 134, 135, 136, 137, 138, 141, 142, 143, 144, 145, 146, 147, 148, 149, 157, 165, 215, 216, 217, 219, 220
Caxton, 145n.
Celestines, 198, 201, 202, 227
Celtic cross, 117, 134, 208
Celtic movement, 16, 45, 46, 69, 79, 109, 186, 229, 230
Châlons, 90
Champagne, Harduin de, 195
——, Thibaud de, 226
Charlemagne, 73, 105
Charles the Bold, King of France, 170
Charles V, King of France, 18, 20, 30, 174, 203
Charles VI, King of France, 19–21, 23, 24, 26, 34, 40, 41, 42, 58, 66, 85, 94, 103, 165
Charles VII, King of France: his illegitimacy, 16, 21, 31, 42, 43, 106, 137, 160; 14, 23, 28, 37, 39, 41, 53, 54–8, 59, 60, 61, 62, 65, 66, 67, 70, 74, 83, 84, 85, 87, 88, 89; coronation, 90–2; 93, 94, 95, 96, 97, 98, 111, 112, 117, 118, 120, 122 124, 125, 126, 127, 132, 139, 145, 147, 155, 158, 159, 162, 163, 164, 166, 167, 168, 176, 177, 183, 184, 186, 187, 188, 190, 194, 195, 198, 199, 202, 203; entry into Rouen, 215–16, 217, 218, 219, 222, 228
Charles V, Holy Roman Emperor, 19, 175, 183n., 189
Charles, Simon, 55
Chartier, Alain, 36, 78
——, Jehan, 37
Chartres, Regnault de, Archbishop of Rheims, 63, 90, 92, 98, 103n., 104, 126, 129, 232
Chartres, 108, 229
Chastelain, Georges, 149
Châteauneuf-sur-Loire, 89
Château-Thierry, 94
Chinon, 14, 35, 37, 40, 48, 54–8, 60, 82, 83, 84, 85, 155, 160, 186, 187, 194, 230
Christ, Order of, 17, 184
Claude, Saint, 156
Clement V, Pope, 16
Clement VII, Pope, 94
Clermont, Count of, 56, 57, 71, 90
Cleves, Mary of, 199
Clovis, King of the Franks, 17, 53, 230
Cochon, Abbé, 146
Coeur de Lys, herald, 167, 168, 179, 187
Colette of Corbie, Saint, 28, 33, 35, 38, 39, 43, 46, 47, 58, 80, 94, 96, 97, 109, 118, 156, 158, 159, 160, 202
Cologne, 165n., 177
Columba, Saint, 229n.
Columbanus, Saint, 229
Columbus, Christopher, 184, 185, 186, 189, 208
Compiègne, 14, 93, 94, 95, 97, 98–9, 132, 144
Comte, Auguste, 221
Constance, Council of, 104
Corbény, 94
Courcelles, Thomas de, assessor at Trial, 138, 141, 219, 227
Courteheuse, Thomas de, 27
Coutes, Louis de, Joan's page, 59, 71, 76, 77, 93
Crecy, battle of, 19
Crépy-en-Valois, 98
Crotoy, fortress of, 110, 111, 155
Culant, Admiral of, 70, 71, 91

Cusquel, Pierre, 115, 145

Dagobert, King of the Franks, 170
d'Ancelrue, Poinsette, 179, 203
d'Arc, the family, 13, 26, 31, 32–5, 37, 41, 163, 199, 215, 216, 219
——, Isabelle, 28, 29, 30, 33–4, 37, 38, 39, 44, 93, 120, 198, 202, 206
——, Jacques, 24, 30, 33–4, 36, 39, 93, 124
——, Jean, 32, 76, 93, 120, 161, 162, 163, 164, 166, 167, 168, 187, 223
Darc, Jeanne, Joan's godmother, 24, 26, 27, 28–9, 34, 36
d'Arc, Pierre, 68, 76, 77, 93, 98, 110, 120, 161, 162, 164, 198, 199, 200, 206
d'Aulon, Jean, Joan's equerry, 25n., 65, 67, 74, 77, 89, 93, 98, 110, 182, 183, 203, 219
Delachambre, Doctor Guillaume, 65, 133, 197
de Luna, Don Alvaro, Constable of Castile, 182, 183, 188
d'Epinal, Isabelle Gérardin, 37
Déroulède, Paul, 222
Desjardin, Master Guillaume, 197
d'Estivet, Jean, promoter at the Trial, 135
d'Estouteville, Guillaume, 217
Dex, Geoffroy, 165
——, Jean, 176
Dominicans, 16, 107, 108, 137, 177, 229
Domrémy, 13, 14, 22, 26, 28, 29, 30, 32–3, 34, 35, 36, 37, 38, 39, 40, 47, 53, 64, 67, 94n.
Drouart, Jehan, 195
Druids, 16, 45, 229
Dufresne de Beaucourt, 21
Du Guesclin, Bertrand, 18, 29, 174
Dun, Saubelet de, 179
Dunois, Bastard of Orleans, 26, 29, 48, 67, 71, 72, 73, 74, 75, 76, 77, 78, 80, 87, 89, 175, 189, 193, 194

Edward I, King of England, 69, 171
Edward III, 17, 18, 40, 42
Edward VII, 224
Eight Beatitudes, Cross of the, 186, 208
Engélide, predictions of, 22
Erard, Guillaume, 132, 133
Eric the Red, 184
Eugenius IV, Pope, 132, 158, 159, 160, 177, 202, 227

Fairies' Tree, 13, 39, 45
Falstaff, 80
Fay, Isabelle du, 205
Felix V, Pope: *see* Savoy, Amadeus Duke of
Fierbois, St Catherine of, 69
Flavy, Guillaume de, 93, 95, 97, 98
Fleur de Lys, herald, 82, 166, 168, 179
Fleury, Cardinal, 222
Folenfant, Georges, 145
Fournier, Berthaut, 166
France, Margaret of, 171
Franciscans, 16, 33, 38, 45, 61, 68, 69n., 73, 79, 90, 91, 92, 96, 97, 104, 108, 117, 118, 124, 125, 141, 156n., 157, 162, 164, 185, 186, 188, 208, 218, 227, 228, 229; Third Order, 33, 35, 38, 43, 46, 48, 54, 58, 63, 66, 67, 70, 76, 79, 96, 104, 105, 106, 155, 185, 201, 227; "voices", 14, 38, 45–7, 53, 55, 64, 69, 95, 96, 97, 112, 114, 118, 124, 125–6, 132, 133, 138, 202

Francis of Assisi, Saint, 107, 156, 183, 223
Fresne-en-Woëvre, 180, 181

Gambetta, Léon, 222
Gaucourt Raoul de, 56, 58, 59, 63, 65, 69
Gélu, Jacques, 54, 64
Germany, Emperor of, 17, 165
Gerson, Jean, 54, 64, 65, 72, 104, 138
Gien, 96
Glasdale, William, 81
Gloucester, Humphrey, Duke of, 117, 216
Golden Fleece, Order of the, 170, 175, 199
Grandes Compagnies, 18, 29, 189
Grand-Failly, Colart de, 179, 203
Graverend, Jean, inquisitor of France, 122, 137, 138, 156, 216
Graville, 91, 95
Grongnait, Sir Nicolas, 163
Guéret, Gilet, 75
Guesdon, Laurent, 145

Hatte, Jean, 167
Henry IV, King of England, 18, 40, 91
Henry V, King of England, 40–1, 42, 73, 216
Henry VI, King of England, 42, 83, 103, 112, 113, 114, 115, 134, 146, 157, 160, 203, 216
Henry II, King of France, 199
Henry IV, King of France, 172
Herriot, President Edouard, 180
Hospitallers, 94, 171
Hundred Years War, 17–18, 33, 40–3, 48, 81, 96, 97, 98, 105, 118, 157, 160, 216

Isabeau of Bavaria, Joan's mother, 14, 19, 20–1, 22, 23, 24–5, 27, 28, 36, 40, 42, 56, 85, 94, 103, 104, 105, 124, 156, 160, 165, 168
Isabella of France, mother of Edward III, 17

James I, King of Scotland, 188n.
Jargeau, siege of, 83, 89, 97
Jaulny, castle of, 186n., 204
Jaulny branch: *see* Armoises
Jeanne-la-Guillorée, 144
Jeanne-la-Turquenne, 144
Jeanne Vanneril, 144
Jerome, Saint, 226
Joan (or Jehanne) the Maid:
Events of her life: birth, 24–6, 37, 203; childhood and education, 26, 36–9, 44–7, 64, 164; her mission, 15, 38–9, 47, 55, 80, 156, 208–9, 228, 229, 230; reception at Chinon, 54–8; questioned at Poitiers, 63–5; at Orleans, *see* Orleans, siege and relief of; given coat of arms, 31, 79, 83–6; at coronation, 90–2; captured, 98–9; imprisoned, 110–6, 136–7, 141; trial, *see* Trial of Condemnation; exile, 155–6, 158–60; reappearance, 136, 155, 156, 160, 162–3, 165–6, 168; marriage to Robert des Armoises, 15, 160, 168–9, 174, 176, 178–181, 197–8, 201–2, 204, 227; death, 158, 206; tomb, 205, 206–9
Characteristics: appearance, 44, 48, 56, 61, 62, 76, 88, 111, 164, 194, 203–4; arrogance, 64, 73, 80, 123, 124; faith, 39, 44, 46–7, 155, 195, 201, 230; virginity, 15, 65–6, 115, 197–198, 226–7
Legend of, 13, 22, 32, 94n., 122, 124, 168. 218, 219, 222–3; Rehabilitation, *see* Trial of

Legend of,—cont.
Rehabilitation; Canonization, 208, 221, 224–5, 226–7
John the Baptist, 164, 186, 203, 206, 229
John II, King of Castile, 182, 183, 188
John the Good, King of France, 18, 19
John Lackland, King of England, 108
John XXIII, Pope, 228

La Chapelle, 95
La Charité-sur-Loire, siege of, 95, 96, 97
Ladvenu, Brother Martin, 121, 131, 142, 143, 146, 216, 226
La Fontaine, Brother Jean de, 125, 126
La Hire, Etienne de Vignolles, called, 14, 70, 71, 74, 118
Lancastrians, 40, 41, 228
La Rochelle, Catherine de, 149
La Rochelle, siege of, 182–4, 187, 188, 189
la Touroulde, Marguerite, 36
La Trémoille, Georges de, 56, 60, 61, 62, 67, 88, 89, 90, 93, 95, 97, 98, 118, 126
le Bouteiller, Raoul, sheriff, 143
Leif Ericsson, 184
Le Maistre, Jean, 122, 125, 126
Leo XIII, Pope, 223, 227
Leprestre, Jacquet, 78, 97, 166, 167, 191, 192, 193
Lesbahy, Jacquet, 166, 193
Liesse, Notre-Dame de, 94, 108, 159, 164, 165, 203, 229
Loches, 87, 167
Loré, Ambroise de, 70
Lorraine, Charles II, Duke of, 48
Lorraine, 13, 22, 32, 35, 47, 144, 161, 163, 164, 170, 172, 173, 176, 178, 189, 196, 201, 202, 205, 209, 219, 222, 224, 225, 228, 229
Louis IX (Saint Louis), King of France, 45, 73, 105
Louis XI, King of France, 188n.
Louis XII, King of France, 203
Louve, Nicolas, 92, 163, 164, 176, 201, 202–3, 219, 223n.
Loyseleur, Nicolas, 123, 129, 130, 133
Luillier, Jean, 36, 77, 78, 88, 97, 193, 232
——, Jeanne, 77
Luxemburg, Elizabeth of Goerlitz, Duchess of, 82, 162, 165, 166, 168, 171
——, Jeanne of, 110, 112, 114
——, John of, Count of Ligny, 95, 98, 110, 111, 117, 157
——, Louis of, Bishop of Thérouanne, 111, 132, 157
Luxeuil, monastery at, 229

Machet, Gérard, 54, 55, 56, 70
Macy, Haimond de, 111, 134, 157, 158, 159
Magna Carta, 108
Manchon, Guillaume, clerk at Trial, 120, 133, 139, 216
Margny, 98, 99
Martel, Charles, 69
Martin V, Pope, 104, 132, 155, 185, 227
Marville, 164, 165, 178, 179, 181
Massieu, Jean, 115, 129, 216
Maximilian of Austria, 19, 175
Mayence, Inquisitor of, 177
Menthon-Montrottier, Pierre de, 157, 158, 159
Merlin the Magician, 13, 39, 230
Metz, 92, 157, 162, 163, 166, 168, 172, 176, 178, 181, 186n., 187, 195, 198, 201, 202, 204, 209
Meung-sur-Loire, 81, 87
Midy, Nicolas, assessor, 136

Miget, Brother Pierre, 131, 220
Mirandelle, Marie-Antoinette, miracle of, 224
Monstrelet, Enguerrand de, 24n., 28, 29, 37, 83, 99, 158, 160
Montereau, 41
Montigny, Jean de, 215
Montrottier, castle of, 158, 159
Morosini, Antonio, 72
Morschoasne, Gilet, 191, 192, 194, 195
Mother-goddess, The, 16, 108, 229
Moulins, 96
Mystère du Siège d'Orléans, 67, 70, 87, 187, 189, 195

Napoleon I, 114, 172, 173, 221
Naviel, Jean de, 111
Neufchâteau, 37, 47, 48
Nicholas V, Pope, 215, 217, 218, 227
Nider, Jean, 177
Novelompont, Jehan de (Jehan de Metz), 44, 48, 54, 63, 67, 76, 93, 98
Norwich, Bishop of, 132
Noyon, Bishop of, 132, 134, 138, 157

Orleans, Charles, Duke of, 29, 36, 38, 40, 43, 48, 59, 60, 63, 68, 73, 75, 76, 77, 78, 82, 88, 116, 118, 126, 159, 165, 167, 198, 199, 200, 206
——, House of, 26, 34, 40, 41, 55, 73, 85, 161
——, Louis, Duke of: affair with Isabeau of Bavaria, 20–1, 23; father of Joan, 14, 26, 39, 46, 58, 61, 84, 88, 112, 168, 205; his murder, 25, 27–8, 29, 30, 40, 41, 69
——, siege and relief of, 14, 36, 38, 39, 44, 53, 62, 66, 69, 71–82, 83, 87, 89, 91, 92, 97, 98, 108, 117, 155, 168, 187, 192, 219; Joan's return to, 77, 78, 192, 197, 206, 219, 224, 232

Paris, 14, 23, 24, 25, 29, 41, 42, 68n., 94, 95, 160, 189
——, University of, 103, 105, 106, 107, 112, 113, 120, 121, 128, 131, 136, 137, 138, 139, 144, 215, 216
Pasquerel, Jean, Joan's confessor, 68, 76, 78, 81, 108, 140
Patay, French victory of, 14, 73, 89
Péguy, Charles, 224
Philip Augustus, King of France, 114
Philip IV the Fair, King of France, 17
Philip V the Tall, King of France, 171
Philip VI of Valois, 17
Philip II, King of Spain, 175
Philippe, Joan's twin, 24–5, 26, 27, 26
Pichon, Jehan, 194
Piri Reis, maps of, 185
Pisan, Christine de, 228
Pius II, Pope, 227
Pius X, Pope, 22
Pius XI, Pope, 84, 228
Pius XII, Pope, 84, 228
Plantagenet dynasty, 17, 56
Poitevin, Jean, 81
Poitiers, assembly of, 30, 54, 62–6, 104, 115, 123, 127, 164, 197, 219, 228
Poitiers, Book of, 65, 126, 194, 227
——, battle of, 18
Porcupine, Order of the, 198–9
Poulengy, Bertrand de, 44, 48, 54, 63, 67, 76, 93, 98, 206n.
Précy, Jehan de, 112
Prelati, Francesco, 188

Prévosteau, Guillaume, 13, 120, 140, 218, 219, 226
Pulligny-sur-Madon, church of, 205, 206–9
Puy-en-Velay, religious centre of, 47, 68, 80, 108, 202, 229

Quenast, Jean, 164

Rabateau, Jehan, 63, 194, 197
Rais, Gilles de, 70, 71, 78, 87, 89, 91, 95, 96, 97, 98, 118, 181, 187–8, 189, 190, 195, 198
Rapiout, 98
Red Branch Knights of Ulster, 229
Rethel family, 171
Rheims, Hermine of, 39
——, coronation at, 14, 53, 57, 80, 89, 90–2, 93, 99, 105, 106, 108, 155, 162, 163, 176, 187, 202, 203, 215, 216, 219
Richard, Brother, 90, 91, 137, 149
Richard II, King of England, 91
Richemont, Arthur de, 98
Riom, 96
Riquier, Jean, 145
Rouvray, French defeat at, 71, 230
Rozmital, Leon of, 189
Rue, Jehan de la, 75

Sabran, Delphine of, 227
——, Elzear of, 227
Saint-Denis, abbey, 24, 25, 26, 96
——, monk of, 24, 25, 27
Saint-Pierre-le-Moûtier, 96
Saint-Pol, Hôtel, 24, 26, 28
Saint-Thibaud of Metz, Dean of, 144, 155, 156, 162, 164, 168, 178, 201
Salic Law, 17
Savoy, Amadeus, Duke of, 157, 159; as Pope Felix V, 165, 182
Savoy, Joan's stay in, 156, 158, 159, 160, 182, 183
Schism, Great, 16, 105, 132
Seguin, Brother, 64
Selles-en-Berri, 89
Sermoise: *see* Armoises
Sforza, Francis, 159, 227
Siquenville, Jehan of, 190
Soissons, 94, 97
Stafford, Earl of, 111
Stewart, Margaret, 188n.
Stuart Mill, John, 221
Syna, Hauviette de, 37

Talbot, John, 73
Tanneguy-du-Châtel, 41
Templars, 16, 29, 91, 109, 134, 171, 172, 184, 185, 186, 188
Thérage, Geoffroy, 226
Third Order: *see* Franciscans
Thistle, Order of the, 17
Thoneletil, Jehan de, 179
Tournai, Guillaume, Bishop of, 170
Tours, 67, 68n., 89, 195
Toutmouillé, Brother Jean, 147, 216
Trial of Condemnation: 13, 23, 37, 65, 83, 97, 103ff., 108–9, 122, 123, 131, 137, 138, 143, 215, 216, 219, 221, 224; falsification of records, 113, 119–20, 122, 127, 131, 145, 164, 217; quotations from, 23, 37, 45, 64, 69, 95, 97, 98, 110, 112, 114, 124–6, 129, 132, 138, 139, 142, 146–7, 164, 208
Trial of Rehabilitation, 13, 16, 22, 23, 32, 53, 65, 108, 113, 120, 122, 124, 129, 138, 139, 140, 160, 208, 215–20, 221, 224; quotations from, 13, 27, 65, 71, 74, 76, 79, 111, 121, 131, 133–5, 140, 141, 145, 146
Trier, 165n., 177

Troyes, Treaty of, 38, 42, 43, 45, 104
——, 89, 90, 104

Ursins, Juvénal des, 66, 219

Valois, Catherine of, 42, 114, 157
Valois dynasty, 17, 18, 19, 40, 41, 65, 105, 203
Vatican, 22, 104, 132, 140, 215, 219, 221, 223, 225, 227
Vaucouleurs, 34, 40, 48, 71, 172
Vendôme, Louis of Bourbon, Count of, 55, 56, 90
Verden, Bishop of, 218
Vergil, Polydore, 145n.
Verneuil, French defeat at, 38, 47
Verville, Béroalde of, 23, 164
Vienne, Colet de, 48, 53
Vigneulles, Philippe de, 162
Villehardoin, 174n.
Virnebourg, Robert, Count of, 165, 303, 223n.
——, Ulrich of, 177
Visconti, Philip-Maria, Duke of Milan, 29, 30
——, Valentine, 29

Wandonne, Lionel of, 99
Warwick, Earl of, 111, 112, 114, 116, 145, 148, 157, 197, 216
Wilhelm I, 222

Xaintrailles, 98, 189

Ysembart de la Pierre, Brother, 121, 138, 141, 142, 143, 145, 147, 216